The Black Dutchman

Book One: Coming of Age

C. Richard Read

The Black Dutchman
C. Richard ReadISBN 978-1-940224-65-7
 This book was printed in the United States of America. Taylor and Seale Publishing, LLC, Daytona Beach Shores, Florida 32118.

Note: Some names and identifying details have been changed to protect the privacy of individuals. Although the author and publisher have made every effort to ensure that the information in this book was correct, the author and publisher disclaim any liability to any party for any loss, damage or disruption caused by errors or omissiions, whether such errors or omissions results from negligence, accident,or any other cause.

This book may be purchased through
Amazon.com and Amazon Kindle
Taylor and Seale Publishing.com
Barnes and Noble.com
Books a Million

Taylor and Seale Publishing, LLC Daytona Beach Shores, Florida 32118 Phone: 1-888-866-8248
www.taylorandseale.com

Dedication

This book is dedicated to my daughters, Robin and Lori. I hope these pages give them understanding as to who they are and insight into the colorful characters who share their blood.

C. Richard Read

TABLE OF CONTENTS

FOREWORD

The Black Dutchman

This is the story of my father, made fatherless at the tender age of eleven months by a court guard's gun. It is also my story, for I am The Black Dutchman.

My dad, George I. Read was raised by his mother who at that time was one of the few black women who didn't work as a domestic servant while her husband was alive. His death changed that. His mother was forced to find work as a cook in a well-to-do white family's kitchen.

Being raised by a single parent, Dad fell into the trap of many children raised in a single parent home. He joined a street gang, skipped school and was on the road to early imprisonment. That all changed when his mother overheard her employer discussing her son's plan to attend college.

"Son; I don't know what it is, or where it is, but you must promise me to find out and go there too."

It took him many years to do so, but eventually he found out where this place called college was. By fortunate circumstances he had found work cleaning a black doctor's lab and through the doctor found out where this place called college was.

Being highly intelligent, the doctor took an interest in the eager boy, and through the efforts of the doctor's friend, (a white Presbyterian Minister) secured a scholarship at Lincoln University, in Pennsylvania for my father..

In four years. Dad graduated *magna-cum-laude* and won the gold medal for science. His life, the life of his family members, and of all who interacted with him, was impacted from his experiences. This is the story of my father and of his legacy.

C. Richard Read

PREFACE

As a boy I remember my father describing the murder of his father, Isaac, by a court guard. Dad said it happened when his father was serving on an otherwise all white jury and had held out for the acquittal of a black defendant (a man the black community felt was being framed). Isaac's position had dead-locked the jury. Dad told me that to remedy that, a guard walked into the jury room and, after some sort of diversionary tactic, calmly blew his father's brains out, ending the deadlock. A white alternate was brought in to replace Isaac, and a guilty verdict was immediately handed down. He told the story often, and in great detail.

When I started writing the story, I opened with the unjust death of my grandfather and the circumstances of his death. The story had been burned deep in my brain as a young boy. I was well into the writing of the story when my nephew sent me two newspaper accounts of that fateful day.

The newspaper accounts didn't match my father's version. After reading the articles, I started to rewrite my opening to match the newspaper accounts. However, when I began the rewriting process, I had second thoughts. First of all, I realized there were inconsistencies in the eye-witness accounts which appeared in the newspapers. That meant there were different versions of what had been seen and heard on that fateful day.

We know rumors develop and grow when facts aren't clear. That simple fact led me to conclude that since the very day the story began, there were different versions of the event. I can only guess that over the years the event became an urban legend and grew to the story my father must have heard many years later as a teen-aged boy, since he was eleven months old when he lost his father.

Given the history of cover-ups, lies and distortions of the truth, the black community automatically became mistrustful of what had been reported. Remembering that my father was only eleven months old the day his father was shot, by the time he was old enough to grasp what had happened, the 'street' version had evolved, and became his truth, became what he believed as he grew into early manhood. That being so, in writing his story I honored his understanding of the truth as he believed it and recounted to his family.

C. Richard Read

CHAPTER 1

The Court House

"Jes' do as I say an' don't be ask'n me no whole lott'a damn questions! Now set yo' watch… I got 9:20. Set your'n to that time, too," Frank Duncan ordered his counterpart. His voice was tight, strained.

"Yeah, yeah, I got it… 9:20," the shorter man replied in a slow, nasal drawl.

Then it happened. The loud banging on the door startled the jurors into silence. It swung open violently, slamming again the room's wall. The hysterical man standing in the doorway was yelling, "FIRE! FIRE!

The jurors turned to the screaming man and jumped up as one. Some bolted for the door, a few just stood, looking frightened and confused, including the black juror. The little guard screamed again, "Didn't ya all hear me, get outt'a here!" He ran to the next room and repeated his alert about a fire.

During the confusion, Duncan's finger tightened around the revolver's handle. In a split second, it was pointing directly at the black man's head. He squeezed the trigger. The explosion was deafening. Blood, bone and brain splattered onto the table. The juror fell forward, this face hitting the table hard. Slowly, the body crumpled to the floor. The gun fell to the floor, making a loud clunk.

"It was an accident!" Duncan screamed. "I was fumbl'n with my gun and it just fell outt'a my belt." The jurors, still clustered by the door, looked back in horror.

As they milled around in confusion, the guard reappeared. "Jes a false alarm. Jes'a damn ol' waste basket fire. Somebody must'a throw'd a match or cigarette in it. Sorry."

"All right, all right," the jury foreman yelled. "Settle down. You all come on back in here and sit down. NOW! You all heard what he said. It was an accident! He…he was jes' try'n to position his gun and the damn thing fell out and went off in all this excitement." The visibly shaken jurors nodded in silent assent.

The foreman, a puzzled expression on his face, looked at the dead man. He turned to Duncan, "We need to go to another room. See if you can find one somewhere." In a few minutes, the guard returned. With an air of self-importance, he announced, "I found one. Jes' follow me." He turned, and walked briskly down the hallway. His haste wasn't reflected in the jurors who followed. They shuffled along like zombies, their ashen faces frozen into expressionless masks. Several dabbed handkerchiefs at the beads of perspiration dripping from their brow. The men's heavy shoes made hissing sounds on the marble floor as they dragged their leaden feet. They entered the new room, Room 7, and took seats. The shock of what they had just experienced cast a pall of quietness over the whole group. Duncan left the jurors and returned to Room 3.

A subconscious need to reaffirm what he had done drew him back. A magnetic urge pulled him to take one last look. He stood at the door for a moment, then, opened it. The bright sunlight flooding the previously dark and dreary room startled him. The early morning clouds had given way to a brilliant yellow light that flooded the deserted room. The sun's bright rays bathed the man's lifeless form in its warmth, momentarily masking the horror that lay on the floor. A casual observer might think the man was lying on the floor, taking a nap, until the gaping hole in his head became visible. Yes, he had indeed shot a man. He turned to leave, but before he stepped out of the room, he glanced back. Without warning, his body began to shake violently; a cold wind had suddenly penetrated his soul. He stood frozen until the foreman's voice echoed down the hall, "Duncan, go tell the judge what happened, you hear?"

He took a deep breath, then, raced down the stairs in search of the judge in charge of the case. "Good," he thought, "he's in." Knocking on Judge Alexander's door, he walked toward a large oak desk, then, stood silently. The heavy faced man sitting behind the desk made him wait several minutes before acknowledging his presence. Finally he looked up from the papers spread in front of him. Peering over his glasses, he nodded his head in recognition, giving the guard permission to speak.

Duncan's heart pounded, his mouth opened, but his voice was gone. His arms waved excitably as his fingers poked the air. "Well what is it!" the judge barked impatiently.

The reprimand snapped him out of his confusion, "Yo' hon'a suh…I was jes' adjust'n my belt in the jury room there, an' my gun, well suh, it fell out to the flo, an went off! An' nex' thing I know'd, the darkie, ahh, Read I believe to be his name, jus' fell ov'a… dead as anything, shot in the head."

The judge's blue eyes bore into the flustered mans for several moments. "Are you telling me the truth, Duncan?"

"On my mother's grave, yo' Honor suh. That's the God's honest truth."

"Did others witness this occurrence?"

"Oh, yes suh', ever juror present, they'll swear to what I jes' tol' you, suh'"

"Very well then, I understand. Accidents do happen. I'll prepare a note for the deceased kin… That would be his wife, if I remember his file correctly. I want her to know exactly what happened."

In the hour it took the janitor to clean the blood and gore from the jury room table, the newly formed jury reached a unanimous verdict in the murder case of Willie Smith, accused of killing John Harold, a white man. In the court room, Judge Alexander heard the foreman read the guilty verdict. Willie Smith was sentenced to death by hanging on the last day of the month.

Shortly afterwards, a hearing was held to determine if Duncan had committed a crime. During that procedure, the two women jurors said they heard a shot, then the sound of a gun hitting the floor. The male jurors said exactly the opposite. The men said they heard the gun hit the floor, then a shot. Duncan was acquitted of any wrong-doing. As a result of this 'accident', guards were required from that day on, to secure their weapons in a holster.

Flies entered the open window of room 3 and began feasting on the flecks of blood and brain the janitor missed in his attempt to leave the bloody scene as quickly as possible. On his way home, Alfonso Pitts found an empty lot and vomited. Even though he had not met the dead juror, he thought of him as a brave man. He had heard through the court house grapevine that the dead juror had held out for brother Willie's innocence.

The clerk found the address: 331 Baldwin Street, across from the University of Chattanooga. As he approached the house, he saw a light-skinned colored woman sitting on the front porch. She was gently rocking back and forth in a high back chair. Standing on the ground, the clerk stopped in front of the woman, looked up and asked, "Are you Mary Catherine Read?"

"Yes, I am Mary Read." For an instant, their eyes met. But, Mary chose to look past the young man's gaze; her eyes found a single rose blossom on a nearby bush. Instinct told her this young man was going to be the bearer of bad news. She just knew it.

Reaching into a breast pocket, he produced an envelope. He pulled out a single sheet of paper and began reading. "This is to inform you of the accidental death of your husband..." Mary's mind froze. She heard nothing beyond those first few words. At the conclusion of the reading, he carefully folded the document and placed it back in the envelope.

Stepping closer, he reached over the rose bush and the porch's banister to hand her the envelope. He turned, and hurriedly walked away.

Mary went numb. Her emotions shut down. She didn't cry, or scream. She didn't make a sound. Instead, her eyes returned to the intricate design of the rose. She sat for a long while before tears came. Slowly at first, then from a deep inexhaustible source, they streamed down her face as she sat, paralyzed by her grief. This woman of the South realized her tears weren't only for her dead husband, but for all of the loved ones the South had taken from her during her short lifetime.

Her mind drifted back to the day the notice for jury duty had come to her husband. How well she remembered the knot she felt in her stomach when Isaac read the notice to serve to her. Inwardly, she cursed that piece of paper. She knew her husband was one of the few blacks in town who could be called to serve on a jury. He had been a freedman, was a property owner and could read and write as well as most whites. Mary also knew that Isaac, having grown up a freedman, believed the South could change. He held steadfastly to the faith that this land, despite having witnessed many cruel and unjust acts, could become a better and different place. He held to this hope because he had occasionally seen another side of the South: acts of kindness and charity. And it was this view he chose to believe in. He had never experienced the lash of an overseer's whip or felt rough metal shackles on his legs. On occasion, this difference created a schism between himself and his wife.

Unlike Isaac, Mary had been born into slavery. She knew the ways of the South and of white folks. She instinctively had a better understanding than her husband of the implications the jury notice contained. For that reason she wanted to say, '"Don't get mixed up in the white man's law." Mary felt, as did most of the town's black folks, that the colored man going on trial was being framed. Everyone knew Willie was considered an uppity nigger by some of the big white folks in town. Now they were going to teach him, and for that matter, all the coloreds, a lesson. She felt he was to be the token colored man on the jury. His presence was to validate the inevitable guilty verdict. It had never occurred to them that one lone black man might hold out against eleven white men.

Everyone knew John Harold was a drunk and could be found lying in the street almost any time, day or night. On this day he had fallen behind Willie Smith's house and split his head on a stump. Willie found John and felt if he didn't report it the police would automatically accuse him of the man's death. For that reason he had gone to the police to report what he had found. It was the biggest mistake Willie would ever make. The police arrested him on the spot for John Harold's murder.

Mary felt the trial was going to be about revenge and power, not justice for Willie. Yet, she remained silent. She knew her husband would do what he felt was the right thing to do. Her feelings were proven right that night.
Isaac and Mary sat side by side in their rockers on the front porch. He took a draw on his corn cob, then, slowly exhaled. The smoke floated lazily upward. "Mary, I won't try to get out of this. I'm going to serve on that jury because that man needs someone to stand up for the truth. Not just for him, but for all of us."

Mary looked at her husband for a moment, then without a word, got up and went inside. Finding her way to the kitchen, she closed the door, took a seat at the table and wept silentLY.

The news of Isaac Read's death hit the colored community hard and spread like wild fire. It was common knowledge that he had never been a slave, but that he owned his own home and had a good job. It was a bitter pill to swallow, a setback for them all. His murder reinforced in their minds the notion that they were at the mercy of any white person -- man, woman or child. They felt white folks had all the rights and this killing showed they intended to keep their power by any means necessary. What few hopes and dreams remained from the Reconstruction era faded even more. Older former slaves shook their heads and said, "..an he weren't never no slave, an da' jes' ups ad kills him like dat."

Human nature, being just that, allowed some colored folks to take a somewhat selfish view. This position was vocalized by a few of Mary's contemporaries

-- women who often walked by and saw her tending her yard, or caring for her new- born baby boy. She was one of the few black women enjoying that luxury. Some of the cooks and maids, in conversation among themselves, could be heard whispering, "Now she won't be so hi' an mitt'y. She gonn'a hab to take her black ass to wuk, jes' lak de rest ob us…hee, hee, hee."

Isaac's funeral was held later in the week, drawing hundreds of people, including a handful of whites.
Mary's son, George Isaac, was only eleven months old when her life changed abruptly. She realized very quickly she would have to seek work to pay the inevitable bills: food, clothes, and the upkeep of the house. She would have to find a source of income, and with her limited skills, her options would be to work for some rich white lady as a cook, or a maid.

After Sunday service at the First Baptist Church, Mary asked several church sisters to keep an ear open about any jobs they might hear of. A few months passed before a sister rushed up to her, "Praise the Lord, Mary, there's an opening as a cook, at the Farr's place, an' not too far from yo' house. They be located on Maple Street, the big white house on the corner. If you gets the job, you could walk there easy. I hear tell he be a banker, or someth'n like that."

"I'm much obliged to you, sister Burton." Mary replied as she hugged the frail old lady.

"They be the Farr's, Mr. and Mrs. John Farr. I sure hope the Lord sees fit to bless you with that job, Mary."

Monday, with her son in tow, without any problem, Mary found Maple Street and the stately mansion. It sat on a slight rise and sparkled in its four-column white majesty. Magnolia and other ornamental trees and shrubs were

MARY READ

tastefully placed around the home. The fragrance of roses filled the air; a fragrance that reminded her of her own home and that brought a smile to her lips. Mary used the side walkway which she assumed would lead to the kitchen's entrance. Walking up to the imposing door, she knocked.

A large brown skinned woman appeared as the door opened. "Yes?" the woman asked sharply.

"Is this the residence of Mr. and Mrs. John Farr?" Mary asked in a small voice, suddenly intimidated by the large lady.

"It is," was the short, terse response.

"I understand there's a cook's job open and I…"

"I'm the cook. Been the cook here for more years than you been on this earth… but you can come in."

"Oh, I'm sorry. Maybe I was told wrong."

" Didn't say there wasn't no job here. Jes' said, I'm the cook. Come, come in and sit ova' there." The self-declared cook pointed to a chair that sat in the entrance-way room, just outside the large kitchen. The cook disappeared through a second door, while Mary took the seat, feeling uncomfortable and unwelcome.

The cook reappeared, opening the door for a tall white woman, rather plain in appearance, WHO carried herself with confidence. She acknowledged Mary with a nod, and a faint smile flicked across her face when she saw the little boy holding tightly to his mother's hand. "How may I help you?" she asked pleasantly.

"I was told there might be a cook's job opening here, but, I guess I was wrong," Mary replied, nodding her head toward the large lady glowering at her from the other side of the room."No, you heard right." The woman interrupted. "There is a job here, not exactly a cook's job, since Amy Lou is still the cook, but we need someone to help her since she is getting up in years." The lady glanced toward Amy Lou who had now turned her back to them and made herself busy but obviously listening to every word being uttered.

"Now, we didn't get a chance to introduce ourselves did we? I'm Mrs. Farr." Then, looking in the direction of the cook, she said "And, that's Amy Lou."

"I'm pleased to meet you both. My name is Mary Catherine Read, and this is my son, George Isaac."

Amy Lou made a grunting sound, pursed her lips, lifted her head up high and walked past the two women, then disappeared into the kitchen and began making loud clanking noises with her pots and pans.

"Let's go outside, shall we?" Mrs. Farr said leading the way out of the door.

Mary and George followed her to a bench that faced a large flower garden. Mrs. Farr sat, then, patted the space next to her, indicating she wanted Mary to sit beside her.

"As I was saying, inside." She began. "Amy Lou is getting up in years, slowing down. Now, she won't admit it, but she is. As a matter of fact, she cooked for Mr. Farr's mother and father, right up until they both passed, so she's…" Her voice trailed off. She turned her large blue eyes to Mary, "When Mr. Farr and I got married; he brought her here to continue on with us." She paused, then glanced at the little boy.

Mary caught her look and thought it might mean she saw George as a problem. "If you do decide to take me on, I promise, he won't be a bother," she added hastily.

"Oh, I'm sure he won't be. I have two sons. As a matter of fact, my youngest is about your boy's age. Now, tell me, what kind of experience do you have?" Mary reviewed her experience as a cook's helper and maid before she married (omitting the fact it began when she was a child slave), adding that in recent years her cooking experience was primarily for church functions.

Mrs. Farr seemed satisfied with what she heard, then began listing all of the Mister's favorite foods, as well as the ones he disliked. Mary nodded in understanding, "I think I can cook the foods he likes to his satisfaction."

Mrs. Farr added quickly, "Right now, you will assist Amy Lou. Help her out as she needs it. Then we'll see what develops." She went over the work hours, her pay and her day off, and then, added, "Just bear with Amy Lou. As I said, she is up in years and used to things being done her way. Can you do that?"

"Yes, Mrs. Farr, I understand, I, I can do that all right."

"Can you start tomorrow?"

"Yes, Ma'am, I can."

The next morning, Mary got four year old George up and dressed. It was still dark as they made their way to the Farr's. George felt since his father's death he was the man of the house, and his mother's protector. When they arrived, Amy Lou was up and stirring.

The kitchen smelled of biscuits, ham and coffee. Mary had arrived a few minutes early, but seeing Amy Lou already up and about, made her feel as if she should have arrived earlier. Then too, the cook's greeting didn't make her feel any better. "Bout time you gets here!" She hissed over her shoulder.

Mary was caught totally off guard, but said nothing. "I fixed a blanket on yonder box for him." Amy nodded to the boy, then, pointed to the wood box in the corner, behind the big stove.

Mary escorted her son to the box."Thank you." Isaac stretched out on the blanket and fell asleep immediately.

"What can I do?" Mary asked.

"You can set the table for breakfast on yonder porch, then you bes' start snapping beans for lunch."

Mary promptly complied. For the coming days and weeks, she found she was more of an observer than a helper. Amy Lou hardly said a word during the course of the day unless it was, "Fetch me that pot." Or, "Fetch me that dish." There was no idle chit chat; when Mary summoned enough courage to ask a question, her answer was short, curt and to the point. After having her ears pinned back several times, she decided it would be safer watching Amy Lou with a keen eye and learning where things were on her own, and to try to find out (without asking) how she wanted to run her kitchen. When Mary used a utensil, she was careful to put it back exactly where she had found it. If Amy Lou spilled anything, Mary was quick to clean it up. After cooking, Mary wiped off the surfaces, washed the dishes and put everything away. However, Amy Lou would not let her near her stove.

Usually, George slept on the wood box until seven, then, had a breakfast of oatmeal and corn bread. Afterward, he would go outside and find the gardener who, like Amy Lou, had been with the Farr family since slavery. Ol' Bob, as he was called, had no family he could claim, and no home, other than the Farr's. When the Civil War ended, most slaves jubilantly left the plantations and big houses. But, Ol' Bob stayed on. As he would explain to little George, "Didn't have no place to go, an nobody to go to. So, I jes' stayed on."

"Ol' Bob enjoyed having the company of little George. The boy trudged behind him like a second shadow; asking question after question. "Why do the bees sit on the flower?" Or, "Why do the seed turn into plants?" The gardener would smile, "Boy, don't you eva' stop run'n yo mouf an ask'n questions? You gonn'a wear ma ears out, sho nuff." His gentle admonition would slow George for awhile, but the sight of an unusual plant or bug would cause him to forget, and his questioning would begin again. On their walk home one afternoon, Isaac told his mother, "Ol' Bob knows everything about flowers and bugs."

Mary stopped in her tracks. "George, children don't call older folks by their first names. That isn't polite. You may call him Uncle Bob, not Ol' Bob, or Bob, is that understood?"

"But little William Farr, calls him those names, an' he's my age. Why is that?"

Mary was embarrassed as she looked down at her bright- eyed son. "George, white folks say and do lots of things different than we colored's do. They live and act different. One day, I'll explain it to you better."

The little boy fell silent for a while, trying to digest what his mother had said. As they walked on for a bit, he said, "Oh, I see."

George and little William became playmates from the moment they met. As the years passed, they became fast friends. When the two of them weren't following Ol' Bob, they climbed trees, ran through the yard, and hid from one another until exhaustion overcame them. Afterward, they would sprawl under a shade tree, giggling, squealing and laughing until their stomachs hurt. Often, when that state of euphoria was reached, the boys couldn't look at each other without bursting into fits of laughter.

The two were only months apart in age, William being the older. But, they were identical in size and height. The major difference was that during the summer, William didn't have all day, six days a week to play or to walk behind Uncle Bob. Twice a week, he was taken away for piano lessons, and on other days, he went off to school for special lessons. Then there were days his mother would call him in to practice the piano for several hours. Often, as George worked beside Uncle Bob, he could hear William reading to his mother. His voice drifted through an open window from a room George had never been allowed to enter.

Amy Lou kept Mary at arm's length for two years, speaking to her sparingly, saying only enough to keep her helper busy, and her kitchen functioning properly. They ate at different times, which further prevented any chance for idle talk or, bonding. Then, one day out of the blue, Amy Lou approached her helper, "Mary, would you sit an' hab a bite wif' me?"

Mary could hardly hide her surprise. "Oh, Amy Lou, I'd love to."

The cook led Mary to the corner table and took her usual seat. Mary sat facing her, all the while wondering what had happened to cause this sudden change. "Mary, my heart is heavy," she began. "I wuz wunder'n if I could talk wif you fo' a bit?"

"Of course you can, Amy Lou. I know what trouble is, and you can talk to me if you like. I'm pleased and honored that you want to talk to me."

Amy Lou began by explaining she had lost her husband before Mary came to work for the Farrs. "He was my only link to my past." She sobbed. "Now, I feels all alone."

"Don't you have family somewhere?"

The large lady dropped her head, "I got's chilln's, but…"

"You do? That's wonderful! Why don't you…?"

" I duz, an I don't. That's what I wants to talk about. I wuz a slave girl in Alabama. This wuz befo' Massa Farr's father bought me. My man an me, now he wuzn't ma huz'ban. But we had two girls, they were look-alikes, 'bout nine year old when a'nudder owner from nudder par ob de state, he come and buys dem. Den right after dat, the massa sells off ma man. Ebber since den, I'z tried to find dem by ax'n any new slaves what wuz brought onto the plantation. Always hop'n I could find a body that may hab seen ma girls, or, ma man. It jus' wuzn't to be. I ain't nebber saw or heard of dem again." Her eyes filled, then, flowed like a silent river.

As Mary listened, the large woman seemed to shrink before her eyes. Sitting in front of her was a small, fragile old lady.

Amy Lou dabbed at her eyes, blew her nose, and finally gained her composure. She continued, "I did met a nudder man, an we got married, proper. But, now, he be dead too. Died jes bfo' you come. I wuz still mad when you come here, I'z sorry I been cross wid you," she confessed.

Mary had felt there was something behind this woman's brusque exterior -- always keeping her at arm's length, never allowing her to get close. Now, she realized the old lady was trying to maintain her dignity, trying to keep her mind and soul together, all the while carrying a deep and hurtful burden inside.

"Ain't nebb'a tol no one bout dis, sept'n ma dead huzban. Yu's de fust one, an I don't knows why I is burd'n you wif ma troubles." Her eyes welled up, and again the tears flowed.

Mary got up and went to the grieving woman. Kneeling, she wrapped her arms tightly around her shoulders. Amy Lou buried her head in Mary's bosom and cried as she hadn't in her entire life. The woman's grief seeped into Mary's soul, and she wept with her. Mary's tears were for Amy Lou, for her lost children, her dead husband and for her own murdered Isaac.

The women's relationship changed from that day on. Amy Lou's attitude toward George changed as well. While she had always been civil to the boy, she never fussed or made over him as other women did. If he was in the room, she hardly acknowledged his presence. Now, she focused most of her attention on him. She began preparing special little cakes and cookie treats. Next, she took over the responsibility of making his lunches. Amy Lou watched him play, and if she felt he was playing too hard, she would insist he come in and rest. Sometimes she would hoist him onto her ample lap and sing him to sleep. Most surprising to Mary, she asked her little boy to call her Aunt Amy.

However, Amy Lou had another shock for Mary. A few weeks later, Mary and George entered a darkened kitchen. In the two plus years she had worked at the Farrs, she had never walked into the kitchen and not seen Amy Lou busy at the stove, or one of the work counters stirring or chopping food. Instead, Amy Low was sitting in her rocker. "Bout time you gets here." She barked. "You knows where everything is, so jes' get to it…and boy, you come on ova' heah and set on ma' lap, and keeps me company."

Mary realized after all these years; Amy Lou was officially putting her in charge of the kitchen. She was relinquishing her long held title of 'cook' and was passing it on to her. Mary felt overwhelmed, realizing she would be solely responsible for all of the food preparation for the Farrs.

Now, when she and George arrived to begin the day, Amy Lou didn't make an appearance until well after breakfast. In fact, she didn't come down until breakfast had been served, the dishes cleared, washed and put away. When she made her entrance, Mary served Amy Lou her favorites: corn bread, two soft boiled eggs and sweet tea.

As time went by, Mary began to notice Amy Lou had to force herself to eat even the smallest amounts, and, an even harder time keeping it down.

Weeks later, coming to work, Mary walked in to a brightly lit kitchen. Looking around, she fully expected to see Amy Lou busy at the stove. But she was nowhere in sight. Not seeing her, Mary called, "Amy Lou! Where are you"? When she heard the entrance-way door open, she turned, expecting to see her new friend. Instead, Mrs. Farr walked through the door, her large blue eyes, red rimmed.

"Mary, I have bad news." She began with a quivering voice. "Amy Lou passed in her sleep last night."

"Oh, no!" Mary said, as her knees gave way.

"Last night, when we saw her, Mr. Farr and I both noticed she looked ill. She's always hated to admit to not feeling well. When we pressed her, finally she admitted to feeling sick, and she looked poorly. So much so, I insisted she go to bed. For that reason I accompanied her upstairs, took her to her room, and put her to bed."

"The poor woman," Mary murmured.

"I kept watch over her until she went to sleep, I held her hand and put cool cloths on her head. She seemed to be resting quite well. Then she started talking in her sleep. She kept repeating, 'Lord, if my babies are with you, let me be with them, too. Oh thank you sweet Jesus.' She may have repeated those words three or four times, and then she just left us."

Mary reached for the nearest chair and sat down. "I'm going to miss her so much. I can't believe she's gone. I guess the Lord thought it was time for her to be with her family. She'll be happy, now."

George's eyes went from one face to the other, trying hard to understand what was being said. He felt sad because they looked so forlorn. Finally he asked, "Does that mean I won't be able to sit on Aunt Amy's lap anymore?"

"That's right George." His mother answered. "She's gone on to heaven. Aunt Amy won't be with us anymore."

"That's not right!" The boy screamed. I'm going to miss her so much." He bolted from the room, ran down the steps, slammed the outside door with such force it shook the stately mansion. His heart wrenching sobs seeped through the upstairs window, adding to the anguish they both felt.

Time, as the saying goes, heals all wounds. For Mary, George, Mr. and Mrs. Farr and little William, that seemed to be apropos. Their lives blended into a pleasant routine. Mary was happy as a cook, while Mr. Farr was pleased with the quality and diversity of the food she prepared. Finally, Mrs. Farr was happy because her husband was pleased with Mary's offerings. Little William and George played hard and enjoyed each other's company. Days, weeks, months, and finally four years went by.

It was a shock the day Mary looked at her growing son and realized he was not only of school age, but, old enough to be responsible to get to and from school on his own. She had delayed sending him because, until now, she didn't feel confident in his ability to do so. Now, she was certain he could. She decided she would walk him there, showing him how to navigate to and from the colored school on his own. As much as she hated the idea, she realized the time had come to send him into the outside world. She realized this was so if he was to grow up and be a man.

"George, you will leave school from the Farr's after breakfast. Then, after school, you will come back here, and when I'm finished with dinner, we will go home together." George listened intently, nodding his head in understanding. What Mary didn't fully appreciate was her son's determination to continue being her protector; walking her to and from the Farr's, was an important part of what he perceived to be his role as man of the house.

Two more years slipped by. George was a good student and enjoyed school. However, at twelve, he began to understand more fully the struggle his mother was having to keep a roof over their heads and clothes on their bodies.

At school a boy pressed George, "I needs a partner, you needs money, so why don't you join up with me?" The young man urged as the two boys stood in the playground. "I been able to help my mama out a whole lot," He stated proudly. The boy's sales pitch opened a whole new world to George. "You ask your mama if you can join me."

Mary was tired; she had had a long day at the Farr's. A last minute invitation by Mrs. Farr had put an extra strain on her that day. Her feet hurt and her back was sore. "Lord only knows why people do things like that." She complained, as she and George trudged home. "If she had told me earlier, it wouldn't have been such a problem."

George was listening, and dutifully replied "Uh huh, I see," every once in a while. But, he had something else on his mind, something he was anxious to share with his mother. He waited until he felt she had fully vented her frustrations of the day. After they walked a few minutes in silence, he said, "Mother, I have a question. Instead of coming back to the Farr's after school, could I help a friend sell newspapers?"

Mary looked at her son with a puzzled expression. "Why would you want to help someone sell newspa'I didn't say that right, mother. I meant to say, my friend needs a partner. We can sell more newspapers if we work in pairs. I can't quite explain it, but that's what my friend says. And, you know what else he told me? He told me on a real good day he can make almost a dollar. His dad is dead, and he helps his mama with the money he makes. And, I know we could use some extra money, too. If you let me, I could help out."

Mary was moved that her son was so aware of their tight money situation. They were struggling, but, she tried not to make their financial problem a problem for her boy. They ate well, she kept him in clean clothes, and, they lived in their own home -- a house her dead husband had purchased and paid off in full. She never mentioned to her son that she didn't have an extra penny at the end of the month from her meager wages. Sending him off to school on his own was a major step towards his independence.

Granting him this request would be an even bigger step. "George, I don't know...where would you be selling your papers?"

"Downtown, on Main Street. My friend has a special corner he works from."

"Oh, I don't feel too good about that." She knew there were roughnecks and other bad elements that frequented that area, too.

As if reading her thoughts, George added, "Mother, my friend says it's safe there. He's been doing it for almost a year, and he makes real good money. His partner and their family moved out of town. So, he needs help, real bad," he pleaded.

Despite her misgivings, the possibility of a few extra dollars swayed her into giving him an affirmative answer.

The first day George came home after selling newspapers, he was able to give his mother fifty cents. He was so proud, he nearly burst with pride. In less than a year, he was giving his mother several dollars a week. It was then, she insisted he keep twenty five cents for himself. Mary was proud of George for other reasons, too. He never 'sassed', or, in any way, showed her disrespect. He usually added an 'um' at the end of any yes or no reply. On occasion, Mary would ask for better diction and demanded a 'yes-ma'am' or a 'no-ma'am', but overall she felt fortunate to have such a loving and devoted son. His newspaper money was truly a help, making her feel all the more blessed.

Their life settled into a pleasant routine: her son, the Farrs, her church. In retrospect, she realized the moments she treasured most were Sunday services and her leisurely walk with George to and from church. During services, she sang and offered praises to the Lord, pouring out her deepest emotions. After services, she felt cleansed, and reborn. That's when her thoughts came into focus, and she could sort out the problems of the week, as well as the coming ones.

Sunday gave them the opportunity to bring each other up-to-date on their past week's activities. These walks together weren't hurried as they were during the work days, rushing to the Farr's. Now, with her son busy in the afternoons with his papers, these Sunday walks became all the more special to Mary.

As they headed home after services, she glanced at her son. What she saw brought a smile to her face. At twelve, he was almost as tall as she was, built solidly, with broad shoulders and muscular arms that almost reached his knees. His hands belonged to an adult male, they were so large. 'What a handsome man he'll grow up to be.' She thought. Finally, she broke the momentary silence. "Son," She began. "I've been thinking. It would be a big help to us if we were to let out that spare upstairs room. It's just sitting there, gathering dust. What do you think?"

He turned his big, brown eyes toward her, his brow furrowed, then after a moment of thought answered, "Yes' um, yes ma'am, that's a good idea. It could be a help, it surely could be."

Mary smiled inwardly at his response since, she had the thought about renting the room for some time. In fact, she had mentioned her desire to do so to the preacher a few Sundays ago. It just so happened when she spoke to her minister, George was across the room chatting with a friend. During the ensuing week, she had forgotten to mention that conversation to him. Now, she was worried. She didn't want that information to come back to her son from anyone except her. She wouldn't want him to think she would make a decision of such importance without consulting him first.

A few Sundays later, the minister took Mary aside, "A sister from a church I'm in contact with, has a cousin coming up from Jackson Mississippi. She may be what you're looking for as a boarder."

"Oh, praise the Lord."

He continued, "The sister said her cousin was to take an evening job at her place of work, and while her employer provides a room, her cousin said she wanted to have a place on the outside, so she could get away from the white folks when and if she wanted to." He pulled a folded paper from this coat pocket. "Here's her address. you can write her and work out the details."

Through correspondence, Mary and the cousin, Gloria Brown worked out all of the necessary arrangements, including the expected day of her arrival in two weeks.

CHAPTER TWO

The Boarder

Mary asked and received permission from Mrs. Farr to leave work early in order to meet her new tenant. For some reason, she was extremely anxious and excited about their first meeting. So excited, she decided to wait for her out on the porch. Sitting in her rocker, she breathed a deep sigh thinking 'Everything is going along so well. Now, things will get even better with the extra income the boarder will bring in.' She turned her face to more fully enjoy the cool afternoon breeze. Within minutes, she dozed off. Involuntarily, she would occasionally shake her head to wake up, only to give in to the warmth and contentment that enveloped her. Finally, she surrendered to the feeling of serenity, and slept deeply.

Somehow she became aware of a presence and struggled to awaken herself. She hadn't heard a sound, yet she knew someone was near. The fragrance of lilac filled her nostrils, so much so, it took her breath away. Mary opened her eyes, trying to focus on the form standing in front of her. Finally, she saw a pair of eyes calmly gazing down at her. She was spellbound by the largeness, the brownness and gentleness of them. And they belonged to a face so gentle, so beautiful, the combination brought a smile to Mary's lips. Her smile was returned by parting full lips, which revealed the straightest, whitest teeth, she had ever seen. The face could have been that of an angel.

Flustered and embarrassed to be caught off guard, Mary explained. "Oh my, oh my, I'm ever so sorry, I must have..."

Sensing Mary's embarrassment, the young lady said soothingly, "Ma'am, it's no problem at all, I made myself at home and poked around your front yard. It's so beautiful, the flowers and all."

As she spoke, Mary tried to understand how it was that she didn't hear the wagon when it drove up, or the driver who must have walked up on the porch to set the two large travel bags near the front door. "I'm truly sorry to have missed your arrival in such a manner. I suppose I was more tired than I realized. Anyway, I'm Mary Read, and you must be Miss Gloria Brown." Mary stood and embraced the young lady.

"Yes, ma'am, I'm Gloria Brown. I'm truly pleased to make your acquaintance, too."

"Thank you, Miss Brown. I'm pleased to meet you as well. I also want to welcome you to my home, and I hope your stay, for however long, will be a pleasant one."

"Oh, thank you, Mrs. Read."

Pride evident in her voice, Mary said, "My son, George Isaac, isn't here right now, but you'll meet him in time. He sells papers every afternoon, and Saturday is usually a long day for him."

"I thank you for opening your home to me. I appreciate it ever so much. And, I do look forward to meeting your son, George Isaac."

Introductions over, the ladies struggled to carry the heavy bags up the steps to her room. The boarder was of medium height and wore a long, loose-fitting dress, yet as she climbed the stairs, her ample buttocks moved the fabric of her dress in a sensual manner. Gloria indicated to her host that she was anxious to see the rest of the house.

With Gloria in tow, Mary proceeded to show her the kitchen, the parlor, the dining room, her room, and her boy.

"Now, I want you to make yourself at home. Don't just stay in your room. You're more than welcome to use the whole house."

"Thank you for being so kind. Would you show me the outside, too?"

Mary was pleased to show off her back yard and the flower gardens. "Now, anytime you wish, come out here and sit if you've a mind to, all right? I want you to feel right at home. You can use the house and yard as if it was your very own."

"I'm ever so grateful for your kindness, Mrs. Read." Later that afternoon, the women finalized the rental details. Gloria paid the rent and was given a key to the front door.

"My employer is sending one of the servants over to pick me up, so I'd better wait out front."

After that first afternoon, Mary hardly ever saw her boarder. Their hours were the exact opposite. The boarder worked well into the evenings and came home when Mary and George were in bed sleeping soundly. It would be two full weeks before George and Miss Brown were to meet.

Some mornings, Gloria, the boarder would get up and look out her bedroom window and watch George and his mother leave for work at the Farr's kitchen. She smiled as she observed the mannerly and manly ways of young George.

At the Farrs, after his breakfast of oatmeal and hot cakes, George kissed his mother and set out for school. He hadn't gone far when he realized he had his lunch bag, but had forgotten his homework. He remembered he had put his books on the hallway hat stand at home. It happened when his mother had called him back to the kitchen to pick up his lunch. That distraction caused him to walk out the door without retrieving his school books.

"Damn!" He swore. I'm going to be in a whole lot of trouble if I don't bring my homework. "Ah shit!" he again cursed aloud. George had picked up the habit of swearing from the older paperboys. He would never let his mother know he used such common and vulgar language. Realizing what he had done, he headed home in a fast trot.

The books were just where he remembered leaving them. After scooping them up, he started to leave. But, the run had made him thirsty. He stopped and put the books and his lunch back on the hall stand. Tip-toeing to the kitchen to get a drink of water, keenly aware of the boarder's late sleeping pattern, he made sure his steps were light so as not to disturb her.

The cool water felt good as it slipped down his parched throat. As he stood drinking from the dipper, he thought he heard a voice, a voice calling his name. 'Nah, it couldn't be.' He mused. But, he heard it again, "George Isaac. George Isaac. Would you bring me a drink of water?"

He thought, 'Oh, oh. I woke the boarder. She's going to be mad as sin at me.' He walked to the doorway and stood at the foot of the steps to make sure he wasn't hearing things. Then he heard it again, this time quite clearly. "George Isaac, would you bring me a drink of water?" The words and tone weren't angry. The voice was soft, sweet, and clear as a bell.

"Yes'um, I surely will," he replied, relieved she wasn't cross with him. Returning to the kitchen, he pumped until the water ran cool. He held the tall glass under the flowing water, allowing it to run over the top. George stopped pumping and wiped off the excess with a dish towel. Trying not to spill a drop, he took small steps as he made his way up the stairs.

He stopped in front of the slightly open door, and waited a few moments. With his free hand, he knocked lightly, but his knock caused the door to open more fully. As it did, the bright morning sunlight filtering through the lace curtains blinded him momentarily. Afraid to move, he stood frozen in place. As his eyes adjusted to the brightness, he sensed the room was different. The boarder had moved the furniture, making it difficult for him to orient himself.

"Mr. George Isaac Read, bring the water over here please."

Following the sound of her voice, he shuffled carefully in that direction, proceeding slowly; afraid he might stumble over the differently arranged furniture. Squinting into the sunlight, he was relieved to pass out of its brightness, and into the shadowy part of the room. For the first time, he could see the bed clearly, as well as the person behind the voice. His senses were assaulted from every direction by the light, her voice, and the fragrance of lilac that filled the room.

"Now, I finally get the opportunity to meet Mr. George Isaac Read." The voice cooed. "Come and set the water down here, please." She pointed to the night table next to her bed, as he moved ever so carefully towards her. "I'm mighty pleased to finally get to meet you, Mr. George Isaac Read. I'm Gloria Brown."

George set the glass down. Once he did, he instinctively took a step back. No one had ever called him Mister in his whole life. "And, I'm mighty pleased to meet you, too, Miss Brown."

"Come, sit here for a spell." Gloria patted the spot next to where she reclined against the headboard. Her body had been covered by a sheet, but the covering slid from her shoulders as she reached for the glass.

"I'm running late for school, I should be going, ma'am," he stammered, suddenly feeling uncomfortable.

"Oh, just set for a spell,. You need to rest yourself. I see you always rushing here or there…just relax yourself for a bit," Gloria said sweetly.

"Well, for a minute." He replied.

Until he sat on the bed he had avoided looking directly at her. Slowly his eyes found her face. When they did, a rush of emotions he had never experienced in his life seeped into every fiber of his being. Her brown eyes were sparkling, unblinking diamonds; her hair was a mass of shiny black ringlets that framed her small, olive brown face. Her beauty bore the richness of an African and Indian mixture. She radiated an overwhelming warmth that made him feel weak. As he took in the rest of her, he noticed her gown was not buttoned at the neck, leaving a clear view of her cleavage. As his gaze traveled further, he saw a dark nipple on a breast that was fully exposed as she daintily took a sip of water.

She said playfully, "Tell me Mr. George Isaac, what are you thinking right now?"

In a hoarse voice he replied, "I really think I better get myself off to school, ma'am."

She laughed softly. Her eyes sparkled even more brightly as she took one of his hands and pulled him back as he attempted to rise. As she did, she glanced down. "George Isaac, you are only twelve, but you have the hands the size of a full grown man?" She said in genuine wonder. Not waiting for a response, she added, "Now wouldn't you rather stay with me jes' a little longer, Mr. George Isaac?"

He heard himself mumble, "Yes'um, I'd rather stay here, Yes'um I surely would."

"Then, like I said, you jes set here and relax."

George looked at her even more closely now as he allowed himself to be pulled back down. He was fixated by her full lips, her small round nose and the smoothness of her flawless brown skin.

Still holding tightly to his hand, she guided it to her seslf and whispered, "Don't I feel nice and soft, Mr. George Isaac?"

"Oh, yes, yes ma'am, it does. You feels real soft." He answered, feeling light- headed.

"Now, Mr. George Isaac, I want you to kiss me. You do want to, don't you?" Her voice was sweet, yet commanding.

His head began to spin. His body felt surges of manliness, deep and powerful, feelings he had never experience before. She pulled him down to her while cupping his face, ever so gently with her other hand. In time, she guided his hands, whispering her desires as she moved them from one sensual spot to another. George was a willing, and apt student.

When they finally spent themselves, Gloria smiled, "Well, Mr. George Isaac, we're sure gonn'a do this some more."

And they met, sometimes three times a week, over the next two years. On those days, George didn't go to school.

#

"Mother, I'm leaving now." George had finished his breakfast of ham, eggs, grits and biscuit in the Farr's kitchen. Mary stopped clearing his dishes off the table long enough for him to give her a kiss on the cheek before he hurried out the door.

It was summer time and Saturday, and he looked forward to a good day of selling papers with his partner Yeller White. He walked fast to meet his friend at the newspaper office where he would pick up his supply of papers.

"Hey, man. What's up?" Yeller called in greeting. He had been waiting or George outside building.

"Not much; white man still in the lead!" George replied with a big smile.

"You can say that again. Hey, I told'em you'd be in fo yo papers real soon."

"Well, you didn't lie, 'cuz here I is here," George teased before he went inside the small office. In a matter of minutes, he returned with a bundle of papers under his arm. "Well, let's get going."

The boys trudged a few blocks and then took up their position. The sky was cloudless and brilliantly blue, and the sun silhouetted their forms as they stood back to back on their favorite Chattanooga street corner. Men, women, and animals moved past them, while horses and mules plodded along pulling wagons and carts with a variety of goods: vegetables, furniture and cord wood. Some carried crates filled with squawking chickens, or squealing piglets. The air was hot, relieved by an occasional breeze which blew wisps of dust that circulated the smell of horse droppings.

Each boy held a copy of the *Chattanooga Daily Times* newspaper in his hand, and waved it vigorously above his head. Each boy had a stack of newspapers nestled between his feet, the papers anchored by a large flat rock to prevent a sudden gust of wind from blowing their papers away.

George's partner, Yeller White was a tall thin boy with a finely chiseled ebony face that glistened from the sweat dripping freely from his nose. George was shorter, and had light brown skin. His face was covered with dark, reddish brown freckles, and his build was square, with arms much too long for his body. Their dress was similar: baggy pants and loose-fitting shirts unbuttoned half way down their chests. Oversized caps, worn low on their heads and pulled to one side in a 'rakish' manner, were their crowning glory. The only difference in their attire was that the tall boy wore no shoes.

"Paper! Paper!" Yeller yelled. "Buy yo' paper."

"Read all about the bank robbery!" George added, calling even louder than his companion.

The boys had hawked their paper for hours and done well. Their stacks were more than half way down, and it was only noon. Maybe because of the heat, or because of the time of day, sales suddenly slowed.

"Boy, it sho' is hot, Piggy." (Yeller referred to George by his street name.) "But you knows what? Bet'cha I sells mo' papers than you duz," he taunted. Getting no reaction, he continued. "Wanna know why? Cuz I can out run yo' nine outt'a ten times, and you knows it."

George smiled, "Yeller, you must be dreaming, that's what."

"I Am not!" Yeller protested.

"Look, Yeller, I can spot you a three step lead and still whup you anytime."

"Oh, yeah, we'll see."

The two loved kidding, never tired of trying to top the other's humor or antics. Like siblings, their time together over the months had given them a deep understanding of the other. Now they mirrored moods and thoughts as twins often did.

The unforgiving noon heat, dust, and smells finally got to Yeller. "Man, I'm hot and tired. I'm sick of this no action shit!"

His partner had no chance to comment, "Tweet! Tweet!" It was the sound the boys had been waiting for. The sharp whistle came from the tall, well dressed white man standing next to a shiny carriage some fifty yards away. A doll-like lady sat prim and proper on the carriage seat, staring straight ahead.

In one quick motion, the boys snatched off their caps and ran as if shot from a cannon toward the elegantly dressed man. Briefly, they matched strides, then, Yeller pulled away. As he did, he yelled, "Watch out forty, let fifty by!"

Yeller reached the man first, and made a graceful, dusty, bare footed slide in front of him. Outrun, George hung back a few paces. With a bow, and an exaggerated sweeping motion of his arm, he offered the paper to the elegant gentleman.

Instead of accepting the paper, the man turned his gaze to the doll-like lady whose bright red hair hung in shiny curls, framing a face with flawless ivory skin. She held a frilly pink, parasol in her dainty fingers to shield her fair skin from the sun's glare.

A smirk crossed the man's face as he pulled a shiny coin from his vest pocket; positioning it between his thumb and index finger...he flipped it into the air. The coin hit the hard packed ground, bounced, then rolled between the two boys, stopping closest to George.

By flipping the coin, the man had violated the unwritten rules of the street. The coin should have been given to the winning runner. However, if one's motive was to impress or, to instigate a 'show' despite a clear winner of the foot race, flipping a coin was one way to get it.

Expecting a good performance from the boys, the man climbed back into the carriage and settled alongside his lady. He licked his lips, as a look of anticipation spread over his face.

Because the foot race was such an integral part of selling newspapers, it was rare to see a solitary newsboy on the streets. The paper boys had learned that white men wanted to be entertained and loved to watch them compete. So, they found that by working in pairs, they could sell more papers than as individuals.

George and Yeller were experienced and knew what was expected of them as they both dove for the coin. However, they no longer fought like two dogs over a bone. Rather, they alternated winning when a coin was flipped. The foot race was real, as it was a competition both boys enjoyed since they were of equal speed.

Because Yeller won, it was up to his partner to put on the expected 'show.' To that end, George screamed in pain when he hit the ground. Then, he began howling like a dog trying to wake the man on the moon. He grabbed his hand, and began writhing on the ground as if it was seriously injured.

Yeller seized the moment, scooped up the coin, and jumped to his feet, then held it high in mock triumph, displaying a grin so huge, it showed most of his pearly whites.

As he walked towards the obviously disappointed man, he quickly changed his demeanor. His face became solemn, and once again he offered the newspaper to the gentleman. However, the man was so upset and disappointed by the turn of events, he refused to look at Yeller.

George, was fully aware of the effect his continuous moaning and groaning was having on his partner, He knew his friend was fighting hard to keep a straight face as he walked toward this pissed off white man.

A gentleman of his status was accustomed to having his way, and getting what he wanted, when he wanted it. He was not used to having his wishes denied by anyone, and certainly not by someone as lowly as this colored paper boy. He was tempted to take out his buggy whip and snap it around the neck of this street urchin, just to teach him a lesson. But, he didn't.

The man's face turned hard, his smirk changing into a look of contempt. Allowing the offered paper to fall between his legs, he flicked his wrists, the reins 'popped,' and the horse broke into a fast trot. The crack of the whip was done so quickly, Yeller had to jump back to avoid being run over by the carriage wheel as it lurched forward. The sudden motion caused the lady's head to bob backward violently, as if it was attached to a spring. Her big, round, blue eyes never blinked. They continued staring straight ahead, and her face remained expressionless, seemingly oblivious to all that had just happened in front of her.

The boys stood shoulder to shoulder as they watched the carriage bounce down the street. Piggy and Yeller wore stone faces as it disappeared, swallowed by a maze of other wagons, horses, carts and people.

Slowly, they turned to face each other, standing almost nose to nose, their eyes boring deeply into the other set of eyes. Now, they waited, and waited, still staring wide eyed into the other boy's eyes; trying to see who would be the first to give in to what they perceived to be a hilarious situation. Finally, Yeller couldn't contain himself any longer. He dropped to his knees, doubled over, and let out an ear splitting howl. In a few more moments, George bent over, and screamed hysterically, too. Finally, they both gulped for air, as their eyes filled with tears of joy.

"Did you see his face?" Yeller asked.

"Yeah man, I saw." His companion answered between deep breaths.

"He was sooooo maaaaad…oooooh weeeee, he wuz mad!" Yeller exulted.

"He didn't get what he wanted for his lady fair, did he?" George added gleefully.

They slapped and punched each other in sheer delight. They had won an important victory; they felt they had outwitted the white man.

The afternoon sun dropped, the heat lessened, and as if by magic, their sales picked up. In a short while, they were down to only a few unsold papers each. Hot and tired, George offered up an idea, "Hey, we've had a good day; we don't have that many papers left, so let's go to the river and take a swim. Then we can do our stuff at the dance competition tonight…we can make more money there, and get rid of the papers, too."

"Sounds good to me man…you right, we can get rid of de few papers while we is dar." Yeller agreed.

The street competitions, held every Friday and Saturday night, were a black custom and lots of fun. Individuals, and street gangs performed against each other. It was a chance to show off, make some money, and earn "bragg'n" rights as to who was the best dancer, singer, or, singing group in town. By listening to the crowd's cheers, and judging the size of tips when the hats were passed, the night's winner was easily determined. The boys would dance to the plunking of a banjo, or the wailing of a harmonica, and sometimes to the 'thunk', 'thunk,' of a jew's harp. On a good night all three instruments, or more, would be present.

Then, the performers could really do their stuff. George and Yeller danced the 'Buck and Wing' and were freely acknowledged by their peers to be the best duo in town.

Their audience was a raucous bunch, made up of black and white men, full of moonshine looking for a good time, ready and willing to whoop and holler for the entertainers. After each performance, the boys passed a hat around the circle of men for tips; often making as much by dancing a few minutes, as they did by selling their papers all day.

Invigorated by their swim in the Chattanooga River, Yeller asked, "Piggy, what say we go over to Elm Street fo' a while. Maybe we gets rid of dez few papers be fo' the dance' begins. Den we ken jes'worry bout putt'n on a good show. What'cha thinks of dat my man?"

"OK, Yeller, let's do that. After all man, yo' ass is blacker than mine, and dat means you is de boss!" George kidded, as he slapped Yeller's back and they laughed at their own humor. George's mother had been a house slave as a little girl. Growing up in the 'big' house on a plantation in Virginia, she heard, and spoke proper English. Now, she demanded nothing less from her son. George, however, would alternate between proper speech and 'street' talk. When around his peers, he used coarse words, but not at home, not in front of his mother. He knew she would yank his ears for such an infraction.

Their ability to work and dance together grew from their initial meeting. By chance, they both showed up to join the 'Snakes,' a local street gang. They went through the gang's initiation of stealing from one of the local merchants, and enduring a bloodletting ritual together. Consequently, they were inducted the same day.

George's father, a freedman, had been shot and killed by a court guard while serving on an all white jury. This tragic event linked George and his companion because Yeller also had lost his father because of a tragedy. His father had worked in the local iron foundry. One day a fellow worker's cracked ladle of molten iron spilled into his shoe, burning his foot off. He was forced to join the ranks of unemployables, and soon became an alcoholic.
A few years later, he went missing from his home. Shortly afterwards, his body was found floating in the Chattanooga River.

As their friendship developed, their ability to confide in each other grew. Both boys shared their deep love for their mothers and the hurt they felt at seeing them struggle to make ends meet. After Yeller discussed his desire to have a paper-selling partner with George, they eventually joined ranks. It didn't take them long to become seasoned paper boys and to be secure with each other as business and dance partners.

CHAPTER 3

The Red Door

As they sauntered toward Elm Street, Yeller draped his arm over George's shoulder, and began speaking softly. "De one thing I knows is, if you's black, get back! If you's brown, you can stick around. If you's yeller… you's mellow. If you's white… you's right!"

Piggy and Yeller laughed as if it was the first time they had heard this self-deprecating humor. "Yeller, you're something else, you really is." George said with a wink.

The boys walked in step, kidding, poking and jostling each other as they journeyed towards Elm Street. They were lost in their own world, oblivious to everything around them. Neither boy was aware of the short, fat, red-faced man, following closely behind them.

"Boys! Boys!" The man called out. "Hold up there, I want to talk to y'all."

The two turned to see if the man was calling them. They felt he was and stopped to let him approach them.

"Now, I can see by them papers you got there you two is try'n to make some money which is fine and dandy, But I'm gonn'a give you all a chance to make some real money. What do you think of that?" He asked, knowing no colored boy would dare refuse a white man's request. Even so, he pressed for a verbal confirmation.

"Yas suh, we would like to make some money… what all duz we gott'a do, suh?" Yeller responded deferentially.

"You all jes' follow me, I'll explain it to ya later." The fat man turned and led the boys down several side streets, finally into an alley which ran parallel to a major and bustling front street.

George and Yeller side-eyed each other as they trudged behind the man. Both felt uneasy, and their steps slowed, reflecting the foreboding settling into their guts.

Sensing their reluctance to follow, the man stopped and turned, "Come on now, we jes' about there." He pointed in the general direction of three doors located a bit further up the alley way. At the same time, he let fly a squirt of tobacco juice with such force, it kicked up a puff of dust.

The fat man slowed, allowing them to catch up as the approached the doors. He stopped in front of the paint-chipped, dull red door, and pulled it open. He stepped aside, then, motioned for them to enter, leaving just enough room for them to squeeze past his big belly.

The boy's eyes opened wide with apprehension as they entered what seemed to be a black hole. The windowless place reeked of stale booze and tobacco smoke. The smells filled their nostrils, making them feel sick, and light headed. At the same time, a wave of fear swept over them. Instinct told them to escape, to turn and run out the door. But, it was too late. The fat man's body filled the open space around the closing door.

The sound of a sliding bolt sent chills through their bodies. They knew only bad things could happen now, and they were trapped.

"Man, we should'a run when we had a chance, Piggy." Yeller whispered.

"Yeah, we should'a." George answered in a quavering voice.

Without a word, the fat man grabbed their arms in a vise-like grip and pulled them towards a dimly lit, hanging kerosene lantern. As they were marched forward, their legs went numb, and their stomachs turned into knots.

As they were led down the center isle toward the hanging lantern, their eyes slowly became adjusted to the darkness. They realized the undefined shapes on either side of them were the forms of men sitting in chairs and benches. As their eyes adjusted further to the darkness, they realized there were still more forms along the sides of both walls. There must be a hundred people in this black hole.

The smoke-filled room was deathly quiet, and the oppressive heat and stale smells caused George to gag. Both boys found it hard to breathe, and their breaths came in short, fast, gasps. An occasional cough floated through the darkness, breaking the eerie silence. The boys could hear their own rapidly pounding hearts beating against their heaving chests.

Once the fat man had them under the lantern, he released his grip. Out of the darkness another man appeared and turned the lantern up. As the circle of light brightened and spread out, the sounds of the assembled men became louder. "All right, let's get the damn show go'n." A voice demanded. Another yelled, "Ya ho! We gonn'a have us a good ol' time today…ain't we boys?"

The crowd's collective voice grew louder and more heated, and the air became a jumble of yells and curses. Nothing made sense to the boys as the crowd worked itself into a thunderous frenzy.

"Ya' all take off your shirts, NOW!" The fat man barked. The boys searched each other's eyes for answers to their rising panic. Their minds were numb; they couldn't grasp what was happening. They stood frozen, unable to think. From the darkness, hands reached out and ripped their shirts off, revealing glistening sweaty bodies. "Now, all you gott'a do is put up a good fight an' you all gonn'a earn yo' selves some real good money, mo' money than ya earns from sell'n them damn papers." The fat man snarled. George's eyes focused on the papers he dropped as he stepped under the lantern's light. Yeller was so confused, he still held his few unsold papers under his arm.

The fat man's voice thundered, "All right damn it, put yo fists up…an' get to it!"

"But mista,' he be ma friend, I don't want to…" Yeller didn't finish. The belt was a blur, and landed squarely on his back. The blow sounded like the report of a small caliber gun. His papers dropped to the floor, "WHACK!" A belt found George's back, then Yeller's. "WHACK!" "WHACK!"

The boys circled each other. Finally a punch was thrown, then another, and another, until the boys tore into each other like the cornered alley cats they'd been forced to become. They fought out of fear, pain, humiliation and terror, afraid not to fight…ashamed that they were.

Their fists made hard smacking sounds. They grunted and screamed from pain as their fists found the nose, jaw, eyes, chest and stomach of the other. At times, they found themselves on the floor from the others punches as of others. they fought with tear-blurred vision.

Blood, spit and snot oozed from their noses and mouths. Lumps formed on their faces as their knuckles found each other's flesh.

After each knock-down, it became harder and harder for the boys to rise. To insure the match would continue, hands reached in to assist the fallen warrior.

They had fought for what seemed an eternity. Finally, Yeller collapsed in a heap. Fearing their fun was over, a man appeared with a bucket of water and poured it over the fallen boy. However, pain, and exhaustion had consumed his entire being. No amount of water would make him recover. Their fun was over for the night.

"To'l ya' the light skinned buck would whup his black ass." A voice taunted no one in particular.

The door from the bar opened, and a tall man appeared, outlined by the setting sun's light that flooded the barroom behind him. "Come on, boys, drinks are on the house," he yelled. Chairs and benches groaned against the wooden floor, as the men stood, pushing their seats back. The shuffling and stomping noises faded as the closing door swallowed them.

The battered and bloodied black boys were of little consequence to these men before they were forced to degrade themselves for their pleasure. Now that they could no longer perform, they were of even less worth. They were nonentities. The boys, didn't count for anything because in the minds of these men, they weren't human beings at all. They were beasts to do their bidding.

George dropped to his knees to move his friend to a sitting position, "Yeller! Yeller!" He pleaded, as he attempted to pull him up, but couldn't; he didn't have the strength. "Come on, Yeller, we gott'a get outt'a here, man." But his friend didn't respond. "Ah shit, I'm tell'n you, we gott'a get outt'a here." He pleaded to the motionless heap.

The fat man appeared from another door and without a word reached under the fallen boy's arms and dragged him to the back. In one motion he unbolted, then, kicked the door open and to pulled the limp form to the alley and away from the red door, then propped him again a wall. George, stumbling like a drunk, followed them into the alley. The fat man ignored him as they passed, and he went back inside.

Kneeling beside Yeller, George shook his friend's shoulder gently, desperately trying to get a response. His heart jumped as the red door opened and the fat man reappeared.

He looked at the pair with dead eyes, then tossed their rolled up shirts towards them. Without a word, he turned, went back in, and closed the door.

George felt relief when he heard the bolt slide to the locked position. He knew that signaled the last he would see of him, and they were free to go, if only he could get his friend to wake up.

"Please, please, man, open your eyes so we can got out of here!" But, there was no response, Yeller was out cold. Not knowing what else to do, George sat next to his friend and began rubbing his hands gently.

Finally, a swollen eye opened. "Oh, man, duz ma head hurt." Yeller mumbled in a barely audible voice.

"Yeller, you gott'a get up, we gott'a get out of here! Come on man, try to get up!" George pleaded, his voice reflecting the fear and panic he still felt.

"All right, all right, I'll try." He whispered. With his friend's help, the battered boy struggled to his feet.

Slipping his arm around his waist, George led him toward the street. "Wait. Can you stand for a second, Yeller?"

"Yeah, I think so…why?"

George guided him to a wall, then released his support. "Here, lean against the building." He hurried as best he could and retrieved the rolled up shirts, then hobbled back to his friend.

The two stumbled out of the alley to a nearby overgrown vacant lot. They pushed through the bushes and low growing trees. A convey of quails exploded from under their feet. “Shit! That scared me.” George swore as the birds flew up, then disappeared at the far end of the field. They continued on until they found a small clearing.

“Here, let’s sit down for a while.” George suggested.

“Ouch! Damn bite’n bugs.” Yeller complained about the attacking mosquitoes.

“Here, put on your shirt, or what’s left of it,” George suggested as he began unrolling the shirts. Two fifty cent pieces fell to the ground. The boys looked at each other, tears welling up in their eyes. “Those damn bastards.” George swore as he kicked the coins away, “I don’t want their fuck’n money.”

“They should all burn in hell.” Yeller mumbled. Then added, “I’d like to shove them coins up that fat son of a bitch one at a time!” He scooped up both coins and flung them into the bushes.

The boys sat in silence, neither one able to find words to express the anger, hurt, humiliation and confusion they felt.

After sitting quietly for a while, George broke the silence that had enveloped them. “I’d better get home, otherwise my mama’s gonn’a be worry’n about me.” He rose slowly to stand on wobbly legs.

“Yeah, me too.” Yeller agreed as he struggled to his feet with George’s help.

As they walked uncertainly to the street, pain from the bruises and throbbing lumps that covered their faces and bodies reappeared with a vengeance. Dried blood had formed irregular splotches on their faces and bodies. At the corner, without a word of goodbye, they separated, each going in the opposite direction.

George entered quietly through his home's front door. He dreaded facing his mother, knowing she would want to know what happened. He also knew he would not be able to bring himself to tell her the truth. What happened to him was too degrading to repeat to any one, let alone his mother. He searched his mind for an explanation. But his brain had gone blank, and he didn't know what he'd say when she asked him about his sorry appearance. "Lord, Lord, what am I going to do?" He whispered, as he continued his search for her.

Glancing around, he noticed a light coming from the kitchen area, and reluctantly walked toward it. The battered boy stopped in the dark shadows by the open door. To buy time, he remained quiet and watched his mom reading her Bible aloud, by the flickering lamp light at the kitchen table.

She heard his footsteps and glanced up to greet him, "Hello, George Isaac." Mary said casually.

"Hello, mother." He answered in a raspy whisper. The kitchen's darkness temporarily masked his bruises.

His mother's eyes instinctively returned to the passage she was reading. "Give therefore thy servant an understanding heart to judge thy people, that I may discern between good and bad.' 1 Kings 3;9.

It took a moment for the image of her son to register because of the dim light. But, she realized there was something terribly wrong with her boy's face. And she noticed his voice didn't sound right. A sense of fear swept over her as she narrowed her eyes and looked again.

"Son,..come here, come closer." She stood in order to see him better. "My God, son, what on earth happened to you?" Mary's knees became weak,. Her body sagged against the table as the light made his face more visible. Shaken to the core, she pleaded, "Oh, son, come here, come here." She pulled him close, and gently rocked him back and forth, back and forth. Her hands found his face as her fingers gently stroked his cheeks, "Now, son, tell me exactly what happened to you."

Confronted with the reality of the demeaning event, a story unfolded in his mind, "Mama, some white boys from the school across the street jumped me… It ain't, I mean, it's nothing, really mama, I'll be fine in no time." He tried hard to sound convincing.

"Were you walking on the other side of the street?" Not waiting for an answer she continued, "I've told you not to walk on that side of the street. Those white boys can be real devils." Her admonition was justified, since, she had witnessed the University of Chattanooga students taunting, name calling, and, even throwing rocks at colored youth who dared walk on 'their' side of the street. "Now this," she thought.

His mother, was a fighter. She wasn't about to let this go unreported, she would definitely talk to someone in authority at the school. Her dead husband hd been a fighter, too, and she wasn't about to let those boys get away with this! "George, we'll go to the school and find out who's in charge and make them aware of what some of their students have done. They should be punished in some way," she said, full of resolve.

"No, mama, let it be. I ain't, I mean, I'm not really hurt bad, really, I'll be good as new in a few days, you'll see. Promise me mama, you'll just let it be." He pleaded.

Mary was enraged, "Son, I just don't believe in letting people get away with things that are just out and out wrong. In this world, you have to stand up for what you… you…you…" Mary's voice trailed off. She could hear her murdered husband saying those very same words to her when she argued with him not to serve on that all white jury many years ago.

She walked to the sink, wet a towel, and had her son sit, then began cleaning the dried blood from his face. "Uhh, you know, son, uhh, you might be right. We might just let this thing be." Her voice was a whisper.

George breathed a sigh of relief when he heard her decision. However, Mary felt revulsion in her gut. She hated the counsel she had just given her son. But while she despised her own words, more than anything, she wanted her son to survive the South and its awful ways. "Now, there is one other thing more, George." She continued.

"Yes ma'am?"

"You must promise me you will always walk on this side of the street. Is that clear? Will you do that for me, son?"

"Yes ma'am. I promise, I will." He said, as a sense of relief swept over him at her decision. Now there was no chance he would be caught in his lie.

George lay around the house for a full week, leaving only to escort his mother when she left in the morning darkness for her job at the Farrs. A few lumps and bruises wouldn't stop him from performing that duty, even though every muscle in his body hurt.

With the week's rest, his strength returned, and his body began healing. After escorting his mother to work, he decided he would poke around town, rather than return home as he had been doing over the past week. With no destination in mind, he headed downtown to check things out.

"Hey, Piggy, what's go'n on man?" The lanky youth asked. "I ain't seen you, or Yeller around fo' a long time." The voice belonged to his gang leader, Snake.

"Hey, Snake, I'm flopp'n, but not fly'n, hopp'n but not high." He retorted.

Snake peered at him closely, "Man, you looks bad, wha's up with yo' face, it don't look right."

"Oh, some white boys jumped me that's all. I'm better now, I'm almost healed," He fibbed convincingly.

"Boy, by the looks of yo' face they sho put a whup'n on you." Snake was referring to the still visible deep bruises on his face. "If you want, we takes care of dem on a dark night, man, just show us where they hangs out. We may gets the wrong ones, but who gives a shit… long as dey's white!" Snake laughed at the thought of dispensing his brand of justice to some white boys on a dark street.

"Nahh, it's been taken care of. They, they're from the school, across from where I live. My mama, she knows the man who runs the place. She talked to him. He told her he would take care of them, probably send them home, you know, so, that's, that. It's all taken care of, man."

"If you say so man. Me, I'd rather kick. But, ok, that's it, huh?" Snake's voice reflected his disappointment. He would have rather had a chance to jump some white boys on a dark night.

"Yeah, man, that's it." Piggy concluded. Very anxious to change the subject, and talk about other things, or, just walk away.

“So, look Piggy, I gott’a go, but, the Snakes, we gonn’a be get’n together Friday, at the shack. See you then.”

They gave each other a ritualistic hand shake, and then went separate ways. George walked a few blocks, then, turned the corner. When he did, he spotted a familiar, solitary figure. It was Yeller; waving a paper high in the air. George hadn’t allowed himself the time to think ahead, to sort out what his feelings might be when he did come face to face with his old partner.

“Get yo’ paper, read about the break in!” Yeller hollered.

George watched his former partner for a few minutes from behind a large tree. Suddenly he felt sick. The emotion of the degrading event overcame him; tears blurred his vision, vomit filled his mouth and spewed to the sidewalk. He turned and ran back home.

It took time for him to recover from the trauma of seeing Yeller, but, after a few days, he became bored staying in the house. He felt like a fish out of water. Going to his closet, he selected a pair of pants, a shirt and put on his shoes. Screwing up his courage, he decided to poke around again. Without any destination in mind he left the house. This time he’d walk in the opposite direction. He didn’t want a recurrence of the event that had happened a few days past. His mind was fuzzy. He wanted to get back to selling papers, but he’d need a partner, and that presented a problem. A walk might help him clear his head. George knew in his heart his friendship with Yeller was dead. He couldn’t face his former buddy, and he realized Yeller felt the same way when he remembered the day he glanced up the street and saw his buddy off in the distance, hurriedly walking away.

As he went down one street, then up another, the angry words his mother would use if she saw idle colored boys on the corner came to him. "George Isaac, idle hands and minds are the devil's workshop. Now you remember that! Those boys are going to end up on the chain gang, mark my words." He would dutifully reply, "Yes, ma'am"

But he knew his mind was anything but empty. In fact, too much was going on inside his. Thoughts of his murdered father, his relationship with Gloria Brown, the end of this friendship with Yeller and the shameful thing that had happened to the two of them, all were pressing in on him. He was grateful Gloria was away for a few weeks and didn't see him all battered and bruised. Thankful he didn't have to lie to her.

For some reason, he couldn't stop thinking about his father. Thoughts of him kept pressing in on his brain. How he wished he could have known him. Wouldn't it be great to be able to ask him questions? He couldn't help but wonder what advice he would offer. What would he have said if he told him about Yeller and himself? Would he be able to discuss Gloria, if he was alive? He shook his head at that thought. Maybe not that, but he would have been able to discuss a lot of other things. He was certain of that.

He knew his father had been murdered, yet he had never allowed himself to think about it. He had never really allowed himself to deal with the reality of the situation head on. He'd never taken the time to try and fully comprehend the actual occurrence, to put himself in his father's place on that awful day.

After his murder, his mother had not been able to explain what had happened to her little son. Over the years she had merely said, 'Your father died and has gone on to heaven.' She couldn't bring herself to try and explain the brutal way he had been killed to such a small child until she felt he was old enough to absorb and handle the reaility of his death. When he became twelve, she revealed in greater detail the actual event. When she explained he had been shot by a court guard, the brutality of it was more than his young mind could fully digest. Now that he was older, he was ready to absorb, the horror of the actual event.

George conjured up the scene in his mind; he pictured his father in what were his last moments. How he wished he could have known what he'd said to those white folks when he held out for an acquittal. Did he have any idea what could happen to him, bucking all of those folks? He concluded, 'He had to know it was dangerous,' confirming his belief that his father was really a brave man.

"God, I wish I could remember him," he cried out in anguish and frustration. But try as he might, he couldn't create a flesh and blood image of him in his mind. All he could see was a blurred image, only the shadow of a man he had conjured up in his own mind. He tried to imagine his voice, but couldn't bring it to life. Was it deep? Did he speak rapidly as his mother did? And his laugh…did he laugh a lot? Was he short or tall? Try as he might, he had to accept that there was not one single specific detail he could remember about him. George felt cheated and sad.

The episode with Yeller had scarred his soul, he saw and felt differently about things now. If he saw a white man approaching, he'd cross the street. Twice he took off running when he spotted a group of white University of Chattanooga students coming toward him near his home on Baldwin Street. He wondered if they were capable of acting out what he had falsely accused them of doing? Thoughts of what was real, and what could become real confused him. He realized he was experiencing feelings of unfounded fears, and he didn't like it. And, try as he might, he couldn't shake them. In addition he felt shame, and he felt he wore it on his chest like a badge for all to see. The humiliation of Yeller and himself fighting like animals was burned into his soul.

CHAPTER 4

Chopick's Mule

He had no idea how long he had been walking, nor did he know where he was. Actually he had walked for over an hour and found himself standing before a big window, in front of a large building. The brick structure sat nestled among a grove of Red Maples. A large sign centered on its front read, Chopick's Ice Cream Factory. Local folks associated the name with two things: the best ice cream in town, and the Jewish owner, Saul Chopick.

The business thrived on the bulk deliveries made to the local eating establishments, stores and hotels. However, to keep his product before the general public, Chopick had an ice cream push cart stationed at the top of the busy John Street hill, one of the steepest hills in town. As George began to notice his surroundings, he saw a hand written poster in the front window, HARD WORKING BOY WANTED. He was so preoccupied with his own thoughts, the words on the sign didn't register. Slowly, their meaning began to penetrate his confused mind: Hard Working Boy Wanted. Finally he realized this could be what he was looking for. As he stared at the words, he became aware there was a face on the other side of the window peering out at him. A little man was mouthing something to him, and making hand gestures. But, he couldn't hear or understand what he was trying to convey. George pressed his face to the glass, trying to make sense of what the man was attempting to communicate to him. Finally, he understood what the man was trying to convey.

He was gesturing to the nearby door, and mouthing, 'come in, come in.' The man's antics, and the total situation struck George funny. When he entered the store, he was still wearing a big smile.

"Welcome, my boy. Come, come in." The man said, with a grin equally as broad as his. "I see you can read, otherwise you wouldn't be looking at the sign, furthermore, you look strong as an ox, so, give me one good reason why you shouldn't work for me? Wait, wait, before you answer tell me one thing, can you count? My guess is, if you can read, you can count! Am I right, or am I wrong?"

George opened his mouth to answer, but before he could, the man continued his monologue.

"And how old might you be? Tell me. No, I'll take a guess. You must be fifteen. No? Maybe sixteen. Am I right? I bet I'm right. Tell me."

"Actually, I'm…"

George was no match for the fast talking man who continued. "Oh, yes, I'm Mr. Saul Chopick, and who is it I'm having the pleasure of conversing with?"

George was totally flustered. He had never met anyone like this, a man who asked question, then answered them himself. The short bald man had totally confused George, but despite that, he found him likable, and nonthreatening. In fact, George noticed there was a mischievous sparkle in the man's eyes. A kind of pleasantness radiated from him. "My name is George Isaac Read, and I'm thirteen years old, sir."

"Ah, you answered some of my questions, but not the most important one… can you count?"

"Oh, yes sir, I can count just fine, sir."

"Well, here's the story. That is, if you're smart and you decide to work for me, and I can tell already that you're a smart lad… and that's why you'll decide to work for me. Now, here's the deal. This is how it would work. I want you to be my new ice cream push cart boy. I'll give you $2.00 in change. If you lose it or can't account for it, I dock you whatever is missing out of your pay… understand?"

George nodded. Although he wasn't quite sure he did understand what the man had just said.

"First, show me that you can make change." Saul reached in his pocket and pulled out a handful of change and started counting. "Here's a dollar in coins, suppose I buy two five cent ice creams, how much change do you give me back?"

Without any hesitation, George counted out ninety cents.

"Good, you did that real good. Now, let's get started. I've got some things to show you." Saul turned quickly, leading George to a back room where an ice cream cart was kept. He showed him how to load and pack ice around the ice cream containers, and how to scoop the various flavors, allowing him to taste each one. "So, do we have a deal? You want the job? I'm sure you do, am I right?" Saul added quickly.

"Oh, yes sir, I do." George replied with a big smile.

"Good, so let's get started. I'll show you where I want you to go." With that, Saul opened a large door "Follow me with the cart." He called as he waited for George on the opposite side of the door he had pushed open. Once George was outside, he closed it, and led the way up the hill.

George followed, pushing the heavy cart, managing to keep up with the little man's brisk pace for a while. However, as they reached the mid point of the steep hill, George stopped to catch his breath. Saul called back, "You'll get the hang of it in no time, it'll get easier every day, you'll see." With those words of encouragement, he continued on, leaving George far behind. The little man charged up the steep incline like a soldier going to war, ready to do battle with the enemy awaiting him at the top.
George gained his second wind, then, began the arduous climb to the top. When, some minutes later he reached Mr. Chopick, he was doubled over to catch his breath and as sweat poured from his face.

Saul made no comment when he stepped from beneath the shade of a large maple tree to show his new hire the exact spot he wanted him to set up. The large umbrella attached to the cart, provided some relief for George from the sun. He had barely managed to get his breath when people came to the cart, requesting ice cream.

Saul stood to the side and observed George scoop ice cream, make change, and interact with the customers. After an hour, he came to his new worker. "Well, my boy, you seem to have everything under control…any questions? No? Then I'll see you tonight." The man turned and hurried back down the hill before George could reply.

At home that night, George fairly burst with pride when he reported his good fortune about finding a new job to his mother. She was equally pleased, happy and proud of her son's accomplishment. Mary rewarded him with a fried chicken, greens and biscuits dinner. "I'll work six days a week for the rest of the summer. And, I'll make as much money or more than I did selling papers." He boasted proudly.

However, the summer turned out hotter than usual, and contrary to what Mr. Chopick had said, the cart didn't get lighter. The thing got heavier as the days wore on. On the hotter, more humid days, he had to make more and more stops to push the weighty cart to the top of the hill. It became a common sight to see him bent over, gulping mouthfuls of air, trying to regain his wind and strength before making another attempt to reach the top.

The sight of George struggling up the hill became such a common sight, people began betting on the number of stops he would have to make before he reached the top. Black folks smiled when the conversation turned to the new colored boy pushing the heavy cart up the steep hill. In fact, they nicknamed him, 'Chopick's mule.'

He worked the cart well into the fall season. Mr. Chopick changed his work schedule to a few hours weekday afternoons, and all day on Saturdays to accommodate his return to school. George had been a diligent worker, not missing a single day once he was hired. He was making more money than when he sold papers. In addition to his pay, there were rich customers who tipped him generously. And, he liked the fact that he didn't have to scramble for it the way he did as a newspaper boy.

One day, as George cleaned the cart after a long Saturday of selling, Mr. Chopick called him in his office. "Well, my boy, you didn't disappoint me. You are indeed a fine worker. However, the season is over, and I won't be needing you until next May. Will I see you then? I know you are a smart boy, so, I think your answer will be yes, am I right?"

"Oh, yes sir. I'll be back, yes sir, I surely will be."

Mr. Chopick gave him an extra dollar, a pat on the shoulder, and then dismissed him with his usual barrage of rhetorical questions. "I'll see you in May? Am I right? You don't have to answer, I know I will, because you're a smart boy."

His parting words made George smile as he left the factory. Despite expecting the bad news, he felt somewhat sad, too. The job had indeed been hard, but it was more dignified than selling papers. He enjoyed meeting the people who would engage him in conversation. Yes. this was a far better job, and he liked the man he worked for; Mr. Chopick was a nice person.

George continued giving money to his mother, in fact, handing her the bulk of what he earned and keeping only a small portion for himself. One day, he decided to set aside a little extra for himself, and began putting that money into a jar. He hid the container under the porch for safe-keeping, and each week added to it. He wasn't sure why he decided to do this, or what he was setting the 'extra' money aside for, but he did so religiously.

It was evening. Mary and George were sitting in the kitchen having a quiet evening, and a delicious dinner of spare ribs, greens and corn bread. "Son, I have something to ask you." She began.

"Yes ma'am?"

"I've been intending to ask you this for some time now." His mother's face seemed more serious than usual. Her eyes were steady and bore into his.

Her voice sounded extra serious. Lord, she's found out about Gloria. Beads of sweat formed on his brow. Screwing up his nerve he asked in a small voice, "What was it you had been intending to ask, Mother?"

"I don't quite know how to say this. It's something I'm not sure of."

This is it! She definitely knows about Gloria. That's why she's having a hard time bringing the subject up. Despite not wanting to pursue it, he did manage to ask, "Ah, what is it you're not sure of Mother?" He held his breath until she spoke.

"Well, son, I heard Mrs. Farr talking to young William. She was saying he would soon be getting ready to go to a place called college."

George's body relaxed for the first time since she initiated the conversation. It wasn't about Gloria. It was about William Farr. Sounding more assured, he asked "What exactly was it you wanted to tell me, Mother?"

"Well, she said it was something he had to do, that is, he must go to this place called college. Now, I think if it's something good enough for young William, I want you to promise me you will go there, too."

"I don't know what a college is, Mother."

"And, I don't know what it is either, son. But I do want you to promise me you'll find out what it is, and where it is and you'll go there, too. Will you do that son? Will you promise me that?"

He was so relieved it wasn't about Gloria, had she asked him to give her the moon, he'd have promised to get it for her. "Yes Mother, I promise. I'll find out what it is, and I'll go to this place called college."

George continued to see Gloria two or three times a week, and missed school on those days. After he left her, he had time to kill. On those days, he would roam the streets looking for nothing in particular, but open to anything. Because he had been a paper boy for so long, he and Yeller where known by many, many people. Among those who had seen them was a gang leader named Snake, the leader of a bunch of young toughs called the Snakes.

They were known as a rough tough bunch with mean tempers, and nasty mouths.

They lived by their wits. Lying, cheating and stealing was all they knew and was the way they got by. Anyone who worked was a damn fool in their eyes. They invited George and Yeller to join them, not because they liked either of them, but because they knew that Yeller worked, and had money in his pockets. George, they felt, would be easy pickings, too. He was younger than most of them, spoke differently and came from a family with money. The gang considered him an outsider to be taken advantage of whenever possible, at least until he proved himself to them.

Mary knew nothing about her son's involvement with those boys. Had she known, she would have taken a cane to him. "No good, foul mouthed ruffians!" would have been her assessment of their kind. George worried every day that she would find out about his association and activities with them. Rightly so, since he knew she had other 'eyes' in the community through her church brothers and sisters. Should any one of them see him with that bunch of ruffians, them, word would quickly get back to her and he would be in a world of trouble.

The Snakes had several locations where they met. One was a remote corner of a field where they would shoot dice. Another location was an abandoned shack. It was used for drinking moon shine and sleeping the day away. A third spot was out in the woods, a place where they stashed stolen goods for personal use or sale.

This day George and Gloria had been together all morning. The sun streamed into her room as a gentle breezed flowed over her body. He leaned over to kiss her as she lay asleep. Slipping into his clothes, he closed her bedroom door quietly, and left the house in search of the gang. He pondered briefly which location to try first and chose the field as the most likely spot. For some reason, he had a vision of Snake on his knees, asking the Lord to bless his dice, *because baby needs a new pair of shoes.* He broke into a trot, and in a short while reached his destination. He smiled when their voices floated down to him from the far corner of the overgrown lot. His hunch was right. As he moved forward, he could see them, some standing, some on their knees.

They spotted him at the same time. "Hey Piggy, what's new man?" A voice called out.

"Noth'n, man. White folks still in the lead!" He replied with a laugh.

"You got that right, brother," Came the reply.

The boys slapped his hands and pounded back as he passed to find a spot between the ones who were kneeling in a circle on the ground. Shorty had the dice. "Come on, come on…seven!" He implored. The dice came up snake eyes. "Ah shit…man, I ain't got no luck today. An' when I do, it's all bad." He got up and sauntered away, shaking his head.

Bam scooped up the dice, "All right, am I covered? Anybody else, anybody else want to cover me? Come on suckers, put yo' money up. I feels hot, so watch out!" He boasted with a big grin. "How's about you, Piggy, you wants a piece of me?" The boy taunted.

"Nah, I'll wait my turn. Then you can cover me, how about that?" There were scattered snickers at this retort. There was a time when he would have been easily bullied or talked into doing it. Now, he gave back as good as he received.

George finally got the dice after Bam crapped out. He rolled several sevens and elevens on this first rolls. He was hot and winning.

"Damn Piggy, what you got, loaded dice?" Bam challenged.

"No, I don't need to cheat like you, Bam. I win fair and square!" George shot back.

"You watch yo' mouth boy!"

"Why, you gonn'a make me?" George snapped.

"You right, I'll make you!"

In a flash, Bam was on George. He put an arm lock around his throat. George tried to pull it away, but couldn't. Soon he began gagging. He couldn't breathe. The two boys rolled around and around in the dirt, their legs flailing. George was feeling faint from lack of air. Finally his hand came up with a fist full of dirt. He flung it backwards into Bam's eyes. Some went into his mouth and some up his nose. The boy howled in pain as he jumped up, trying desperately to get his breath and the sand out of his eyes and nose.

"Hot damn, that was all right, Piggy." Snake said, admiring the defensive move Piggy had made on Bam.

"Damn it! Somebody gets me some water befo' I goes blind." The hapless boy pleaded as he stumbled around, tripping and falling over the legs of the boys sitting on the ground.

"Fill this here in yonder stream!" Snake ordered, as he gave one of his members an empty whiskey bottle. When he returned, Snake had Bam lie down as he slowly poured the water into his eyes. After a second bottle, the dirt was flushed out. Finally, the boy opened his eyes.

"Damn, that hurts. You fuck'n Pig you."

"You started it!" George snarled.

"Dat's right! Dat be's de end ob it. Yo' got's dat?" Snake ordered.

"Yeah, I hears you." He answered. But, under his breath muttered, "But I ain't gonn'a fo get it tho."

"I heard dat. Now shut yo trap!" Snake yelled.

The boys reassembled, forming the traditional circle. The dice were returned to George who continued his hot streak. After he completed his turn, and pulled in the winning pot, Snake, the biggest loser, jumped up, "It's too hot in dis damn field, let's go swim'n!"

"Yeah, let's go!" The others answered.

"Last one in is a toad's wart!" Snake challenged as he took off with his long legs. In a fast dash, he led the group to the nearby Chattanooga River.

As the boys approached their favorite secluded spot, they shed their few ragged clothes on the run. Most were buck naked by the time they reached the river's bank.

Without breaking stride, they dove into the seemingly slow-moving water. However, the river ran deep, with strong currents that could easily sweep an unsuspecting person away. To make matters worse, none of the boys swam well. Most played around in the shallows, happy just to cool off. Some ventured off by dislodging one of the numerous logs wedged against the shore. Jake, one of their members,had hung on to his log too long and was swept out to mid stream where the current was swift. He was never seen again. Later that day, the Snakes held (their version of) a memorial service in the shack to pay tribute to one of their lost members. They drank a bottle of moonshine, and slept the rest of the day away.

George and Snake were among the few that had mastered the art of staying afloat by 'doggy' paddling. They had ventured out further than any of the others when

Snake turned to his companion, "Hey Piggy, lets grab dat log an take it out to de middle, den, swim back. I bet ya' I can beat yo' black ass. Wat'cha say to dat?"

"That sounds good to me my man."

The two youths found a log. Together, they pushed and paddled it out to a deeper part of the river. On the count of three, they let go, and headed back to shore. Paddling furiously, they looked like two drowning animals as they splashed, coughed and fought their way back to the bank. Once their feet hit bottom, they scampered up the sharp incline and fell to the ground. Their dark bodies glistened from the dripping beads of water. Proud and exhilarated by their accomplishment, they lay side by side laughing and arguing as to who had won the race. "Piggy, how come, yo' boy Yeller don't be come'n around no mo'?"

"I ain't seen him in a dog's year." George answered evasively, "He just stopped be'n my paper partner and come'n around." George lied.

"If you duz see 'em, tell him to bring his black ass to the shack. He still be one ob us. He still be one ob de Snakes."

"I will, next time I see him."

In minutes they both fell into a deep sleep.

George began dreaming. He was running home from the Farr's after saying goodbye to his mother. It was raining harder than he could ever remember. Thunder claps boomed in his ears. Fear consumed him as lightning bolts hit all around him. He felt the rain pelt his face, hitting so hard, he thought he would go blind. His feet made squishing sounds as he splashed through puddle after puddle. Finally, he turned into his yard. Approaching the house, he took the steps two at a time. Pushing the front door open, he scrambled up the stairs. When he reached Gloria's door, he stood before it, frozen. in place. Water pooled around his feet. Despite his fears, he pushed the door open.

The room was bare. Even her bed was gone. The dresser had none of the familiar sweet smelling bottles. Even the wash stand pitcher and bowl were gone. The familiar lilac fragrance was missing. In its place, a stale musty odor assaulted his nostrils. He went to the closet. It was empty. Lord have mercy, she was gone! She had left without so much as a goodbye.

George bolted to an upright position, blinking, and rubbing his eyes as he looked around. Snake was only a few feet from him, his chest rising and falling in perfect rhythm. "Oh, man. It was just a dream, or was it?" He was totally confused. Finally, it came to him; he had been with her this morning. Remembering the pleasure they'd shared, an involuntary smile curled his lips. Now, he felt better.

He put on his shirt and pants, Snake was sleeping so peacefully, he decided not to bother him and headed home. Halfway there, he realized something was wrong as he absent-mindedly patted his pants. Then, it came to him; his pockets were full of money before he went to sleep. He jammed both his hands into his pockets to confirm his fears. They were empty! "Damn it! Shit! One of those bastards picked my pockets clean. I'll be a son of a bitch!" He yelled as he punched his fist into his open palm, again and again. "I'll find out who took my money. I swear I will." He had been looking forward to giving his mother some extra money.

During the next several weeks, he never mentioned his missing money to anyone in the gang. He knew the guys would laugh at his stupidity for leaving the money unguarded. It was dumb to leave it rolled up in his pants, lying out in the open while he and Snake showed off swimming. Yeah, he'd been just plain dumb.

A week after his dream, Gloria told him she was going home to visit with her mother, but she promised she would be back in a couple of weeks. With Gloria gone, and no job, he skipped school altogether. He felt he had nothing to look forward to except the companionship of the gang. He followed them wherever they went and participated in whatever activity they chose to indulge in. It might be shooting crap, or, it could be stealing fruit from a merchant, or, just drinking moonshine, and sleeping the day away. It all depended on Snake's mood. Now, he had to find them in order to spend a day doing who knew what.

They weren't in the field, so, he headed for the shack. His second guess was right. As he approached the run-down structure, he heard their voices. One of the boys standing out front saw him approaching, "Hey, Piggy, what's go'n on man?" he shouted.

"Hopp'n but not high, flopp'n but not fly'n"

After giving each other their gang-hand shake, George entered the shabby building. The boys were sitting on boxes and broken chairs around an old table, playing penny poker. They all had serious faces.

One boy, Snags, looked up, and a smirk crossed his face, "Well if it ain't Chopick's mule. How's the mule feeling today?"

"Shut your mouth, Snags. I ain't nobodys mule! You got that?"

"The more I looks at you, the more you looks like a mule." The boy taunted.

"Yeah, you ugly ape, the more I look at you, the more I think you're the shit face that stole my money!" George snarled.

"My. My. Ain't we in a hump today?"

"Hold it! Just hold it!" One gang member yelled.

"Stop dis shit! I gots other things on my mind… like gett'n up some drink'n money," Snake added, but it was too late.

George rushed Snags, knocking him off his box perch, pummeling him with both fists. They rolled on the dirt floor, cursing and screaming. George's fury was without limit. It took Snake and two others to pull him off. "Stealing my money while I took a swim, you piece of dirt!"

"Stop dis crap, Both of ya!" Snake screamed. "How de fuck do you know who stole your money?"

"Because the fuck face is always on me. I know his type. He's sneaky an' always trying to out-fox me," George retorted.

"Any ob des suckers could'a done dat, so cut de crap, Piggy! Snags, go sit ova dar. Piggy, you sits ova here." Both boys took seats at opposite ends of the shack, breathing heavily, and glowered at each other.

Snake began pacing around the room, "Now, let's gets to some serious stuff. We gonn'a get us some moon. So, dig in, an' put up!" He took off his cap and went to each boy. "If yo don't puts in, yo sho in hell ain't gonn'a take out, if you gets my meaning." The youths, dropped in nickels and dimes. Piggy put in a quarter. The boys smiled when they saw the quarter go in.

George saw Snags drop a nickel in. "You cheap piece of shit, you can give more than that! What you putt'n in ain't your money anyway…but you gonn'a hold'n on to it, huh?" He said derisively.

Snags jumped up to challenge his tormentor, but Snake pushed him back down. That's enough Piggy! You too, Snags, jus' take it easy, the two of you!" Snake began counting the money he'd collected as he headed for the door, "Be back befo' you all counts to ten." Outside, he broke into a trot and went down the dirt path to make his purchase.

The tension hadn't subsided inside the hot room. Some of Snag's friends decided to see if they could get a rise out of George. "Hey Piggy, you eva have a woman?" One boy asked in an idle manner. "Bet' you ain't never had none," Another boy chimed in.

"I have so." He snapped.

"When was the last time, boy?"

"When I last got some, aint none of your business!" George replied defensively. "But, I've had more 'stuff' than any of you apes have, that's for sure."

Judging by his response, the boys felt they were onto something. So, the taunting continued, until Snake returned. As soon as he walked through the door, he caught the drift of the teasing, but chose to ignore it.

Uncorking the bottle, he took the first swig, then, passed it around. The bottle went from mouth to mouth. Some rubbed it in a circular motion, as if that somehow made it more sanitary. In a short while the bottle was empty. Soon, its fiery contents began to take effect.

Snake jumped up, putting his face inches from George's. "Nigger, I heard what you told the boys. Talk'n all big about gett'n it . Man, you wouldn't know what to do wif it if'n it was give to you on' a plate, and we knows how you likes to eat!" The reaction to Snake's barbs was instant. The gang members fell to the floor laughing.

"I would so know what to do" Piggy replied, sounding defensive in spite of himself.

"Oh yeah!" Snake replied, "We gonn'a see how big a liar you is." The leader grabbed his arm then led him outside. The others followed as snake marched them down back alleys and through empty lots. They walked for blocks and blocks, looking like a rag-tag army, following their leader. Finally they stopped in front of a large frame house ,on a nearly deserted street.

"You got some money, Piggy?"

"Yeah, I got some money, why?"

"You got a dollar?" Snake pressed.

"I told you I got money, I got a few dollars."

"Let's see it."

George reached in his pocket and pulled out several bills. Without hesitation, he pressed one into Snakes hand. "See?"

He handed it back. "Well, what'cha wait'n fo,' go in a buy yo' self a wom'n. We be wait'n right here." With Snake's encouragement, the other boys playfully pushed George up the steps to the front door. Snake knocked, then, fled down the steps, leaving the confused boy alone. The leader and the other boys took up their vigil under a big tree across the street, big huge grins on their faces.

George hadn't a clue what was on the other side of the door. But, Snake's words, "Go in and by a wom'n." swirled around inside his head. Suddenly, the big door opened.

A large brown skinned woman with fancy jewelry in her ears, and fake pearls around her neck, glared at the hapless youth. "What's you want boy?" She snapped.

Mellow music from a piano floated through the open door. Off in the corner, a fat black man sat at an upright piano, playing, humming and singing along with his own plunking. He seemed to be playing as much to himself as to the assembled women in various stages of undress inside.

George tried to answer, but nothing came out of his mouth.

"Well? What's you want? I ain't got all day, boy."

"Ahh, I, I, I want to, I want to buy me a woman."

"You want to what?" The seldom surprised madam replied.

"I, I want to buy a woman." He managed to repeat, this time with a bit more self assurance. It wasn't what he felt he should say, but it was what Snake had said he was there to do. He had heard there were places men went to buy sex, but he didn't know what the protocol was to make the request in a proper way.

The madam was so surprised, she took a step back. Some of the women sitting around in various stages of undress, heard the conversation, got up to peek at the youthful voice they heard requesting a woman It wasn't what he said that caused her to step back, so much as the combination of his words, his obvious youth and the seriousness with which he made the request. The lady's eyes got large and her mouth curled into a gold toothed smile. Well, you say you wants to buy a woman? Well, we ain't got no woman for you to buy. What you gonn'a do, buy her and carry her home like a sack of potatoes?"

"No, ma'am, that ain't what…"

"Now, we duz have lady's what will stay with you for a while fo' a price…that what you got in mind, honey?"

The ladies were all watching and listening to this exchange, and enjoying every minute.

"Yes-um, that's what I mean, a lady to be with me for a while. Yes-um, that's it."

The madam's eyes narrowed. "Lord, have mercy. I do believe this here child is serious. Boy, you better get yo' hind parts outt'a here, you jus' a child. Now you get out of here and go back home to yo' mama."

"But you don't understand." George protested. He didn't know which would be the biggest embarrassment – being laughed at by the ladies standing behind the madam, or the gang across the street if he were to be turned away.

To be more assertive, he reached in his other pocket and pulled out a hand full of coins and bills. "I have money, see?" He pulled his hand out so quickly, the money fell to the floor. The coins rolled this way and that, a few bills floated down to the floor, settling at the madam's feet. The madam stood speechless, flustered by the boy's determination. George stooped and began retrieving his money. By the time he had retrieved his money and stood up, one of the girls had walked over and stood within inches of his face.

"Boy, you do thinks you's a man? You really thinks you can handle a woman?" She challenged.

"Flo! You ain't serious is you? You can't..." The madam said in disbelief.

"I sure is serious. He ain't noth'n but talk, anyway."

Deciding it might be a good joke, the madam said, "All right then. Give me two dollars, boy." She stuck out an open palm.

George peeled off two dollars, and handed the money to the madam. She stuffed the money into her bosom and stomped off.

Flo winked at the other girls as she took George firmly by the arm and led him towards the stairs. "Don't hurt her now, boy," one of the girls said in a loud whisper as he passed. Half way up the stairs the woman took his hand, thinking he might get cold feet and flee. She looked forward to having fun with this man-child. "My name is Flo, what's yours?" She felt she should at least try to make this young thing feel more comfortable, and at ease as they ascended the stairs.

"My name is George Isaac, My friends call me…" He stopped mid-sentence, he didn't want this woman calling him, Piggy. Instead he coughed, hoping to cover up his omission.

Flo noticed his ploy, but went along with it, not knowing what name he was attempting to cover-up. She led him to a darkened room where the shades were tightly drawn on both windows. The room contained a large four poster bed, with several pillows casually thrown on it. It was positioned right in the middle of the room. She ushered him in ahead of her, then latched the door. She felt devilish and wasn't about to let her prey escape. There was an oak stand with a pitcher and a straight back oak chair in the otherwise bare room. Flo wore an amused look when she muttered to herself, "I bet this ain't gonn'a take long." She sat on the far side of the bed. "Well, wat'cha wait'n on? Get yo' self ov'a hea."

The taunts of the gang and the mocking looks of the women downstairs had embarrassed him. Now that it was just the two of them, he felt at ease. Flo took his slowness as a sign of shyness, or that fright had set in. She looked at him, and cooed, "Come on now, don't you be nervous, Flo gonn'a take real good care of you…promise, an I ain't gonn'a hurt you one bit."

"Ma'am, I ain't one bit nervous."

Surprised by his reply, she raised up to take a look at the boy. Flo had had experience, but he was a boy though built like a man, a strong muscular man at that. She understood first timers and knew the wonder, the mystery and anticipation they brought. If they were nice to her, she would try to repair their self-esteem, comfort them, and try to give them a second chance. However, if they had been mean she would rub it in and try to do damage to their egos. "How old are you, George Isaac?"

"Thirteen, soon be fourteen ma'am."

She had guessed sixteen by his size and build.

"Thirteen! You're only thirteen?" She bolted up. "I thought you wuz at least sixteen!"

George didn't respond. He walked to her side of the bed and turned toward Flo. His eyes were steady as he gazed into her shocked face. She was surprised by his lack of shyness and gentle aggressiveness. Despite her misgivings, she reached for him, but he took her hand away. She looked up at the earnest face above her; this man-child who seemed tender and caring as he kissed her. Only her long-dead husband had ever reached her soul this way. Never, ever had anyone since she had become a professional reached her this way. Now, this young rascal was actually making her feel she was not being used.

They stayed together for a long time.

The knock was sharp and insistent. "Flo! Flo! Wat'cha all do'n in there? You know how long you all been up here?" the madam called through the door.

Flo was slow to answer. Both she and George had fallen asleep. Raising herself up partially, she looked at the still sleeping youth, smiled, then answered, "We be out in a bit." Her voice sounded drowsy. Gently, ever so gently, she shook George until his eyes opened. He looked so peaceful she hated to disturb her young prince. As he turned toward her, she kissed him lightly on the forehead. "Wake up, Mr. George Isaac. We got to go, but we gonn'a see more of each other, what you say to that?"

With a contented smile, he answered, "I'd like that, I surely would." I like you a lot Miss Flo, I really do."

"I want you to know, I'm gonn'a talk to the madam. I want you to understand, you're sure nuf, a good, gentle man, Mister George."

"Thank you Miss Flo. I'm glad I met you. I look forward to seeing you again real soon. Well, I guess I'd better get going now. But, if you say it's all right, I'll be back."

"Honey, it's more than all right. I needs you more than you'll eva know, boy." George had no idea he had awakened something vital in this woman who had resigned herself to a life of numbness and feeling worthless. She had given up on ever receiving any semblance of human warmth from a man again. "I gotta ax you a question, Mr. George."

"You do? What is it?"

"How did a young thing like you ..."

"Miss Flo, maybe one day I can tell you more."

"All right, I won't ax you no more, at least fo' now." She answered with a knowing smile. "Well, let's go down. I'm sure the girls is gonn'a want a report." Flo held George's arm tightly as they walked down stairs. Her subtle smile made her look like a blushing bride. She exaggerated her hip movement as they descended the stairs, fully aware every eye in the room was on the two of them.

"Well, what was it like, Flo?" One of the girls called.

"You all wuz sure gone a long time." Another girl questioned.

"Girls…I'm gonn'a tell you someth'n. This here boy, well, he be a sho nuff man, an can come see me any time."

"Well, ain't that something. Nex' time, I'm gonn'a see fo' my self ," another girl replied.

"Uh, uh. He be mine, an I'll scratch the eyes outt'a any body that thinks otherwise. An, I don't be play'n." Flo said, making sure her claim on him was crystal clear. She planted a kiss on George's lips, then, escorted him to the door. The girls laughed. The piano man interrupted his playing and raised a glass in salute to them, then, without missing a beat, continued plunking out a soulful blues tune. His small, chunky, diamond and gold-banded fingers, moved effortlessly back and forth over the keyboard.

When he stepped onto the front stoop, he realized for the first time it had been a couple of hours since the gang pushed him up to the door. The sun had dipped behind the distant hills. None of the boys remained. They'd grown tired of waiting; the joke hadn't worked out as they'd planned. As he headed home, he had a bounce in his step. The tune the piano man played came to his lips. He whistled it loudly all the way home.

Several days passed before George caught up with the gang. He guessed they would be in the field shooting craps, and he was right. Snake was the first to spot him coming through the fields. He yelled, "Well suh, in the flesh, an' in person." Prompting snickers from some of the others as they elbowed one another, trying hard to cover their own embarrassment at the turn of events of the other night. Then too, they weren't blind. They saw the swagger in his stride, and the smirk on his face. They knew he thought he was really hot stuff.

George knew he had them where he wanted them for the very first time. He was always being made to prove something to be one of them. Now, he had made them look bad. Until now he had never thought about it, but he was sure not one of them had ever been with a woman. Of course they wouldn't admit it. But, he was pretty sure. As he approached them, a smile crossed his face; he remembered their jovial attitude when they pushed him up the steps to what they were sure was going to be total embarrassment for him.

He chuckled, because none of them would ever really know. Now that he was giving the matter serious thought he realized they were nothing but all talk, even Snake. Despite his being sixteen and the gang leader. Snake (he realized for the first time) was all bluster, trying to fool his members with his 'attitude,' an act he used to cover up his own cowardice. He acted tough around the boys, but the few times they were around girls, George remembered Snake couldn't find his tongue.

George was in control of the situation and intended to have fun with his new- found power. Walking to the circle of boys, he took his time breaking in among the kneeling players. Dice always passed to the left, so, he knelt on the right side of Shorty, the boy holding the dice. He knew all eyes were on him, and he knew each guy there had a question for him. Comfortably positioned he began looking from face to face until he'd made eye contact with every one there. "Bet you suckers want to know what happened, don't you?" George asked mockingly.

Knowing they'd lost control, and to a person anxious to know, they said, "Yeah, yeah, we wants to know what happened."

George cleared his throat, glanced around before he spoke, "First you have to understand there were about ten women there; and, each one better look'n than the other one. And man, they were dressed so you could see what you were gonn'a get." The boys let out collective sighs, and a few, 'oh man,' as each drew imaginary pictures in their minds. "Now, you all keep quiet and I'll tell ya what happened." George commanded.

"Yeah, you all keep yo moufs shut! Snake ordered; anxious as any of his gang members to hear the details.

"It was like this…I paid the head lady after I see the woman I want." He lied.

"Yeah?" the boys answered as a chorus to encourage him on.

"Man, she was the best look'n one there, too. I tell the head lady she's the one I want. Then I points to her and say, 'Woman, I want to be with you!' Man, you should'a seen how she walks up to me. Real slow, move'n her hips jes' so. After she comes over, she takes me by the arm, and walks me up the steps to her special room, jes' the two of us. An you should'a seen what she was wear'n, woo wee. All see through stuff, man! She was sure nuff one fine look'n lady. She weren't no coal scuttle blond, neither."

The boys were all transfixed, hanging on his every word. Snake became impatient with Piggy's long pauses. "Then, wha'cha all do, damn it?"

"Now, let's see. What did we do next?" George feigned forgetfulness as he scratched his head and looked up to the sky. "Oh, yeah, she sat her fine frame on the bed, then, she took her gown off and…"

"Oh, come on man…stop the shit!" Snags yelled.

"Then, I takes my clothes off…and, and."

"Yeah? Yeah?" Several boys whispered. Their eyes were big and their mouths hung open. George had never enjoyed anything as much as he did this moment. "Then I gets into the bed…"

"Yeah? Then what?" A dry throated voice asked.

"Then I talks to her, sweet and nice…"

"What you say to her?" A boy asked.

"I tells her, 'you is sho beautiful…' and then."

"Yeah? Den what?"

"Now we gett'n to the best part of the story." He stopped and slowly looked at each face in the circle. "You boys really want to know what happened next?"

"Yeah, damn it, what happened next?"

"Well, I moves real close to her, and I put my hands on her and then…you know what?"

"What, damn it! What!" Several boys yell.

"Well, suh, I moves even closer to her and then I… I…I…fall asleep, and so does she." George leaned forward as he and doubled up over with laughter. As soon as they realized they had been suckered, they jump on top of him and pounded him. While they rolled on the dirt Piggy gasped, "You damn darkies, you so big and bad. Take your hind parts there and pay your money and find out for your damn selves!"

Three weeks passed. Today he was going to spend the morning with Gloria. He had escorted his mother to work, had breakfast and was looking forward to seeing her. Trotting home, he took the stairs to her room two at a time. Standing in front of her door, he knocked lightly. It was already slightly ajar; his soft knock caused it to open more fully. "Good morning, Miss Brown," He said, peering in as it swung inward. It took a moment for reality to sink in, the room was empty. The closet door was open and it was bare as a bone. His mouth dropped. This had to be another dream, only this time he knew it wasn't. She was gone.

What had she said or done that caused him to foresee this day in his dream. Maybe it was what she hadn't said, or done, that caused him to know this day was coming.. There had to have been signs; otherwise that omen wouldn't have come to him in his sleep. He must have had a gut feeling this was going to happen. "Why couldn't she at least have said goodbye! How could she just up and leave? After all we had shared, how could she do this to me? Not a note, not a soft goodbye whispered in my ear. No, she just walked away." His anguished words echoed in the empty room.

Several weeks passed before the gang decided to spend a day at the river. Once there they broke into several groups. A few jumped in the water and splashed around. Some sat on the bank and exchanged jokes. Snake and George challenged each other to a race. They swam out to a log they selected then back as fast as they could. Snake grinned when he got the water out of his eyes and realized he had beaten his rival. "Told ya, I'd whup yo'." He boasted.

"Luck, my man. Just plain luck."

They walked away from the rest of the guys, Snake found a spot, stretched his long body out in the cool grass, closed his eyes and promptly fell asleep. George walked on a bit further, went behind a bush and relieved himself. As he did, he noticed he had a problem. He had heard women could make men sick down and immediately he wondered, "Did Gloria or Flo make him sick?" Suddenly he panicked. He called out, "Snake! Snake!...man you gotta' look at something!"

"Piggy, what's wrong wit you? You done gone plum crazy?"

He was in such a panic, he didn't hear a word Snake said.

"Something's wrong with me, man. I'm all swollen'

Snake wouldn't look directly at Piggy.. "Man, yo' got a sickness, yo' needs to see a doctor."

"I don't know no doctor to go to!" George complained.

"Shush yo self! Ma mama, she usta wuk fo a colored doctor 'fo she died, I ken take yo dar." Snake felt important, he knew something Piggy didn't, and Piggy needed him in a very different way.

In a tight, small voice, George replied, "You'll take me there?"

"Sho nuff, I takes you dar right now."

Snake led his frightened companion to a part of town he'd never been to before. The houses were big; the streets lined with large shade trees. White picket fences stood like rows of soldiers, guarding the well-kept yards and flower gardens. "Dis, be the doc's place." Snake said with authority. Taking the walk way that led toward the back, he went up the steps to a side door and knocked. After several tries, he turned to his friend who had a worried look on his face. "Maybe ain't nobody home."

"You sure this is the right house?"

"'Cousre I'm sho!" He snapped, irritated. "Been here mo' times than you swatted flys! Tol ya, my mama wuk'ed fo' de doc. Ain't nobody home. We bes' come back tomorrow." He descended the steps, and led the way out of the yard.

"I just thought…maybe we should try another door." George pleaded. Panic had set in and he was desperate to find out what was wrong with him. "Maybe we should try another door." He repeated to his friend, who was now walking away.

"Na, we bes' come back tomorrow."

They were half way down the walkway when a deep voice called, "Boys, what is it you want?"

Snake turned, and headed back the flower lined path toward the tall, elegantly dressed, brown skinned man, standing just outside the open door. George was close on his heels.

"William Jones, is that you, boy? Well, as I live and breathe…you sure have grown."

"Yes, suh, Doctor Bletso, it be me."

"   Well, it sure is good to see you young man, it's been some years…not since your mother's funeral. What a pity her passing, such a fine woman she was, too. And you, how've you been?"

"Jes' fine, doctor, jes' fine."

"That's good. So, what brings you here today?"

"It be's ma friend here, he got a sickness," Snake said, pointing to George's groin area.

"Oh, I see. Well, you boys come on in and we'll see what the problem is." Glancing at George, he asked, "and young man, who might you be?"

"My name is George Isaac Read, sir."

Doctor Bletso offered his hand, "Pleased to meet you. I'm Doctor Bletso. Come, both of you can follow me." He led them down a long hard wood hallway lined with impressive pieces of furniture, and clusters of paintings in ornate frames, some, so large they stretched from the floor almost to the ceiling, taller than a person. The doctor pointed to a chair placed next to a door outside one of the many rooms off the hallway. "William, you take a seat here." The doctor opened a door opposite from where he had seated Snake. He held the door open, "George, you go in and take a seat. I'll be right in." Turning to William he asked, "How are you making out since your mother passed? You were to go live with an uncle as I recall."

"Yas suh, that's what I done. I be do'n jes fine, doctor, yas sur, jes fine." He lied. The uncle, a drunk, had thrown the boy out after a month. William, finding himself on the streets, learned to survive by his wit. He also formed bonds with other cast away boys, quickly becoming their leader. Because of his long, lanky body, and slithering walk, the group named themselves after him. Deciding his walk reminded them of a snake, they dubbed themselves 'The Snakes.' The boys survived by stealing, gambling and hustling.

"Good, glad to hear that you're doing well, William. Well…I guess I better take a look at your friend." The doctor entered the room, closing the door behind him. He saw George nervously fidgeting on a chair, looking at the books that lined his office walls. "Young man, you did say your name was Read?"

"Yes, sir, I did, that's my name."

"Would your mother's name be Mary?"

"Yes. Sir. That's my mother's name."

"Well, I never had the opportunity to meet her, but I did have occasion to meet your father, Isaac."

George's heart leaped. "You did?"

"Yes, he attended a meeting at which I spoke. He was a very impressive man, your father. It was too bad what happened to him, really a shame. It took courage to do what he did. You should be very proud of him, George."

"Oh, I am sir. I'm very proud." George thought, "Maybe one day he can tell me about my father. Oh, I hope so."

"That's good. Now, you sit right there, I'll be right back."

Talking to the doctor calmed him somewhat. Feeling more relaxed now, he allowed his eyes to take in the room. Wherever he looked, he saw books. There were more books in this one room than in the library at the colored school he sometimes attended.

The doctor returned, "George, come with me." The boy followed and entered the room. "Now stand over here, stand in front of me." The doctor said, motioning.

The boy headed toward the doctor as his eyes took in the room. It was all white, filled with tables, cabinets, glass vials, jars and metal instruments. It dazzled his eyes; there was so much to see. He walked to the doctor now seated on a stool and stood like a statue, not knowing what to expect.

"All right, let me look ."

The request embarrassed him, but his desire to know what was wrong, outweighed that fleeting emotion. He complied with the doctor's request, and waited for an answer.

"Ummm, I see, well…I think I can fix you up" The doctor said, after a cursory look. "George, you haven't been circumcised. Now, what I mean by that is, the skin around the head of your penis needs to be removed. If you don't pull the foreskin back when you pee, it sometimes gets infected. I'd say that's what happened to you. Also, when you pee, you should pull the skin back and you must wash that part of your body every day and keep it clean. Understand?"

"Yes sir, I think I do. I mean, is it serious? Am I really sick down there?"

"No. Just an external infection; It's not serious, but, it must be taken care of. We can fix that up. I'm going to circumcise you."

The doctor immediately read his face and realized he had no idea of what he was talking about. He added "What I'll have to do is cut the foreskin away. Here, get up on the table and lie back. We might as will get to it." He made no mention as to how painful the procedure would be.

And it was. It was the most painful experience of George's life. He screamed as the doctor snipped and cut, crying until he had no more tears left. The doctor put a salve on the open wound, and allowed him to rest. After a couple of hours, he called William in, "You're going to have to help your friend home. He's sore right now; he'll need someone to lean on along through here." Turning to his patient, he placed his hand on the boy's shoulder. "George, you should stay in bed for a few days, then, you come back and see me again. I'll want you to put this salve on it in the morning and again at night. Can you do that?" he asked, handing the boy a jar of ointment.

"Yes sir, I can do that."

When George got off the table, his legs were hardly able to support him. Snake was so upset at the loud scream he had heard. He couldn't stop shaking as he offered his arm. Obeying the doctor's orders, he led Piggy to the door.

The doctor followed and watched as this patient gingerly went down the steps. "You're going to be sore for a few days," He cautioned, "Then you'll be good as new. Now, don't forget, I'll need to see you in, oh, I'd say three days."

As the boys slowly went down the street, Snake asked, "Man. What did the doctor do to you? You sounded like a stuck pig! I swear, I started to take off."

George didn't reply, "Help me man; hold me so I don't have to put all my weight on my legs."

Snake slipped his arm around his waist, trying to lift him as he walked. "Is dat some better?"

"Yeah, that's a lot better. Shit man, I ain't never hurt like this in my whole life."

"Well, what de fuk did he do to you, man?"

" He did what he called a circumcision. He cut the skin off of my 'thing'."

"He did what?" Snake screamed in disbelief.

"Like I said, he cut the skin off the front of my dick!" George was in a foul mood and didn't feel like explaining in greater detail. "Man, just help me get home so I can lay down."

Snake was even more shaken now that he could picture in his mind what had been done to Piggy. As they neared his house, Snake made an understanding offer, "I bes' leave you off here. I don't want to run into yo' mama, an' hab to hear her mouf'n off on me, tell'n me I should get a job and all."

"Thanks for your help, man. I mean that."

Snake looked embarrassed,. He wasn't accustomed to receiving praise, or words of appreciation. "Weren't noth'n, yo'd do the same fo' me, right?"

"You bet I would." George said in all honesty.

Snake turned and started running. He had a lot to share with the gang.

When his mother found him in bed, he explained he had an upset stomach. He was too embarrassed to tell her what had really happened. Mary was actually happy to see her son slow down and rest, he was always on the go. Yes, she felt this illness was definitely a good thing. "By the way George, Gloria Brown has left us and won't be coming back."

"Where did she go, Mama?"

"Back to Jackson, Missippippi. She was sorry she didn't get a chance to say goodbye to you, son."

"I'd liked to have said goodbye to her, too." He said in a monotone voice as he tried to put his finger on his feelings. Was it sadness, disappointment, betrayal? As he thought about it, he realized it was every one of them.

On the day George was to go see the doctor, he thought it would be fun to see the gang first. However, out of bed, the soreness returned when he attempted to walk. He decided to head for doctor Bletso's office instead. He felt he had enough energy to get there, but not much more.

George went to the doctor's back door and knocked. A maid opened the door. "What you want, boy?" The maid snapped.

"I came to see the doctor. He told me to come back today."

"Are you sure, boy?"

"Yes ma'am. I was here a few days ago, and the doctor…"

"I thought I heard your voice, George." Nodding he said, "It's all right Barbara, he's a patient of mine. Come on in, son, I'll be with your shortly, I have another patient right now, so, I'll put you in here for now." The doctor ushered him into a room that was unlike any he had ever seen. It had human skulls, bones, skeletons and other odd items. "Don't touch anything, but, look around all you want," he said as he closed the door.

Finally, the doctor returned, "Well, how's my young patient today?"

"Some better, sir, but I'm still sore down there."

"Did you follow my instructions?"

"Yes, sir, I did."

The doctor nodded in approval as he looked at the circumcision site. "You're healing just fine. Give it a few more days and I think you'll forget the past few day," he said with a smile.

As the doctor examined him, George's eyes went to the book-lined wall. He began thinking, anyone who had so many must be a person with knowledge and information. He realized this was the opportunity he had been looking for. Screwing up his courage he said, "Doctor, I have a question I'd like to ask you."

Somewhat surprised, the doctor looked up. "You do? What is it?"

"Well sir, I made a promise to my mother, and I want to keep that promise, but I don't know how to do it."

A bit confused, the doctor pursued his statement. "What was the promise you made, George?"

"You see, she asked me to promise I'd go to a place called college. And I said I would."

"Well, that a very fine thing you did, George."

`"But, I don't know what it is, or where it is. I just don't know how to get to this place called college," the boy said in total earnestness.

In spite of himself, the doctor smiled, "Oh, I see. You promised your mother that you would go, but you really don't know what college is…well, I think I may be able to help you with that problem."

George became so excited at the prospect of receiving an answer, he interrupted, "You see, my Mother works for Mr. and Mrs. John Farr. They're real rich people. Well, my Mother said she heard them talking, and they're going to send their son to a place called college when he's older. My Mother said it must be a good place, otherwise, why would they send their son there? That's why she made me promise I'd go there, too."

Covering his mouth and dropping his head to hide the smile he couldn't suppress, the doctor said, "George, I can tell you what it is and how to get there, too."

"You can?"

"Yes, yes I can. But before I do, I need to find out a few things about you. I'll want you to come back here in four days. Then, we can talk in greater detail about your promise to your mother. Is that agreeable with you?"

"Oh, yes sir, it is." He became so excited about the coming meeting with the doctor he forgot his soreness for the first time in days.

The time passed quickly. Today he would see the doctor and get answers to his question. He'd gotten up, dressed, and was waiting outside for his mother. When Mary finally appeared, she noticed how excited her boy was. "My son, you're an early bird, this morning. You're stomach feeling better?"

"Yes, ma'am, it's much better," he said, almost forgetting that had been his excuse for staying in bed. George wanted to tell his mother he was going to find out where this place called college was, but he didn't. He knew how much this good news would please and bring joy to her, but he decided he'd wait until he had spoken with the doctor and had the full answer. As they walked to the Farr's, George was quiet, but his mind was racing.

"Is everything all right son?" She could tell he had something weighing on his mind.

"Oh, yes. Everything is just fine. I was just thinking, that's all."

"Do you want to talk to me about it, son?"

"No, not now, but I will, real soon, he answered with a smile.

Mary respected her son and didn't pursue the matter further.

Once breakfast was over, he broke into a fast trot and headed to the doctor's house and its back door. He knocked, and waited for someone to answer. He couldn't remember when he had been so excited.

The maid wasn't hostile when she opened the door this time. In fact, she said, "Well, good morning young man." The doctor must have spoken to her, because her attitude was totally different.

"Good morning, Miss Barbara," he replied with a smile.

"Follow me." She said, "You sure came early. Doctor ain't hardly had a chance to finish his breakfast. It might be a while before he can see you. But, I'll let him know you're here." She led the youth to the room with the bones, skulls and vials -- a room he liked very much.

George sat on a stool, anxious to allow his eyes to feast on the interesting items placed about around the room.

After a bit, he slid off the stool and walked from one display to another, careful not to touch anything. It was one of the most exciting places he had ever been. His exploration was interrupted when the door opened and the doctor came in.

Doctor Bletso was fully aware that today was an important one for the boy. In his own way, he was as excited as the early bird he found poking around the room. He went to the boy, extended his hand and received a surprisingly firm and vigorous hand-shake in return. Sensing the boy's anxiety, the doctor said, "Good morning, George. It's good to see you."

"It's good to see you, too, sir."

"Come with me. We'll talk in my office." He turned and led the way.

Offering George a seat, he stood, leaning against his desk. "Remember I told you I had some checking to do before I gave you an answer to your question?"

"Yes. I do remember, sir."

"Well, I've done just that. I went to the colored school and made some inquiries about you."

Suddenly, George felt uncomfortable and cornered. He wasn't prepared for this turn of events. His eyes grew large and he felt his face flush.

"Do you know what I found out? Do you know what they said about you at school?"

"No sir. I mean, yes sir. I mean no sir." He knew he had not made the best of impressions on his teachers, and his attendance record was awful. In fact, this year's would be the worst because he had been seeing Gloria and the Snakes. Trying to put on a brave face, he managed to say, "Yes, sir. I would like to know."

"They told me you hardly ever come to school, but you were still managing to get 'C's. I was told you could be an above average student if your attendance was what it should be. Do you know what average means George?" Without waiting for an answer, he continued, "Average means ordinary. Remain average and you won't be able to live up to the promise you made to your mother and go to college. You must become an 'A' or at worst, a 'B' student. You can't get to college being ordinary, George. Simply put, college is a school of higher learning. People go to college to become a teacher or some kind of professional person. You will have to study, study, study. Should you want to become a doctor, or a lawyer, you'd have to attend school even more years than the four required to get what is called a bachelor's degree. Do you understand what I'm saying to you George?"

The boy nodded, trying hard to digest all that was being said. He couldn't follow everything, but, he did know college was a school, and he'd have to get his grades up to fulfill his promise. "Yes sir, I understand some." He responded.

"I'll help you, but you'll have to demonstrate to me, starting now, that you've got what it takes to buckle down and get those grades up. Are you ready to get started?"

"Yes, yes sir I am."

"Your teachers told me they felt you would be college material if you were to get serious. Understand, George, most colleges will not allow you to come unless you have a background in mathematics, languages and some science. Right now we won't worry about that since the colored school here doesn't offer those courses, but we'll solve that problem at a later date. So, as you can see, you have lots to overcome to live up to the promise you made your mother. Now, I'm going to ask you to make me a promise. Are you ready to do that?"

George's head was spinning. But he knew he was on the right path to fulfill the promise he'd made to his mother. And that promise was the most important thing in his life. "Yes sir. I am," he answered.

"You're not to miss one single day of school from now on. Is that understood, young man?"

"Yes sir, I understand."

"Secondly, you're to bring me your report card. I want to see 'A's and 'B's from now on, is that clear?" The doctor's voice was stern.

"It is, sir."

"All right, since you made me a promise, I'll make a promise to you. If you do what I've asked, I'll promise you that I will see to it you will get to go to college. Is that fair?"

George could hardly contain his joy, "Oh, yes sir. That's fair. Yes sir, it surely is."

The doctor extended his hand. George took it in his, while he felt he was about to dismiss him. But he wasn't ready to leave; he needed more information from this learned man. "Doctor," he began in a small voice.

"Yes?"

"Just where is this place called college? I sort of understand what it is, but I still don't know how I get there."

The question brought a fleeting smile to the doctor's face. "George, there are colleges all over the country. In fact, you live across the street from a university. That's similar to a college, only it offers more advanced, or higher degrees than colleges do. But that school is for whites only. There are no colleges here for colored students, so, we'll probably find one in another city, or even another state. Does that help you understand a little better?"

"Yes sir, I understand some better."

"Let me explain it this way, George. I wanted to be a doctor; therefore, I had to go to college, then on to a medical university where I had to study for a long, long, time. After I completed all my courses, plus other work, I graduated with a diploma that states I am a licensed physician. By the way, George, have you thought about what you want to become?"

"No. Sir, I haven't."

"Well, young man, it's something to start thinking about. You could be a doctor, a minister, a lawyer or a teacher. Once you decide, then that's what you'll be preparing for when you go to college. Are things a little clearer, now?"

"Yes, yes sir, I do have a better understanding, now."

A few days passed. George was nervous and in conflict. Did he have the ability to bring his grades up? He felt he had enough information to tell his mother he would be able to keep his promise. He now knew how to get to college. But, he decided to wait until he saw if he could bring his grades up. The doctor seemed to think he could, but, he wasn't as confident. He had never really studied or applied himself in school, had never made an effort to learn. Now, he'd wait and see if he could. He reasoned once he knew he could, then, he'd tell her. He couldn't afford to take the chance that his mother might find out about his being absent from school during the past few years. Even though the doctor had quickly discovered his poor attendance record, he didn't raise the questions his mother would. Her knowing would expose his relationship with Gloria, and the Snakes. These were things he didn't want to ever have to attempt to explain. Lord, she would kill him if she ever found out. No, he reasoned, he'd wait and see how he did in the grade-improvement department first.

Mary began noticing a change in her son's behavior. He was staying home nights, even on weekends. He seemed to have a new interest in books. She also noticed he had begun writing in his note book with an earnestness she had never witnessed before.

In what seemed no time at all, he was issued a report card, the first one since the doctor and he had had their discussion. He never shared it with his mother since she had no knowledge of such a document. Having been a slave, she had no concept of such a thing as a report card. His heart was pounding before he opened it. He couldn't believe his eyes; he had managed to pull his grades up to all 'B's. George was proud of himself, proud for what he had accomplished. When he shared it with the doctor, he beamed with pride as he saw the doctor's face reflect approval.

"George, do you know what this shows me? It shows me you are capable of all 'A's, and that's what I want. Spend more time with your books, my boy. That's how you will be able to raise your grades."

The young man felt a wave of nervousness sweep over him. He thought he had just preformed a miracle. Now he was being asked to perform another. But he didn't verbalize his fears to the doctor, nor did he complain. Instead he heard himself answer, "Yes sir, I can do it."

"Good. Now I have something I want to offer you, George."

The boy looked at the doctor, wondering what new and impossible request he'd make now. "Yes. Sir?"

"I want to offer you an after-school job, with your mother's permission of course. Are you interested?"

"Oh, yes sir!" he could hardly believe his ears.

"All right. If you take it, I'll want you to come here right after school, and on Saturdays, too. You will keep my laboratory clean and do other things that I'll explain to you as you become familiar with the laboratory and my other needs."

"When would you want me to start?"

"As soon as I can clear it with your mother. Here is what we'll do. I'll give you a note to take home. Does your mother read, George? If not, you can read it to her."

"She knows how to read, sir."

"Good, have her read it and you can let me know what she says. How's that?"

"I'm sure she'll be pleased, doctor."

"I'll pay you a dollar and fifty cents per week."

"Thank you doctor, I appreciate what you're doing for me."

"George, you have a long hard road ahead of you, I'm sure there will be times when you will have anything but thanks for me." He dismissed George with a pat on the head.

Mary told her son to say yes to the doctor's job offer. In a matter of weeks, when her son came home from the doctor's laboratory, he was full of stories about his work. Mary absorbed them with a great thirst. She even began prodding him for more and more information. details; she didn't want him to leave a single detail out. However, her curiosity was not without motive. She couldn't wait for Sunday in order to tell her church sisters about the important job her son had working in the doctor's laboratory. If she felt he wasn't going into enough detail, she would pry and probe until she felt she had every ounce of information. Then she would embellish the story as she retold his exploits in detail to her friends. No matter how simple the answer, in retelling the story, whatever her son had done became magnified and a hundred times more important.

In a short time, Doctor Bletso saw promise in George. No matter the task he assigned to the boy, it was done to perfection. The doctor decided to see how much responsibility he could handle, reasoning the best way to find out would be to push him as hard as he could in order to see what he was made of.

As soon as George finished one task, the doctor would assign him another. In a brief time, he had moved from sweeping floors, to learning how to clean test tubes and vials. Shortly he was allowed to fill vials and jars with compounds that the doctor used to formulate prescriptions. The doctor gave him books to read, and when George least expected it, would question him to see how much he had absorbed. George responded to the extra chores and reading assignments with a cheerful smile and ready answers. The boy's quick mind and work ethic convinced the doctor he was definitely college material.

George was proud and excited when the doctor gave him a white laboratory smock to wear as a reward for his excellent work. Had he shared that bit of information with his mother, she would probably have wanted to deliver a sermon to the whole congregation. George witnessed some of his mother's behavior, and out of embarrassment began to keep more and more of his achievements to himself.

Early Saturday morning, George was in the basement laboratory performing one of the numerous tasks the doctor had written on a pad for him to complete. The assignments were listed in the order in which they were to be completed. George heard the doctor's familiar footsteps coming down the stairs, then the sound of a second set. He stood up as the doctor approached him. "George, I want you to meet someone," the doctor said, turning toward a tall, thin, white man trailing behind him. "This is Reverend Marion Mansell."

George approached the minister, who had extended his hand. After a brief hesitation, he extended his own. He had never shaken a white man's hand before.

"I'm please to meet you, sir."

"And I'm pleased to meet you as well, young man. The doctor has been telling me some very good things about you."

"The Reverend is a Presbyterian minister. His church runs a school in Rogersville. That's over in the north east corner of our state. Its' a preparatory school for colored boys and girls, and it offers mathematics, languages and science courses that you can't get in the school here. Remember, I told you these are courses you will need before you can be admitted to college."

George was all ears as the doctor spoke. He felt a joy he had never experienced before. Each day he felt he was taking a step toward realizing the promise he had made to his mother. "Will I be able to come home on weekends?"

"I'll let the Reverend answer that."

"No, once you get there, you will be there for the whole school year, son."

"I've been telling the Reverend about your promise to your mother, your improved grades and the good work you're doing for me. Based on all those factors, the Reverend thinks he will have a full scholarship available for you. All you have to do is keep your grades up."

George wasn't sure he understood everything being said, he certainly didn't know what a scholarship was, but everything seemed to add up to the fact that he was getting closer to keeping his promise. Now, he thought, he would share the good news with his mother.

At dinner that night, he told his mother everything he understood. He explained he might have to go off to a preparatory school before he could be accepted at a college. "I don't know quite what it is, but the Reverend said I would be able to get something called a scholarship, and he would be working closely with Doctor Bletso to help me get into college."

Mary sat in rapt attention, savoring every word flowing from her son's mouth. When he'd finished his explanation, her only comment was, "Praise the Lord." She got up from the table, walked to her son and kissed him on the forehead. "Son, I think I'm going to bed early tonight, and son…thank you." Her hand found the top of his head and she patted it gently.

In a few minutes George heard her bedroom door close.

If Mary's initial reaction to her son working for the doctor could have been described as prideful, the knowledge that her son would be attending college verged on overbearing; a feeling held by her church sisters. "Yes," She would say, "My son is mixing medicines, and taking tests to go to college!" Before long, the sisters would flee if they saw Mary headed their way with that special gleam in her eye.

A year passed before George realized he hadn’t seen Snake, or any of the gang. He’d been too busy with school for anything other than an occasional visit to Flo. He kept her abreast of everything that was happening, and she proved to be a good listener. Flo understood his determination to do better in school. He felt free to reveal his deepest thoughts and concerns to her. Their relationship grew deeper with each visit. Unlike Gloria, there was an ease with her. He could, and did discuss anything with this understanding woman.

When he thought back to his days with Gloria, he realized all they had in common was sex. She really hadn't cared about him as a person; in fact, he concluded she wasn’t a loving person at all. When he looked deeper, and it hurt him to do so, he recognized their relationship had been nothing more than a mere convenience for her.

The difference with Flo was she felt he was a special young man. She was proud of him for who he was, and for what he was trying to accomplish. She enjoyed George in ways she had never enjoyed a man before. This man-child coming into her life had been a blessing. Flo had said to him one day, “ If you was older, I’d march yo’ up to the altar, sho, nuf I would and make you and me legal as ken be.”

Flo, like his mother, couldn’t keep her pride in him to herself. She kept the girls informed about his job, his plans to go off to a special school, or anything else she was aware of. Through Flo, they felt they knew George, and had a special stake in him and his accomplishments, too.

Over time he became a special person to them. The girls loved to tease him, yet they respected what they saw as a special bond between himself and Flo. They would make mock advances, and Flo would play along and put on a display of defending what she claimed as hers. "You old hags, keep yo' hands off'n my man. He be mine alone," she would tease.

On day he asked between deep breaths, "Miss Flo can I ask you something?"

"Sho. You gonn'a ask me to marry you?"

George laughed, "When I come back from school. Will you wait that long for me?" He teased.

"No. Hell, I'll be an old hag by then. You better marry me right now!" They both laughed. "All right, now, what you wants to ax me?"

She began tickling him until he laughed so hard he couldn't breathe.

He began visiting her no more than once a week. In a way, he had no choice. The doctor kept him busy and he knew he had to keep his grades up. But, he willingly went along with the heavy schedule, fully aware of the prize he was determined to win.

As he headed home, he looked forward to a quiet evening of study. When he entered the house, he was surprised at the sight of a small, frail, black lady sitting on the living room couch. Mary heard her boy come in, and met him as he stepped into the living room. "George, meet your Grandmother, Fisk. She's going to be living with us for a while."

George went to the little lady and gave her a gentle hug. "I'm so glad to meet you, Grandma. Mama spoke of you often; she wondered what had happened to you."

Mary added, "We lost track of each other when I married your father and we moved up here from Jackson." She took a seat next to her mother. "Your Grandmother found us when she heard one of her church members say she stayed with a Mary Read in Chattanooga."

George stammered, "Was it a lady by the name of Gloria Brown?"

"Why yes. Dat be's the lady's name. Miss Gloria Brown." Grandma Fisk answered smiling.

"I tell you, it was a miracle." Mary said as her head moved side to side, "It was God's work, that's what it was." Her eyes closed and her hands assumed a prayerful position.

Grandma added, "Amen, praise the Lord!"

George now knew where Gloria was, and he couldn't help but wonder if she ever thought of him. He had mixed feelings as he thought about her for the first time in a long while. As he compared his relationship with Flo to the one he had with Gloria, he realized how really special Flo was. He was grateful the Snakes had pushed him up the steps that afternoon.

He sat in awe as he looked at the little black lady sitting on the couch. She was only the second relative he had ever met. The first was his father's only known living relative, a cousin, Roland Hayes who was making a name for himself as a singer. He had visited them briefly. But, after he left, they never heard from him again. George was too young to actually remember the visit. It only seemed real because his mother mentioned it often.

Mary had no brothers, or sisters, making Grandma very special to him. Whenever he had a spare minute he would spend it with her, wanting to learn as much as he could about her life in general, especially her life as a slave. And, Grandma was equally enthusiastic about spending time with him, enjoying their walks together. That gave her a feeling of closeness as they talked about one thing or another. She became even more impressed with her grandson as the days went by; it seemed he knew almost everyone. George ,on the other hand, enjoyed showing her off to anyone who stopped to talk. She was a special source of pride to him.

As they walked slowly down a side street, he recognized a familiar face coming towards them.

"Hey. Piggy! How you do'n man? Long time no see!" It was one of his old gang members.

"How you do'n Shorty? Oh, I want you to meet my Grandmother."

"Pleased to meet you, too ma'am." Shorty said, removing his cap and nodding his head respectfully.

Grandma smiled and nodded in recognition of his greeting, but made no attempt to engage him in conversation.

"Wha,cha do'n wit yo' self man? You don't come'n round no mo, how come?"

"It's a long story man. I'm busy with one thing or another. Hey, how are the guys doing and how's my main man Snake?"

Shorty looked at George for a moment. Disbelief showing on his face. "Man, you really ain't been around. You ain't heard?"

"Heard what?"

"We wuz at the shack one day, and ottt'a de blue, de police come, they grabbed all of the guys and puts dem on the chain gang."

"They took Snake too?"

"No, Snake weren't there. But a week later Snake, he got stabbed to death in a crap game. He wuz play'n wit some grown men, an he wuz win'n big off'a one dude.

Well, this dude, he gets mad, sez, 'no young punk gonn'a make a fool outt'a him. Pulls out a knife and puts it into Snakes heart. Kilt him dead, man."

George suddenly felt ill, but maintained a stoic attitude. He tried to end the conversation quickly and finally said, "Well, I guess I'll be see'n you around, man."

"Yeah, Look, you should come around. Some of us, we still be hanging at the usual places even tho Snake ain't with us no mo."

"Sure, shorty, see you around." George said as he and he and grandma walked away, George remained quiet for a long time. His mind was racing. Lord have mercy, he had gotten away from the gang just in time. Had he been there the day the police came and put them on the chain gang, everything would have come out, his mother would have found out what he had been up to for all those years. It would have hurt her so badly and made him so ashamed he wouldn't have been able to look her in the eye.

Grandma broke the silence. "George, now jes' who be dat boy?"

"Grandma, he's a friend, but I don't see him anymore."

"Dat's good son, cuz dat boy, he spells trouble, you bes' stay away from em."

"You're ever so right. Don't you worry none grandma. I don't see him anymore."

"Good, son. Good."

After they resumed their walk, George asked, "Grandma, can you tell me what it was like to be a slave?"

Grandma turned toward him. "Sho son, I can tells ya, it were hard. Ya see, we wuz slaves in Virginn'y. My massa, Fitts. He were a mean man. He would wuk us from ken see, to kan't see. One day I wer so sick, I couldn't move outt'a ma bed. Massa he hear bout dat, and he come into da quarters wit a single tree. An' he beats me outt'a ma bed. Sez I wuz jes' fak'n be'n sick; dats' how he fus' come to take notice of me."

"Weeks later, he come look'n fo me. He tuk me to a cabin he kept jes' fo his use, and der, he had his way wit me. Dat's how come yo mammy come out so light skinned. When I start show'n, he took me outt'a de fields, an' lets me wuk round de yard. Dis wuk were not too hard, neither. He lets me do dat till yo mammy were born, till she be 'bout five years old. Den, he puts a house servant in charge ub her, an he sends me back to de fields. Den, I only gets to see my child once in a while. But yo mammy…she was raised by dat lady, mo dan by me, raised up in de big house."

"Yo mammy, she us'ta play wit his fo real gurl chile, fo a few years. Den, da let her wuk in de house, do'n laundry and help'n clean. Later, da lets her work in de kitchen. She learn quick, too. Dat's why she be such a good cook. Now, you hear how yo mammy speak? She roun' white folks so much, she speaks, an ax jes like dem."

"Grandma if you were slaves in Virginia, how'd you end up in Mississippi?"

"It were after the Civil War. We wuz wuk'n in de cotton field in de hot sun, outta the blue some up North, white soldiers come walk'n by. Da sees us wuk'n in de fields, so da yells, "Yo all gett'n paid fo de wuk yo all do'n?'

We yell back, "Slaves don't get no pay fo' wuk."

"Well, don't yo all know we won de war, de war is obber, you all is as free as we is!'"

George looked at his Grandmother in awe. "What did you do then, Grandma?"

"Well, we jes puts our hoes down, goes back to de cabin an picks up some things; clothes, a few pots and pans what to cook in, den, we jes starts walk'n. Den, I ax'd which way to Mississippi? Dey sez its South, an' we should head norf. Myself, yo mammy an a few mo say, we wanna go find kin folks whut wuz sent dar by our massa. Dat's whur ma Pappy were sent. So, we breaks up…most ob dem, da go norf, a few ob us, we goes South. Along de way, I finds a pistol on de battle fields. I brung it wit me. I'll show it to you when we gets home."

"How long did it take you, Grandma?"

"It took a long, long, time. It were hard. Didn't keep no account'n of the time. But, it be ova a month, close to two, I rec'n. We stops here and der, wuk'n fo food an' a place to lay our heads and ta keep our bodies and souls together. Some of de ones whut starts off wit us, stays where da finds wuk, da rest ob us, keeps on go'n. We walks, walks till we ends up in Jackson. I found wuk der, an in time yo mammy, she meets up wit Isaac, yo daddy, en den, she marries em, en goes off wit him…an we jes loose trak ob each odder."

They had walked and talked for over an hour, totally lost in their conversation, George glanced to the side where she should be, but she wasn't there. He spun around, horrified to see her standing in the gutter, arms at her side, head bowed. "Grandma, what are you doing?" At first she didn't acknowledge his question. Finally she raised her head, then, looked in the direction of the white woman who had approached and passed them.

"Grandma, you don't have to get off the side walk anymore." However, his pleas fell on deaf ears. No matter how many times he reminder her, she continued to do what had been beaten into her since she was a little girl. He finally stopped trying to change her in that regard.

Sunday's church service was over. George and Grandma sat side by side in rockers on the front porch, he reading a book that doctor Bletso had loaned him, and she sitting quietly observing him. When he looked up from the book, Grandma asked in a soft voice, "Son...what do those little dots tell you?"

"Grandma, those little dots are letters, and the letters, put together make words. A lot of words put together, one after the other tell a story, just like you told me stories about slavery. Only instead of telling the story by talking, these dots tell the same story on the pages of books. These words tell me different things that I want to learn about. Do you understand?"

"I think so, Maybe you reads to me some?"

George went into the house, returning with a fifth grade reader. Opening the book, he read a simple story. "Do you see what I mean now, Grandma?"

She peered over glasses perched at the end of her nose. Clearing her throat, she asked, "Son, you reckon you could learn me about what dem little dots say?"

"Yes Grandma. I can teach you what those little dots say." Getting up from his chair, he knelt before her. Taking her gnarled hands into his, he kissed them tenderly.

A year later, George boarded a train for Rogersville, Tennessee and Swift Memorial College.

CHAPTER 5

The Bradleys

Rogersville, Tennessee could be described as a mere speck on the map. It boasted a population of a few hundred white and colored souls. There were no particular neighborhood boundaries that dictated where people lived. Folks lived interspersed: a black family here, a white family there. It was as likely a neighbor would be of the opposite race as one of your own kind…and on occasion, whites rented from colored folks.

Tilts Bradley was a brick-mason and owned a one-story wooden house on the edge of town. He rented a cabin located at the back end of his property to a hillbilly family, John Bear, his wife, and six children. He and his clan came from one of the nearby mountains where most of his kin still remained. John did odd jobs around town, but more important he was the town contact for the sale of his brother's moonshine to the local town folks.

Tilts was fully aware of what John did: however, that didn't bother him one bit. "The man pays his rent on time, and he don't keep me up nights. So, as far as I'm concerned, he's all right in my book,"was his response when neighbors gossiped, or when someone might be critical of John and his brother's activities.

Once, John's clan was having a battle with a rival group of hill folks. To protect their inventory of moonshine from possible destruction, Tilts let them bury (under cover of darkness) hundreds of gallons of the stuff in the muck of his hog pen for safe keeping. This was done without his wife Mary's knowledge. She would have had a fit had she known such an activity was going on her property.

Tilts, his wife and five children lived comfortably. He worked hard and maximized every opportunity that came his way. His main source of income was from his trade as a brick mason. He specialized in laying up chimneys. Locals knew a chimney done by Tilts would be trouble-free and draw well. Because of his reputation, Tilts never had to look for work. He was as busy as he wanted to be.

In addition to his regular income, he raised hogs, chickens, and maintained a garden large enough to keep his family well supplied in 'put up' vegetables and enough tobacco to keep himself supplied in smokes, and 'chaw'.

The buildings on his property were an even weather-beaten gray bleached to this hue from the sun, wind and rain, giving his property an overall neat appearance. The two brick chimneys he had laid at opposite ends of his house and the bright red tin roof were the most distinguishing features of his home.

The property was situated well back from the main dirt road, positioned in such a way that a stranger could easily miss the wagon trail that led up to it. A fence separated his property line from the adjacent property. Tall grass that grew on both sides of the fence acted as a camouflage for the trail to his home. Tilts liked being somewhat inaccessible, reasoning it made it harder for someone to sneak up on him, or his family.

He was a tall, big boned, brown-skinned man with a bulbous nose, and deep set honey-colored eyes that always had a mischievous twinkle. He was a hard worker, but he liked to laugh and have a good time, too. His main sources of pleasure came from his children. He liked nothing more than to assemble them on the porch while he sat in his high back rocker, and held them spellbound with fanciful stories. There were five in all, four girls and a boy.

The sun's last rays had just disappeared behind the rugged hills behind their house, the fire fly's flickering lights became brighter and brighter with the passing of each minute. The assembled children wore expectant looks, reflecting the knowledge they were in for a special treat. A small voice called out, "Papa, tell us the ol' haunted house story tonight!" "Yes. Papa! Tell us the haunted house story." The other children would echo.

Tilts, surveyed their faces as he leaned forward in his rocker, took aim, then, let fly a squirt of tobacco juice between two of the girls. The girls knew instinctively to move and turn their bodies aside quickly when Papa wanted to spit. He then began speaking softly, almost in a whisper.

"De ol haut house, hits haunted yet
An no body lives dar...no you bet
Standin up dar on de black oak hill,
An every thing about it so quiet and still
Caint hear an owl or whippor-poo-will
Members dat place long time a-go
En hern tell ob it logng time befo
Folks caint libe dar! No sir-ee
Folks whut own hit offers hit free

Some goes dar en ez meny comes away
En de gurn en comin am on de same day
Night settles down en de jes caint stay

Thems white foks whut tries hit you know
Nebber ben a nigger inside de do'
Floors may sway wid diamons en gold
If left to de nigers hit'll nebber be stole.

Aint nebber hear tell of but one cullard man
Whut made up his mind fer to try his han-
'ed he sorta tuck it on de 'stallment plan
Yes-suh! Jim Jones wuz de gennamins name
An fer a niger you could call him game,
Least wise if you listen to whut he say
'bout de number of uf enemies he gwin
ter slay.

He brag so stout, en he boast so strong
Dat folks all believe whut he say 'fore long
En 'gree wid him whuther right er wrong.
Bout dis time when his fame spred roun'
As a man 'mungst men what would stan his
ground
De owners of de haint house call on him

En he say, "Dey tells me Jim,
Dat you is a man whut knows no fear,
An Ise come all de way ober hyar
Been searchin' from fur an near.
Jim, 'nowledged de fack-den de man he say;

If Jim go to dat house en stay fur one lone
Nite to prove to de foks dat all haint talk--
Nothing but jokes, he'll git a hundred dollars
Or his picture in de paper jes fer to show.
De bravest man de world ebber no"

It aint writ how Jim feel 'bout dis
But here came a chance he jest couldn't miss!
To prove that he could stan his groun-
Take his claim all de time he wuz bragging around

En he went! I'll give him his jues!
But he fooled 'roun de gate lak' he couldn't get
through
En tuck in de house from dat pont of view,
Den Jim he say, "De corntrack read I believe
Dat I stay at de house an nebbeer will leave
Fum nine or ten o'clock at nite
Plum on thru twell plum daylite.
But! Hit dont say stay in de house you see
So a seat on de steps will about suit me.

So Jim tuck a seat on de steps and smoked
An thought'bout haint tales bein' a joke
An tried to smile at de joke-but failed.
Fur de thunder rooled en de win hit wailed.

Den cum uh crash in dar on de flo
En sumpin e'nuther run a'gin de do.
En his har uncurled when he heard a shout
De spirits am up en walkin about!
Man on de steps-you'd best lite out!

Den Jim he say, "Ise looked fer hants
En hants I's foun-But I won mix wide
Kase dey got no sense."
Wid dat he set his foot on de fence
En stepped out in to de elements!

Jim Claimed atterward dat he never did run
When folks sorta tease him to have some fun
But a man whut seed de way he was gwine
Said he had to run sidewise to deep from fly'n

Yas suh! De ol' house looks all right
Likes you look at hit now in de broad day lite.
But when nite settles down en clouds hang low
En de wailin and wind commences to blow
En haints gin tar prowl-hits time to go!

The children squealed, laughed and giggled with delight. By their response a stranger would have thought they had never heard the story before. In truth, they had heard it, as well as most of the other stories he told countless times. Yet, they never tired of hearing them, and he never tired of telling and retelling his yarns. The children loved the intimacy they shared during those moments, feeling a part of something uniquely theirs as a family.

"Tell us another story Papa?" Anchrum, the son asked.

"Please…please." The girls chorused.

"No, no more tonight, you hav' ta get up early for church…so it's off to bed you go."

There was no mumbling, or protesting; Papa had spoken. The girls got up from their porch seats and made an informal line as each gave him a hug and a kiss on his stubble covered face. He gently patted each one on the head as they marched away and went to their bedroom door. Anchrum, standing on the ground said, "Good night Papa," and headed toward the back of the house.

"Good night, son."

The girls went to their minimally furnished bedroom; two double beds pushed together with just enough space between them to stand while making up the beds. A large dresser with an assigned drawer for each girl's use, and a wash stand completed the furnishings.

Rosa, the eldest, was responsible for the girl's bed-time preparation. Each night she laid out their night gowns and brushed the hair of her two youngest sisters. Lena, less than two years younger than Rosa, did her own.

As Thelma, the youngest, washed up, Ada and Lena, played with their own home-made sock dolls that had spent the day resting against chicken feather pillows, all lined up in a neat row.

Ada decided to put her doll to sleep, and placed it next to her on her pillow. "I want you to put your doll to bed, too Lena!" Thelma commanded from her bed.

Lena scowled at her sister, "No, my doll isn't tired yet. She wants to play some more."

"Rosa, make Lena put her doll to bed!"

"Rosa isn't my mother. She can't make me!" Lena replied defiantly.

Rather than placate Thelma, or challenge Lena, Rosa took a different tact. "Would you girls like me to tell you the haunted house story that Papa told?"

"Oh, yes, yes!" they all replied.

Rosa smiled, "All right, as soon as Lena is through washing up, I will, but you'll have to wait until then." She was pleased to have been able to avoid a fight between Lena and herself.

After Thelma finished washing, Rosa helped her baby sister empty the wash basin outside.

Ada and Lena were able to manage washing and cleaning up on their own. After Rosa sponged off, the others put themselves to bed. Rosa slept with Thelma, and Ada with Lena. They had just gotten into bed when their mother, knocked and opened the door. Mary was a tall, attractive dark brown woman. Her features and hair bore her Cherokee heritage; her color reflected her African blood. She peered around the room to see that they were tucked under the covers. Satisfied, she squeezed between the beds and gave each girl a good night kiss. "Good night girls, sleep well, see you bright and early for church. Did you say your prayers before you went to bed?"

Rosa answered, "Oh, I'm sorry, we forgot."

"Well, we will have to do better than that, won't we?"

The girls threw off their covers, jumped out of bed and quickly knelt by the foot of the beds, then said a short prayer. Prayers said, they jumped back into bed.

"Good night Mother." They responded.

"Good night girls."

After a few minutes, Rosa whispered, "You all be real quiet and I'll tell you the story, how's that?"

The girls agreed they would.

Speaking softly, she repeated Papa's story of less than an hour ago, word for word, inflection and dialect, just as he had told it. The girls muffled their laughter by covering their mouths and burrowing their heads deep under the covers. Telling the story in secret caused even more laughter to erupt as one girl after another began giggling for no reason other than they were feeling totally silly. Finally, Rosa spoke up, "All right, that's enough. Mama will hear us and start yelling. Anyway, it's time to go to sleep. Remember, we have to get up early." A few last second giggles broke through the darkness, but within minutes, the children were all sound asleep.

Anchrum had washed off outside. In the Bradley household, men and boys didn't wash indoors as long as the weather was reasonably mild. Once he dried off, he found his mother in the kitchen and gave her a good night kiss before putting himself to bed in his tiny room located off from the kitchen.

Mary finished up her kitchen chores, then, went out to the porch to join her husband. She found him sitting in the dark, smoking his corn cob pipe. She took a seat in the smaller rocker positioned next to his. "Tilts Bradley, I do declare. I wish you would stop telling our children those God-awful stories. It jest ain't right filling their heads with such nonsense. You tell your stories to your friends, you tell them to strangers, you tell them where ever you go. Can't you at least spare the children?"

"Awe, Mary, it don't hurt them none, just something to laugh about that's all. An' Mary, I ain't ignoring ya. It's like I been tell'n ya, if I thought it did them harm, I wouldn't do it." It was one of their marital rituals. She would fuss whenever he told the children stories, and he would defend himself by declaring it harmless fun. She knew he wouldn't stop, as it was ingrained into his very soul. He would spin yarns anywhere he could find a willing ear, or, as sometimes was the case, an unwilling one. Tilts had earned the reputation of being one of the greatest story tellers in North East Tennessee.

Mary knew he wasn't going to budge, so she changed the subject. "I put up two dozen jars of tomatoes today. You can start bringing in string beans on Monday."

"All right, I'll pick a bushel before I go to work. That should hold you for a while. I have a new chimney to lay up, but I can do it a'fore I leave. If ya need's more, ask Rosa and Anchrum to pick 'em when they get home from school. Now, I don't want you go'n out in that hot sun, Mary. You let the children do the pick'n if you need more."

"No, I won't. Anyway, I think what you pick will be enough for the day."

The big man turned his gaze to his wife, "You know you look mighty pretty, Mary, you know that, don't you, honey?"

"Now you hush."

"It's the way the moon light falls on your face and hair."

"Oh, you stop that sweet talk, Tilts Bradley."

Without another word, he reached over with his large, rough masons hands and skillfully pulled out the pins that held her hair in a bun. The removal of the pins caused her thick black hair to fall down to her waist. Tilts stood, took her by the hand, and led her to the bedroom.

Much later, he watched Mary's face as she slept peacefully, her features bathed in the brightness of the moon's light. He rolled over on his back, and stared at the ceiling, thinking how content he was with his life, and his family. He treasured moments like this, allowing his mind to wander wherever it pleased. It was one of the ways he'd come up with ideas for a story or yarn. Sometimes he would take an actual event, and reshape it in his mind. Once he did that, he'd try it out on some unsuspecting person, watching to see what part of the story evoked laughter and what parts didn't. He'd tell it until he got the kind of response he wanted. If it didn't evoke enough laughter, he'd tinker with it until it did. Everything was grist for his mill. One true event became a ditty, rather than a story. It happened like this.

John Murray, the local constable was known as a bully. He loved to beat up on people, white, or black, it didn't matter to him. And, he didn't need any provocation, just opportunity. One night Constable Murray ran into little Sam Brown on a lonely dark street. First, he verbally abused Sam; then, he commenced to whip him with his billy club. What the constable didn't know was, while Sam was a little man, he was also powerfully built. In fact, he was stronger than any two ordinary men.

This morning after his encounter with the little man, Constable Murray didn't report to work. The reason he gave was that he had been jumped by two or three hooligans, and beaten badly.

The truth eventually surfaced and became known to the community at large because of Sam's sister. He came home after the altercation to pick up a few possessions before he left town for good that night. As he packed, he told May Bell, how Murray started a fight with him; began hitting him in the head with his club for no reason at all. Sam managed to take Officer Murray's club and gun away, and tossed them into the bushes. After he disarmed the constable, he methodically put a hurt'n on him with his fists. Normally a peaceful man, and slow to anger, Sam was quite the opposite once he was wronged. Then, it took an army to hold him down. Unfortunately for Constable Murray, there was no army to come to his rescue.

The truth of what happened that evening became known because Rosa and her father were working in the garden when a neighbor came by and asked. "Tilts, you heard the latest about Constable Murray?"

"Nah, I ain't heard noth'n new about that no good scoundrel. Why?"

"Well, Murray ran into Sam Brown in a dark alley and decided he was go'n to put a whupp'n on him. Seems he didn't know anything about little Sam Brown, cuz nobody in his right mind would take on Sam. Shoot him, yeah. But try'n to beat Sam with a stick? Well, that there weren't too smart." The man filled Tilts in on every detail of the story as it had been relayed to him.

As the neighbor spoke, a big grin spread over Tilts face, and soon he began singing;

"Constable Murray was the bully of the town,
Till little Sam Brown, just mowed him down!"

Rosa had been all ears as the story unfolded, and laughed at her father's ditty. That night she sang it for her sisters. The next day, she sang it to some of her school friends, who sang it to their friends and family members. Soon, almost every child in Rogersville knew it. From that day forth, Constable Murray's life was never the same. Whenever children, (black or white) saw him, they sang how 'Little Sam Brown, just mowed him down!' Then, would scamper away; laughing at the way his face contorted, and turned red.

Tilts had been anxious and proud to be a father, and because Rosa was his first born, loved doting on her. He'd spend every free moment he could with her. As a tiny infant he'd carry her around the yard, showing her the flowers and the fruit trees, all the while, talking to her as though she were a much older child.

As the years went by, he involved her in as many activities as possible. He shared his interest in gardening and hunting. Without any encouragement from her father, Rosa tended to be a tomboy; she could climb a tree, skip rocks on the river as well as any boy, and was fascinated by snakes. But, she had no interest in learning to shoot. She would sit contentedly next to Papa when he went hunting, enjoying the quietness and solitude of the woods, and listening to his explanations of its many wonders.

He understood the habits of the birds, lizards, snakes and the animals they observed. Sometimes he would stop mid-sentence to point out an animal slipping through the forest shadows, or raise his rifle, take aim and shoot a squirrel. He'd explain. "Of course you can just shoot 'em, or you can hit the bark under their head. If you do it right, the shell hit'n the bark acts like a small explosion an, it sorta stuns 'em. When they drops to the ground, all you gotta do is knock'em in the head. That way the meat don't get all shot up." On a good afternoon, they would return with six or seven, enough for a good squirrel potpie.

Rosa was so mindful that many of her father's habits annoyed her mother, she often counted the ways: The story telling, his love of guns and knives, his use of swear words, and tobacco. Worst of all, she saw purple when the subject of his raising and fighting game cocks came up, the latter two being high on her list of sins. She remembered the time she scolded Papa for showing her brother Anchrum how to pull an ordinary pocket knife out of his pocket fully open. Papa demonstrated to his son by putting a bean in the slot the knife blade dropped in into, causing the tip to stick up a tiny bit. When he pulled the knife out, he'd hook the blade's tip on this pants. As he drew his hand out further, the knife's blade was fully open, and exposed.

Mary thought teaching her son such a thing was an absolute disgrace. Rosa however, found the instruction clever, and admired her father's resourceful mind.

At age thirteen, Rosa began attending Swift Memorial College full time. As a gifted, bright and eager student, she skipped grades throughout her early school life. She would routinely end up the youngest in her class. Her freshman class at Swift was no exception. Until college, school had always been easy. Now she found her courses required extra effort. And she had to devote more time to study to keep her grades up. To that end, she found it helpful to prepare for tests and reports by studying with her class mate and cousin, Annie Brice.

Cousin Annie lived a mile from Rosa, it was a walk she looked forward to since the road was remote, and rimed with a variety of fragrant wild flowers and a haven for birds and small animals. With the demands of school, house chores and her little sisters, she seldom had time for herself. The trip to Cousin Annie was fun. The route to her cousin's house was more of a trail than a road. She loved listening to the sounds of nature, and the walk gave her the opportunity to let her mind drift, and to day dream. Their occasional get-together was a special treat.

This morning Rosa had gotten up early to do her Saturday chores before heading off to Cousin Annie's. After her arrival, the girls spent several hours questioning each other in order to prepare for their upcoming tests. In time, both felt confident that they had mastered their subjects. Finally, their brains became fatigued, and the girls decided it was time to enjoy the little time they had left before Rosa had to leave. They got up from the kitchen table and went outside and sat on the porch swing. They relaxed for a while, laughing, talking and sipping iced tea. Finally Rosa said, "Well, I'd better get back home to help Mama with the children."

"All right cousin; let's hope we do well on our tests." Annie said as Rosa departed down the front steps.

"I'm sure we will." Rosa answered happily.

Rosa was lost in her own thoughts as she neared a small foot bridge. She saw two white men approaching from the opposite side. She gave them no thought, and without hesitation stepped onto the bridge and continued on towards them. As they approached, the men laughed and blocked her path. "I'd like to do you, you little b.....!" One of the men muttered, as each grabbed her firmly by a breast. Rosa screamed as she broke free and ran as fast as her legs would carry her back home. Her reaction prompted more raucous laughter from the men as they watched her tear up the road, screaming hysterically.

As she ran up the path to her house she screamed, "I've been raped, I've been raped!" Her mother was outside hanging clothes when she heard her daughter's screams.

"Child…what's wrong?" She had never seen Rosa in such a state.

"Mama, oh Mama, two white men, they raped me!"

"Shhh. Shhh child; now you come over here to your Mama, and tell her what happened."

Tilts had come home early and had been nodding off on the porch, in his rocker, half awake, half asleep, when Rosa's voice broke into his consciousness. The words 'rape', and 'two white men', snapped him fully awake. Without hesitation, or waiting for any further explanation, he burst into the house, fire in his eyes.

Meanwhile, Mary was trying to get the details of exactly what had happened. However, Rosa was sobbing and crying hysterically, unable to find her voice, unable to answer any of her mother's questions. The only sounds she was capable of making were deep, wrenching sobs.

Tilts kept loaded shotguns over all three of the houses doorways. If he heard a noise at night, he had only to reach up, grab a gun, open the door and step outside, ready for anything, without ever breaking stride. On this occasion, he did the reverse; he opened the screen door from the outside, reached up and pulled the gun off the wooden pegs "Come on, Rosa, you show me the sons of bitches that raped you!" He grabbed her arm in a firm grip, then, led her down the path to the main road leading to town.

As he rushed away with his hysterical child, Mary pleaded, "Now, Tilts Bradley, don't you go off and do something foolish!"

With Rosa in tow, Tilts headed for the courthouse square in the center of town. The square was where local men congregated to pass the day in silence, or in conversation, smoking or chewing tobacco. By custom, the white men sat on the benches facing Main Street, the colored men sat on the benches facing the two side streets. Huge trees provided ample shade for both groups. Most of the men wore battered straw hats and faded bibbed overalls. Some had red handkerchiefs tied loosely around their necks. The white men varied in skin tone from beet red to pale white. The colored men offered an assortment of skin tones from white, to brown, to yellow, to jet black and shades in between. All together, the men presented a pallet of colors as the sun's light filtered through the shade trees, and down on them.

As he paraded Rosa past the white men he hissed, "Jes show me the bastards and they're dead men!" Tilts demanded as they walked past the line of white men. Some looked up, not having the faintest idea why Tilts (whom most knew) was dragging his daughter down the street, a gun cradled in his arm. One man who knew Tilts, looked up as he approached and in his Tennessee twang asked, "What's going on Tilts…ken I hep ya?" Tilts didn't answer, instead, he continued on past the men.

"I don't see them Papa. I don't see the men. They aren't here."

Without another word, Tilts turned and headed home.

Mary's heart had been pounding ever since her husband headed to town with her first born. She didn't know how much longer she could wait for him to return without tearing her hair out. She felt her heart would surely jump out of her chest. She'd taken up her vigil on the porch, straining for a glimpse of them, praying with all her heart and soul that he would return unharmed, and even harder that Rosa didn't see the men she said had raped her. Finally, she spotted them walking up the path to the house. "Thank you Lord for answering my prayer," She murmured softly.

"We didn't see them today, but by God, I'll take her out every day till we see 'em." Tilts roared.

"Now Tilts Bradley, you ain't gonn'a do anything but get yourself killed, and cause a lot of trouble. Anyway, I need to talk to Rosa. You jes' get outta here for a while."

Tilts heeded Mary's admonition, then, headed for the indoor cabinet where he kept a bottle of moonshine. He poured himself a half a water glass, went back outside, sat in his rocker and sipped his drink.

Mary brought Rosa into the dining room and sat her down. Taking her hands, Mary began, "Now, Rosa, tell your Mama exactly what happened. Tell me everything those men did to you." Mary had noticed when her daughter burst into the house screaming. "Rape!" her clothing had no tears or dirt spots on them.

Finally, somewhat composed, Rosa began. "Mama, I was crossing the little bridge, down by cousin Annie's and these two men…" her lips began to quiver, and her voice broke.

"Yes child, now what did these men do to you, exactly, I must know."

Clearing her throat she began again, "Well, they blocked my way, so I couldn't pass by them. Then they started laughing, and saying things, nasty things."

"Then what, child?"

"They grabbed my breast. Each one did. Each one grabbed it real hard."

"What else did they do?" Mary said, trying to sound calm, dreading to hear what else they might have done. "Did they do anything else, or was that all they did to you?"

"That's exactly what they did. Then, I broke free and ran just as fast as I could."

A look of relief passed over Mary's face. "They didn't touch you anyplace else?" What you told me, that's all they did. Is that right?" Mary pursued.

"Yes, Mama, that's right. That's exactly what they did."

Mary sighed a deep sigh of relief. She realized how close her family had come to a fatal disaster. She thanked God Rosa had not seen these men at the court house square. "Rosa, what those men did to you was not right. They had no right touching you. But, you were not raped." Mary proceeded to have the most difficult conversation she had ever had with her daughter, and she also let Rosa know what could have happened to her father, had she seen those two men.

Rosa went to bed older, wiser and shaken to her very core, fully aware her ignorance could have caused the death of Papa and the destruction of her entire family. As she lay in bed sobbing, her sisters crawled into bed with her, and smothered her with their warm bodies, each child trying in her own special way, to comfort their the comforter. As they cuddled, Lena hummed a soft lullaby. Before long, the youngest ones fell asleep. Soon, exhaustion overtook Lena and Rosa, and they, too, finally slept.

During the night Rosa dreamed animals from the forest had broken into their house and taken Papa away. She tried to chase the animals in order to rescue him, but her legs wouldn't move; they were stuck fast in mud. His screams awakened her from the nightmare. She sat up in bed fully awake, realizing her fright was based on a dream and wasn't real. She said, "Thank you Jesus, thank you for looking after us today. Thank you for being a merciful God." Finally, she surrendered herself to a peaceful sleep.

Time has a way of healing all wounds, and, the episode with her father eventually faded to the point where she didn't have the recurring dream about the forest animals, or, dwell on that awful day during her waking moments.

Two years passed, and Rosa had entered her third and final year at Swift. She looked forward to graduation and starting her career as a teacher.

Today in science class she wondered if she would be one of the persons her instructor, Mrs. Downs, would call on to give the assigned homework report. The thought has just entered her mind when she heard her name called: "Rosa Bradley, we will now hear your report."

Rosa walked to the front of the class. She felt confident because of the long hours she had spent on her assignment, feeling she had honed it to perfection. As she walked to the front, she reviewed all she had learned in her public speaking class. While she was a confident and good speaker, she didn't always know what to do with her eyes. Her instructor had stressed the need to appear to make eye contact with the audience, especially when giving a written report. She reminded herself to look up from the paper and in the direction of her classmates. Since she knew the subject well, she would pick a spot in the back of the room, above every one's head and focus on it. She tried hard not to make eye contact with an individual. If she did, it wasn't for long. She found it could be distracting.

Rosa began her report by looking up from her papers often, even looking around the room at times. All the while her body language exuded confidence. Half way through the report, she realized the eyes of one boy had been riveted on her and she found it troublesome. He had been observing her intently since she first began her report. She tried hard to ignore his fixed stare, finding it unsettling. Now she was becoming annoyed. Deciding she wasn't going to allow him to make her feel uncomfortable, she'd stare right back at him.

As she spoke, her eyes traversed the room until they found his. Now she thought, 'I'll turn the table on him and make him feel uncomfortable; I'll give him a dose of his own medicine.' Rosa had seen him in a few other classes, and remembered seeing him doing odd jobs around the grounds. The one thing that impressed her about him was that he seemed more mature than the other boys. As she examined him more closely, she noticed his eyes were brown, extremely large, perfectly round and bright, and, despite her staring back at him, his eyes never moved from her. For a full minute, she returned his gaze. Then, something happened; she lost her train of thought and had no idea where she was in her presentation. She was momentarily confused, and had to look away from the boy to gather her thoughts. She took a deep breath to compose herself and tried to pick up where she had gotten lost. For the rest of her presentation, Rosa ignored the young man's side of the room.

After class, the same youth stood waiting outside the classroom. He moved forward when she came through the door and fell in step with her as they walked down the hallway. Then he said, "That was an excellent report you gave.You must have been up all night preparing it." He concluded.

"No," She replied, shaking her head, "I don't find science that hard…it's one of my easiest subjects. But Latin, now I do find that really hard."

The boy smiled, "I must say it shows, I mean your grasp of science. Oh, by the way, my name is George Isaac Read, and you're Rosa Bradley, correct?"

"That's correct." She answered, flattered that the young man knew her full name.

Outside they walked down a hedge lined path and continued to chat easily about school. As they did, Rosa realized for some reason she was attracted to this young man. If someone were to press her to give a specific reason for her attraction, she'd say it was the ease with which they could talk. She knew she'd like to see him again, and as if to find a way to do that, she asked, "Do you go to church, George?"

He replied, “I did when I was home. I haven’t attended since I’ve been here.”

“Would you like to come to church with my family, and me this Sunday? I attend the First Baptist Church.”

“Yes, I’d be pleased to accompany you to church, Rosa,” He smiled inwardly, hardly able to contain his surprise and pleasure at the invitation.

“Fine. Then I’ll see you there Sunday morning at eleven O”clock.” Rosa replied, pleased that she had the nerve to ask him.

They said their good-byes, then, went separate ways.

Rosa had no way of knowing George had been watching her for the past two years. He had a working scholarship, and sometimes got to class at the very last moment. To avoid causing disruption, he would take a seat near the rear of the room and somewhat out of sight to his classmates. But, he had a full view of them, and she had been his main focus. He was fascinated by her quick mind, ready smile and womanly body. Despite his initial attraction to her, this had been his first conversation, and now that they had had an opportunity to talk, he was even more impressed with her. As he walked away he thought, ‘One day that girl will by my wife, and the mother of my children.’

George arrived at church early. He stood off to the side and received friendly smiles, and good mornings from some of the regular attendees entering the building. Several church members recognizing him as a stranger, offered, “You’re welcome to come in son” as they walked by.

“Thank you, I’m waiting for someone.” He replied politely.

It wasn't long before he saw them coming. Rosa, her mother, and he assumed her three sisters, and a brother, but no father. He wondered why. He hoped the reason for his absence wouldn't be tragic as in his case.

It was difficult to suppress his pleasure as he watched Rosa walking towards him. She looked beautiful in her Sunday best: large white hat, frilly dress and gloves. He was totally smitten by her grace and charm. Rosa greeted George, then introduced him to her mother and siblings. Once inside the church, Mary made sure Rosa was able to sit next to this fine looking young man. After services, Mary invited George home for Sunday dinner, and the opportunity to meet her husband, Tilts.

Neither Rosa, or her mother had mentioned why her father wasn't in church, just that he would have a chance to meet him later in the day. George thought maybe he was crippled like Yeller's dad, and home bound. He thought it unusual for the head of the family not to attend church with his family.

After services, Mary and the children walked ahead of Rosa and George, giving them some semblance of privacy as they trailed behind.

Once they entered the yard, he saw a tall man sitting on the porch, smoking a pipe. "Howdy you all." The man called out.

"Hello, Papa." The children answered as the younger ones rushed forward for hugs and kisses.

"Who's that ya got there with you?"

Rosa answered, "Papa, I'd like you to meet a classmate of mine, George Isaac Read."

Tilts stood and offered a hand to the youth. "Good to meet ya, son."

"George, I'm going to change and help the little ones change, but I'll be back shortly. Meanwhile you and Papa can get acquainted."

"Come son. Let's take a walk." As they headed to the back it became crystal clear why the big man wasn't in church. He wasted no time in launching into his philosophy, and the code by which he lived. "Son, I believe a man has to make at least two big choices in life. He's gonn'a have to choose a religion or a faith to live by, and, he's got to choose a wife. Mark my word, son, those are gonn'a be the most important decisions you will ever have to make. You'll see, one day you'll face those choices. Can't no one do that for you, neither."

"I never thought about it quite like that, sir; but I understand your point." George said in complete honesty, wondering why the conversation had headed to those subjects so quickly.

"Since the rest of the family had gone inside to change, why don't we just walk around some?"

"I'd like that, sir."

"Now, back to what I was say'n about religion. Ya, see. I can sit in the woods and worship God. I don't need no man made box to sit in ta talk to Him. And I don't need no middle man ta talk to Him for me. My wife, she don't agree with me, but she has a right to her thoughts. And I have the same rights, too."

George nodded and smiled at the man's logic. He liked this big, frank-talking man.

Tilts walked him around the house to his garden, pointing out the various vegetable he was growing, as well as the flower beds that bordered his house and garden. He told George with a certain amount of pride about the hog pen, and how it had been used to hide moonshine. "Now let me show ya something I bet you ain't never, ever seen before." He led him to the small building where he kept his game cocks. They were confined to small cages, eight in all, neatly stacked, one cage on top of the other. "That's what I do with my Sunday mornings. That's where I wuz today. It upsets the wife, but I ain't gonn'a listen to no man what don't get his hands dirty do'n an honest days work, while he asks me to hand over my hard-earned money to him. No Siree. How's that help'n God?"

George didn't know if he was expected to respond, but he gave a noncommittal answer, "I see your point, sir."

"Maybe one day, I'll take you so you can see my roosters fight."

"I'd like that, sir."

After leaving the shed, Tilts began pointing out his prize flowers, arranged neatly in beds, and borders around the property. George felt it was as if he had returned to his childhood and was walking with Ol' Bob, the Farr's gardener. George remembered the many hours he had spent soaking up information about nature. Because of the time he spent with the gardener, he was able to converse with Rosa's Dad as an equal, impressing the older man tremendously with his knowledge.

Tilts turned to the boy, "I live by a simple belief,. Ya wann'a know what it is?"

"Yes. Yes sir, I do."

"A man that knows nature, knows God. That's my belief. And my boy, I'd say right off, I believe you know God."

George didn't realize it at the time, but he had passed Tilts' 'test' with flying colors. He decided then and there, if the boy asked, he would be allowed to visit Rosa.

#

Earlier in the morning while his family slept, Tilts had gotten up, gone to his game cock coop, selected two of his prize roosters and put them in their carrying cages. Tilts loved Sundays. This was his day. He wasn't going to sit like a mummy in a box, wearing fancy clothes. He worked hard during the week, and this was his day to enjoy.

He walked to Jim Johnson's about a mile down the road from his place. Tilts arrived at his destination at about the time his family was getting up to prepare for Sunday Service. A few men were already milling around Johnson's barn. One spotted him coming up the path. "Howdy Tilts, I see you come prepared to get your birds killed!"

"Ya been drink'n moon so early in the day, Charlie. Ain't nobody got better fight'n birds than me, so if you're smart, you'll put your money on my birds."

"I'm gonn'a hold you to that Tilts." Charlie retorted. Tilts continued on into the barn. A couple of dozen men, black and white, were already inside, standing in a circle around the pit. Most were farmers, but among them were a few store owners and professionals. They stood out in the crowd because they wore white shirts and neckties.

When the men saw him, they greeted him with a chorus of "Howdy Tilts!" The circle opened to allow him through. "Hey there, Bradley!" A rough voice called. The red faced man's cheek was puffed out by a wad of tobacco.

"Hey there, Bonner. How you do'n? Your rooster ready to get his ass kicked?"

"You wont't be show'n your face in these parts after today, Bradley," was the good humored reply.

"Don't talk stupid Bonner. Is your brother bring'n one of his skinny ass'd birds to get slaughtered, too?"

"Nah, he ain't coming today, he's feeling poorly."

"Now, you tell him to get better, an' nex' week, he should bring his worm infested birds so mine can prove to you two, you don't know noth'n about breed'n good fighters. You tell him that, you hear?" Tilts said with a wry grin.

"I"ll tell 'em. I damn sure will, Tilts."

The people that had crowded into the barn began moving aside to make way for big Jim Johnson as he headed to the dugout circle. He was a giant of a man, black as coal, with a mouth full of gold teeth. He stepped into the pit, "We bes be gett'n started soon. Furst off, I wanna tell ya, we gonn'a meet at Bill Smith's place nex' time. An' you all remember, don't be runn'n off at the mouth, an tell'n folks about it unless you know fo' sho they be trustworthy. Got that?"

Murmurs of "Yeah, we know." "We don't want to get the damn law down on us…now do we?" A chorus of

"Noooo's" Echoed back.

"Now, let's get go'n. We got seven fights lined up fo' today. Tilt's Bradley an' George Bonner is fu'st up."

Tilts reached into his cage and pulled his rooster out. He was a brilliantly colored bird. His head turned quickly, nervously. He knew instinctively he would be in a battle for his life soon. Tilts took his charge to the pit and stepped down into it. Bonner entered from the opposite side with his bird.

"Naked heel" Bonner shouted.

"Naked heel it is. No Gaffs!" Tilts answered.

Coming together, each man thrust the two birds back and forth, beak to beak. Then, the referee shouted the words the men were waiting for, "Ready, pit!" On that command, the birds were released onto the pit floor. Like two, small enraged bulls, they charged each other.

Jumping high in the air, their hackle feathers fanned out like porcupine quills, the birds grabbed each other's beaks. After a few leaps into the air, they released their holds, all the while emitting shrill battle calls. Chest to chest, they brought their legs up to their own chests, then, released them down as swiftly, and as often as they could. Each bird's spurs pointed outward, trying to catch their opponent's body. Their wings flapped furiously for balance, each bird's feet were blurs as they slashed at the other's body. The two combatants presented an awesome sight, the sounds were blood curdling, and the combination of the two worked the audience into a frenzy.

They hooted and hollered, using the birds' owners' names to identify their choice, "Come on Bonner, kick Bradley's ass!!" "Kill Bonner's bird, baby!" "I've got five dollars on you, don't let me down, Bradley!" "Tilt's bird is shit, put him in the ground!" others yelled. The men shouted, cursed, and cheered depending on how the events unfolding before them was going, and how it affected their wagers.

The early morning hour didn't stop the men from uncorking the moonshine Johnson sold. The effect of the alcohol became evident as some of the men became louder, and more aggressive.

"Damn it Jake, stop yell'n in ma' ear!"

"Well, move your lazy self so you won't hear me!"

"You want me move, why don't you move me?"

Sensing trouble, Johnson walked over to the two men. "You all jes' calm down! Ya' hea' me?"

Jake looked up, "All right Jim, don't you worry none, every thing's all right."

"Good. See that it is." Jim replied as he walked away.

The birds fought for twenty minutes, and while blood smears covered their feathers, neither one seemed to have an advantage over the other. Then, Tilt's bird struck his opponent squarely, and both spurs landed in the other's chest. The bird let out a blood-curdling squawk before it dropped on its side. Blood oozed from its mouth. Despite its victory, the bird continued to attack his fallen foe. Tilts stepped in, grabbed his bird and returned it to its cage.

Bonner quickly scooped up his mortally wounded bird and went outside. Neither man acknowledged the other. Tilts however, walked over to three men he had wagers with and collected two dollars from each.

"Tol' ya' Tilt's bird would kill that scrawny bunch of feathers." A voice taunted.

Two more men with birds entered the pit, and another battle started. The next two combatants dueled for over an hour. Tilts' second cock was severely hurt and lost his match. Being loyal to his birds, he brought it home, and attempted to nurse it back to health. Healed, the bird might fight again. However, if he was too wounded to enter the pit again, he'd take the bird out into the woods, and release it; giving it a chance to survive on its own. Tilts would never use a bird that lost a match as a breeder.

From that first Sunday, until the conclusion of the school year, George met Rosa's family at church and accompanied them home after services. Mary had given

George a standing invitation to join them for Sunday diner, an invitation he gladly accepted.

Aside from the good meal, Sundays meant time with Rosa. They enjoyed taking walks, or sitting on the porch swing. However, time with her, didn't mean time alone. One or more of Rosa's sisters were assigned to go along on their walks or were assigned to play nearby when they sat in the swing or strolled around the yard

George was serious about Rosa and wanted to plan their future after he graduated from Swift, and, hopefully, from college. The school year would end in a few months, and he wasn't sure what the future held for him. He knew he would be leaving Rogersville, but beyond that, he had no idea what lay ahead. In deep thought, he walked down the campus path trying to sort out his future, wanting very much for it to include Rosa. Off in the distance he saw two men waving at him, calling his name. He strained to see who it could be. Finally it came to him, it was Doctor Bletso, and Reverend Mansell.

"George! George! We've been looking all over for you." The doctor explained. "How are you anyway, my boy?"

"Just fine, thank you."

"You look very well," The Reverend added.

"We've been getting good reports about you from the school. Straight A's. We knew you could do it." The doctor said beaming. Turning to his companion he said,

"The Reverend here has something to share with you George. Tell him Reverend."

The minister looked as if he were ready to burst if he didn't get to share the information he had quickly.

"George, we have been able to get you a working

scholarship at Lincoln University in Pennsylvania. You will be able to achieve a bachelor's degree there."

"Does that mean I'll actually be going to college?"

"Yes, it does, George. It will mean you will be able to fulfill the promise you made to your mother," Doctor Bletso said with a big grin. "That is if you are interested." George lost his voice, as a broad grin spread across his face.

The joy showing on his face was answer enough. The three embraced and danced around in circles. Passing students looked at the celebrating men in wonder.

With this new information, he wanted desperately to share the good news with Rosa, but whenever they saw each other at school, there were constant interruptions. There was never time or opportunity to have a meaningful conversation. He decided he'd wait until Sunday. He knew the conversation he wanted to have with her would change his and hopefully her life forever.

Sunday finally rolled around, services ended, and now he'd have a few private moments with Rosa. Mary and the children led the way back to her house, while George and Rosa hung back as far as they could without drawing any undue attention to themselves. Despite their efforts, however, Lena joined Rosa and George and asked if she could walk with them. She liked him as a big brother and wanted to share some local news with him. "Of course you can walk with us." Rosa responded to her sister's request.

George was unhappy about the turn of events but didn't let on. Rosa wasn't pleased either, but she was sweet and courteous towards her sister. George realized the opportunity to share his good news would have to wait a bit longer. After they ate, he asked if he and Rosa could be excused from the table. Tilts sensed the boy had something on his mind and gave them permission to leave. However, Lena followed shortly afterward and assumed her role as chaperone, but this time she kept some distance between herself and them.

As they walked down the trail to the main road, Rosa allowed her hand to 'accidentally' touch his, igniting a small explosion, causing an exhilarating feeling that neither one had experienced before. They stopped and turned to each other.

Lena stood at a respectful distance. She realized something special was happening. In order to make herself seem less visible, she turned her back and began humming softly then began playing with imaginary animals. She had mastered the art of making herself less intrusive in what was a most difficult role for her.

"Rosa," George began, "I've been accepted at Lincoln University. I'll be going there this fall." His heart was in his mouth as he spoke.

"Oh, George, That is the best news I've heard in a long, long time. I'm so happy for you. I'll miss you, you know that. But, I know what this means to you."

"Thanks Rosa. Now, I have a question to ask of you."

"You do? What is it?"

"Will you wait for me? I mean, will you marry me after I graduate?"

They looked into each other's eyes, much the same way they had that day in class. He wanted so much to hold her in his arms and press her close to him. Instead, his arms hung straight down by his side. He had never mentioned his love for her, and she didn't expect him to. There had been an unspoken understanding between them.

Somehow they knew there was a special connection since their first conversation. Ever since that day they knew they belonged to each other, and they knew one day they would marry, and spend their lives together. Rosa took his hands, smiled and said, "Yes!" Eleven year old Lena, sensing the importance of the moment, turned away when they kissed for the first time.

"George, I have news, too."

"You do? What is it?"

"I've been accepted as a teacher for a school up on Hawkins Mountain. I'll start the first of the new school year."

"What great news. And I know you'll be good at it too. You are so talented."

"Some of the students will be older than I am." She added.

"Does that scare you?"

"Not really. Mother thinks she can make me look a good ten years older." Rosa replied with a big grin.

"Then that should take care of that problem." He added with a smile.

George's face took on a serious expression, "I don't know how often we will be able to see each other in the coming years. I suppose we will have to just wait and see how that works out, but we can write each other and…"

"George, I'll wait for you for however long. So, don't you start worrying about anything. That's a promise. Look, we're both going to be busy; you will be adjusting to a new school. Plus, with classes and all, you will be very busy, and the same will be true with me; I'll have classes and a whole school to run. I think we have to face the fact that we both have to be patient. I think the time will pass quickly. But I don't mind. Do you?"

"No, no. What you said is real. We each have our own paths to follow for a while. Then that path will lead us back together again. That's how I'm going to look at it."

"I like that. That's how I'll look at the coming months and years, too. We are on paths that takes us apart, but, will lead us back together again in the end. Yes, I can live with that." Rosa said with a smile.

After graduating from Swift, George journeyed back to Chattanooga to see his mother. In September he took the train to Pennsylvania, and Lincoln University.

Mary knew she had work to do to make her sixteen year old daughter look older so that she would get the respect of the children she would be teaching, children that in some instances would be her age, or in a few cases, older. She decided to start with Rosa's hair, trying different styles. Finally she said, "Rosa, a part in the middle and a bun in the back makes you look the oldest."

Rosa allowed herself to take a peek in the mirror, and quickly agreed. "You're right Mother. That's how I'll wear it from now on."

`"With the full length dresses I made, and the high top shoes, none of the students will ever guess your age." Mary added with a smile.

"When I look in the mirror, I can't believe it's me." Rosa replied, pleased beyond words.

"You know, since some of those children will be as old, or even older than you, Rosa, so you must carry yourself like a proper lady. That way they'll respect you."
"Yes, Mama, I will."

That night, sleep wouldn't come. She realized this was going to be her last night at home for almost a year. Tomorrow, she'd begin her career as a teacher. Mixed feelings soon overwhelmed her. Thoughts of leaving her little sisters and brother, her sweet mother, and of course her Papa. Oh, how she would miss him. Then feeling of anxiety flooded her mind. Would she be a good teacher? Would the children listen to her? Her only comfort at the moment was in the knowledge that in four years, she would be Mrs. George I. Read.

Still, she tossed and turned, unable to find sleep. Without realizing why, she began to feel comforted as Papa's voice drifted through the window, into her room from the porch. He was singing, "For an old man he is old, for an old man he is grey, but a young man' s heart is full of . . . ." softly to himself:

Rosa drifted off to a peaceful sleep.

Tilts, always an early riser, arose even earlier this morning. Slipping out of the house quietly he walked to the back and leaned against the gate post of his garden. The feeling he was experiencing could only be described as eerie. His eyes couldn't focus on any single thing as they scanned the garden; rather they jumped from one plant to another, seeing nothing more than a blur of abstract shapes and colors. And his mind was doing no better. It wouldn't, or couldn't settle on one single clear rational thought.

This was the moment he had dreaded for years. And it can't be said he hadn't attempted to prepare for it. By attempting to steel himself for this moment in advance, he felt he would have a handle on his emotions, when the day arrived. But those early attempts at mental preparation melted away as the hour of her leaving came closer. Now that the day had actually arrived, any resolve he had been able to muster had evaporated. This was real. He knew once his little girl climbed on that wagon, and headed toward her new life, she would always return as a visitor. She would never ever be a part of his family. That thought ripped his heart out. Tilts could always control his mind, but today all he could do was have one miserable thought after another. It was the sound of a screen door closing that jolted him out of his depressed state.

Tilts looked up and caught a glimpse of Rosa stepping out on to the porch as she looked this way and that, trying to locate him.

"Rosa, come round back, I want ya to look at somth'n," he called.

She stepped off the porch and walked to the back. She found Papa busy examining a rose blossom. "Rosa" he began, his eyes deliberately avoiding hers, "These here blossoms are more full on the bush than usual, don't you think?"

As she examined the bush, she nodded, "Yes, they do seem to have come in better than last year. Yes, they are much, much, fuller, Papa."

"I thought so." Without another word he toured the yard with her, enjoying the bounty their hard labor had manifested in the colorful flower beds scattered throughout the yard. Finally, they returned to the garden. With his daughter now at his side, the lush vegetation was no longer a blur, everything now came into sharp focus.

Tilts made small talk about bringing some of the vegetables in for Mary to put up, then, spoke of the bugs that were chewing the bush beans. After a half an hour the tour was over, and unlike himself; he had run out of conversation.

The sun was rising; people were stirring in the house. The time had come for him to say goodbye. Clearing his throat he said, "If you ever need me, send a letter and I'll be there. You know that. Now you take care."

"I will, Papa. I know you would come for me, no matter what."

Tilts nodded, leaned over and kissed her on the forehead. Holding her tightly by the shoulders for a brief moment, he released her, turned abruptly and walked off into the nearby woods. He felt unsettled that Rosa was leaving home, but, not fearful. Despite her being only sixteen, she was more mature than many grown women he could think of. Considering he was such an emotional person, the calm that was settling over him seemed almost contradictory. He realized that was based on the fact his brother Jim and his wife Bertha would be looking after her. Both were good, hard working, salt-of-the- earth country folks, folks who held the same values he did. They were people you could trust with your life. As he thought about it, he realized he was doing just that, trusting them with something more precious than his own life. As he walked deeper into the woods, he began to feel more secure in the knowledge that his Rosa would be in good hands. He found a tree, plopped his lean frame on the ground, leaned against it, took out his pipe, and lit it up. He would sit there until he knew she was on her way.

The forest's quietness and coolness enveloped his body and in a short while he surrendered himself to its tranquility, and slept.

Rosa had taken a seat on the porch when she heard the clatter of the wagon coming up the lane. She looked up to see Uncle Jim's big frame rocking to and fro, on the flat bed wagon as it pulled into the yard.

"Whoo. Whoo there!" He called to the two big mules, stopping them alongside the house under the shade cast by the big oak tree that stood majestically in the front yard. Jim was several inches taller than his six-foot-two brother Tilts. He was thicker in the shoulders and chest. But there were similarities; Their green-gray eyes, their prominent noses and their copper skin tones, stamped them as brothers. Then too, both had the ability to give a devilish look, or make a comment at the most unexpected times, and you would find yourself being taken in by a joke.

Jim saw Rosa but pretended he didn't see her. Looking past her, he called out as loud as he could, "Hello! Hello! Anybody home? Mean to' say I've been travel'n fer hours, and ain't nobody here to greet me?" He tried hard to suppress the grin spreading across his face.

Mary scurried out of the kitchen door. "Now you know we're home...just sitting on pins and needles looking for you! Why don't you get down off that thing and let me fix you some eggs and biscuits?"

"Howdy, Mary, and you too, Miss Rosa. I seen ya right along, jes' thought I'd ignore ya fer a while. You sitt'n there all prim and proper, look'n like a regular grown-up woman. I ken hardly believe my eyes."

"Hello, Uncle Jim. It's good to see you, too."

"Mary, your biscuits are always tempting, but Bertha fixed me some travel'n food, enough fer both ways. Maybe another time. Ya see, the Missis ain't feel'n too well, so I bes' be gett'n back as soon as I can."

Anchrum came out carrying two large traveling bags. "Well, hello there young man. You've grown up to be a regular young gentleman."

Always shy, Uncle Jim's complement brought a slight smile to his face. "Good to see you too, Uncle. Should I get the mules some water?"

"Ya read my mind, young fella. Fetch them each a bucket."

Anchrum set Rosa's two bags on the wagon, then headed to the back of the house for the water. In a matter of minutes, he returned, setting a bucket down for each of the two thirsty animals, bracing his legs against them so they wouldn't in their haste to drink, tip them over.

"Now, let me take a look at ya girl." Jim rocked back on his seat and pushed his straw hat even further back in disbelief. "Last time I seen ya, you weren't nothing but a skinny girl. Now look at ya, Rosa. You make a might purty sight. My brother must be proud as a peacock!"

Rosa was flustered by her uncle's praise but tried not to let her feeling show. "Thanks for the compliment, Uncle Jim," she replied simply. "Shall I get up on the wagon?"

"I reckon so. Like I said, I 'm anxious to get back to Hawkins mountain so I can look in on your Aunt Bertha. She was feel'n poorly this morning. So…"

Rosa stood, carefully stepping down from the porch, trying to assume the role she had accepted as a teacher. Her dress reached down to the top of her high lace up shoes, and she wore a blouse with a high collar adorned by a gold broach. Her abundant black hair pulled into a tight bun. She also carried a purse. Her tom-boy days were to be put away for now.

Jim, still in a state of disbelief said, "I'll say one thing, you make a fine looking young lady. You look for the world like a grown-up woman. Them kids you gonn'a be teach'n won't never know you're fer shur true age. I'm tell'n you straight. Mary, you've done a great job of put'n years on her."

"I explained to her, if the children know her true age, they wouldn't give her no respect at all. That's why she's going to have to carry herself like a woman at all times." Mary added.

"Mary, I don't think you need to worry one bit about that. She ain't gonn'a have no problems at all, so you jes put your mind to ease. Now, Mary, I don't want to rush, but we bes' be getting on our way, as soon as the mules finish their drinking."

All of Rosa's siblings were lined up on the porch. They all had the saddest aces, each one no more than a blink away from tears. As she made her way to the wagon, she hugged and kissed her sisters, assuring them she would be back for visits. Finally she came to Anchrum. She hugged him as hard as she could, and then, kissed him on the cheek. He stood woodenly, his arms hanging down by his side. As she held him, he whispered, "Bye Rosa, you take care." His eyes reflected the deep, unexpressed love he held for his sister. Rosa understood his feelings as he looked briefly into hers before he turned and disappeared into the house.

Having done her crying last night, Mary was now able to hold back the flood she knew would come when this moment came. She was determined to be strong in front of her children, especially in front of Rosa. Mary hugged her tightly. "God be with you child," she whispered as she stepped back.

Jim reached down to help Rosa up on her seat next to him. "Well, we bes' be going. Now you tell that brother of mine not to worry none. We'll look after her as if she was our own young'n. You tell him that for me, Mary."

"I will, Jim. Well, safe travels, and tell Bertha to feel better."

Jim glanced back at the bags and tipped his hat to Mary and the children. Then he snapped the harness, yelled "Giddiap mules!" On command, the two animals lurched forward.

The wagon hadn't turned onto the main road before Ada and Thelma let out mournful howls. Mary looked at the children, but instead of offering them comfort, scurried into the house to deal with her own emotions -- emotions she thought she had rid herself of the night before. For once she thought of herself. The children, she knew, would comfort each other. She had confidence in Lena and knew she would assume Rosa's role as big sister and comforter. For now, she was going to her room and treat herself to a good cry.

Without hesitation, and fighting back her own tears, Lena began soothing Ada, and Thelma. In a few minutes she had them laughing at her funny antics. Meanwhile, Anchrum had gone into the house, taken his rifle from the corner of his room, and disappeared into the woods. It would be a while before the house would return to normal with Rosa gone.

Now on the road, the homestead out of sight, Rosa no longer turned to get a last glimpse of her family. The mule's sharp hoofs made klickety, klack sounds and kicked up puffs of dust. The two figures atop the wagon swayed in unison as the wagon bumped down the road at a good clip.

Sensing Rosa's sadness, Uncle Jim began a monologue, talking nonstop for over an hour. Sometimes making sense, sometimes not, he just wanted to keep her distracted. The impact of leaving home, he realized had begun to overwhelm her. However, his persistence paid off; eventually she began listening, and responding to his meandering conversation. Finally she became totally engaged, and they talked about everything and nothing all the way back to Hawkins Mountain.

The sun's rays were getting longer when Jim turned off the main road and onto a rutted dirt lane. "Well, we're jes' about home, Rosa. Bout a mile up that lane, and we'll be there."

"It's been a long time since I've been here, but I do remember this lane. I remember it because of the way the trees grow over the road, as if you're entering a cave." Rosa exclaimed, as she looked up at the thick overhead foliage.

"The rains have been hard on the lane. It's such a steep grade, the water jes' flows down so fast it makes the ruts deeper, and deeper, each time we get rain." Jim said, shaking his head sadly, wishing he could in some way make the next mile a bit smoother for his young companion.

The mules had had an easy trip until now. The main road has been smooth by comparison, just a few steep inclines here, and there, but the lane was a different story – a sharp uphill climb all the way to his house, steeper in some places than in others. The mules had to bend their backs and pull harder, especially when a wheel dropped into a deep hole, causing the wagon to temporarily get stuck.

“Hold on now Rosa, it’s going to be a bumpy ride from here on out.” Uncle Jim warned.

“I’m fine Uncle, Jim. I think it’s sort of fun.” Rosa laughed.

”Well, I guess it’s better to have a sense of humor about it, than to get all worked up over it.” Jim said with a wry smile.

After an hour of drops, bumps, and lurches, Jim’s face broke into a broad grin. “Just around that there bend, Rosa, and we’re home.”

His two coon hounds verified that home was close by. Their deep voices broke into a chorus of rich ‘awooo’s, awooo’s’ as the log homestead came into view. The chained dogs leaped, and spun in excitement at their master’s return. The barking brought Bertha rushing out of the house. Her smile revealed a gold rimmed front tooth that gave her face an extra bright countenance.

“Hello, you two! Oh Rosa, it’s so good to see you, child! And aren’t we quite the lady. Lord, child, you are a fine looking young thing!”

“Thank you Aunt Bertha, you’re so kind. And I’ve missed not seeing you for the past months. Are you feeling better? Uncle Jim said you were under the weather when he left this morning.”

“I’m still not myself, but I’ll survive.”

Jim jumped off the wagon, helped Rosa down, then, he gave his wife a big bear hug. Bertha took Rosa by the hand and led her to her room, one of two small bedrooms off the main room which served as kitchen, dining room and sitting room. Bertha had a large stone fire place that Tilts had laid up for them years ago, and another chimney that their wood stove was hooked to. “I always liked your home, Aunt Bertha. It’s so comfortable and snug.”

"You know, the Lord didn't bless us with children, but we added this room just in case we were. Well, he didn't, so, I'm pleased it's here for you."

"You and Uncle Jim would have been good parents, too." Rosa added thoughtfully.

"We like to think we would have been. But, man makes plans, God makes the decisions. Your uncle Jim and I, well, we've accepted that. Now, I want you to freshen up, take a rest, then, I'll fix us up some fried chicken. How's that, Rosa?"

"That sounds like a good idea. I think I could use a nap, Aunt Bertha."

The sounds, and the smells of chicken frying, and fresh biscuits baking helped Rosa to awaken with a smile. She dressed and came out into the main room. Aunt Bertha had just begun to serve the meal. "Come, sit child. We'll be ready in just a few minutes."

Jim had washed up and put on a fresh shirt. He looked handsome as he towered above his wife while holding her around the waist. "She's some good cook, I'll tell ya Rosa."

"Oh, I remember on my last visit. Aunt Bertha cooked up some venison, the likes of which I never tasted before."

"Jim knows flattery works on me." She said with a coy smile, "But I accept yours for what it is, Rosa. Honest appreciation."

The meal was eaten in relative silence. Eventually Bertha broke the quiet. "Well, are you ready to see your school tomorrow morning after breakfast?"

"Oh, I can't wait. Having the job and the school is like a dream come true," Rosa said wistfully.

The night slipped by quickly. After breakfast the three walked the mile single file, Jim leading the way. As they walked, Uncle Jim said, "You see that fence running along the side of the road, there on the left side?"

Rosa nodded.

"Well, that there fence goes some below our house, clear on past the school fer quite a ways. Now, there is a story about that fence you should know. The school sits on about an acre of land on the other side of it. But, for you to get to your school, you're gonn'a have to climb the fence, and cross land that belongs to a family by the name of McMullen."

"Does he object? I mean, will it be a problem for me to cross his land?"

"No, honey, don't you fret none. Jes' hear me out. Some years ago the McMullen's had a falling out with a family by the name of Barrow. A member of the McMullen clan caught a Barrow trying to steal a hog they had hung out to cool after butchering. That led them to start shoot'n at one another. Then, they got to stealing, or shoot'n game on the other's land, just for devilment. They both had more land and game than they could ever use. But, I guess it gave 'em something to get all riled up about. Nobody got killed, but a couple of men folks on both sides got winged, and laid up for a spell. To try and settle matters, an' to put an end to it, the McMullen's decided to put up a fence, then vowed to shoot dead, any Barrow caught on their side of it. It took years to put the fence up, but by god they did. Over time both sides still took shots at one another, but luckily, nobody got killed. This went on for years and years."

"I find that an almost unbelievable story, Uncle Jim."

"Well, it's true. One winter a plague of some kind killed off most of them on both sides. But that fence still stands. What few members of the families that are still alive are too old, or too feeble to fight anymore. Now, the pity is, for you to get over to your school, you're gonn'a have ta climb that fence every day."

"What about the children, Uncle Jim? How are do they manage?"

"Rosa, only a few old Barrows and us, are the only ones left on this side of the mountain and on this side of the fence. We ain't got no children, and all the colored children live on the other side of the fence. So, they don't have ta climb the durn thing every day ta get to the school. There's a settlement of coloreds on that side of the mountain. They'll be coming to your school, the whole bunch of 'em. They's quite a bunch, all mixed up, Indian, colored and some white in their blood lines. Most have straight hair and range in color from white to high yeller, to brown. The common name amongst them is Brice, Ford and White."

"Couldn't the McMullen's put a gate up, so we could get to the school without climbing the fence?"

"Oh, yeah, he could. We asked him years ago. He said he ain't cutt'n no hole, or putt'n no gate ta make it easy for no colored person. He said, he's be'n nice as it is, 'cuz he lets us cut across a small piece of his land ta get ta the school house." Uncle Jim stopped, and pointed to the fence. "Well, here we are, there's your school. Come here Rosa, peek through the fence. You'll get a better view of it from here."

Rosa went to the stacked logs and looked through to see a gray frame building on the far side of a weed covered field. "It looks like a sturdy building." Rosa announced, as the reality of the building and its significance sank in. She added, "In fact, it looks like a castle in a fairy tale to me."

Jim and Bertha smiled, then Jim added, "Oh it's a good structure, I don't' know about a castle, but I do understand what you're saying, child. Now, I'm gonn'a show ya how to get over this here fence, nice and easy. I know it looks hard, but you'll get the hang of it in no time." The fence, a good six feet high was made by stacking small logs in a zig, zag pattern with fork-like points poking out where the logs ended. Jim started climbing the fence. "Now, ya gotta be careful not to get your clothes caught on the log ends; that's why you should climb up near the middle."

The women watched as Jim climbed, than, descended on the other side. "All right ladies. You first Rosa. Give it a go."

Being a tomboy and tree climber all her life, it was no problem for Rosa to navigate. She climbed it with ease and came down the other side with no problem. Bertha, not as young, or agile, took a bit longer, but was able to climb navagate the fence as well. With everyone on the other side, Jim led the way to the school.

Bertha produced a key and opened the front door. Inside, she handed the key to Rosa. "It's your school now Rosa." The school smelled musty and dusty. "I think the first order of business is to let some fresh air in." Bertha said as she began opening window.

The desks had been left in a disorderly pattern around the room; books were strewn about on the floor, as well as children's clothing thrown here and there as well. "Well, I see my work is cut out for me." Rosa said as she looked about.

"Don't you fret for one minute," Bertha said. That's why we're here. We gonn'a roll up our sleeves and have this place all nice and shiny, and clean in no time."

"I see the wood box is empty, and the stove needs a cleaning. While you ladies start inside, I'll bring in some wood, then, I'll help out with the cleaning."

Within a few hours, the desks were lined up in neat rows, the shelves and furniture dusted, the floor swept and mopped. As the three stood admiring what they had accomplished in such a short time, Rosa spotted an empty jar. Without a word she took it outside, and returned with a bouquet of wild flowers. "Now, that does liven up the place." Bertha announced.

"Yes, yes it does." Jim acknowledged. "Well, Miss Rosa, day after tomorrow is the big day. Are you a little nervous?" He teased.

"Yes. A little bit. But more anxious to just get started." She replied.

Jim looked at her with a serious expression. "Rosa, these here children you gonn'a be teach'n. Well, they can be a wild bunch. Some, as you know, is older, and some a lot bigger than you. But, if you stand your ground, you'll do jes' fine, I know you will. Now, if things get too rough, you jes' tell your uncle Jim, and I'll handle whoever it is. You hear me?"

Rosa smiled, "I hear you, Uncle Jim, and thanks."

In the wink of an eye, the big day arrived. Rosa walked to school and in no time found herself standing in front of the fence. Looking at it from top to bottom, she said, “Fence, I do believe we are just not going to get along. Anger welled up inside her at the thought of having to climb the dumb thing every day, especially now that she was all dressed up and neat as a pin. She wanted very much to present a dignified image to her students. Her mood changed briefly as she thought of how proud Papa and Mama would be if they could see her now, ready to start her career as a teacher. Without any real effort, she negotiated her way over the fence, followed the path and made her way through the field. By staying in the path, she saved her freshly polished shoes and dress from the weeds, burrs, and stickers that grew in abundance throughout the field. She was very determined to look just right for her students.

Inside, she looked around to make sure everything was as perfect as she could make it. Satisfied, she pulled out her chair and took a seat behind her desk. She had arrived a half hour early, now all she could do was wait for the children. At eight o’clock they began entering the room. Rosa looked at each one closely as they came through the door. Despite being warned by Aunt Bertha and Uncle Jim, she was surprised at how old some of them seemed to be and how big a few of them were, both the boys and the girls.

The children returned Rosa’s scrutiny with their own. They were, of course, trying to size up the new teacher as much as she was them. Was she tough? Could she be run off as quickly as the last one had been? Smirks crossed the faces of some as they looked her over. One student laughed aloud, remembering the day he had let a large toad loose in the class room and the teacher flew out the door.

With the children all seated, she began, "My name is Rosa Bradley and I'm your teacher. You will address me as Miss Rosa. Now I want to get to know who you are." Pointing, she chose the youngest-looking child. "We'll start with you young lady, and please stand when you speak."

And so it began. The youngest child was eight; the oldest of the twenty students (Florence Brice) was seventeen. Rosa smiled to herself when Florence, feeling prideful about her status as the oldest, volunteered that bit of information.

The first day proceeded well. The children hadn't yet figured out the new teacher, so they remained watchful, and on their best behavior. They knew there was time to look for what could be a weakness they could exploit later on.

Relying on the students and what they told her their grade levels were, Rosa handed out books she felt would be appropriate. She knew that in time she would be able to tailor the books to their real capabilities as she got to know each one of them better.

In a few days it became evident to Rosa that there was a kind of kinship between most of her students; they were either first, or second cousins, brothers and sisters, or aunts and uncles. As a group, they tended to be strong-willed, raw- boned, tall, and handsome.

Some weeks later, on his way to school, Buddy Brice, a year younger than his sister Florence, spotted a garden snake over a foot long in the path. He grabbed it, put it in his side coat pocket, and continued on. His gait quickened, and there was a bounce to his steps as he neared the school. Today would be his day to 'test' the teacher.

The children were performing various tasks as the morning class progressed. The small ones practiced writing, the middle grade children were reading, while the older ones had become involved in a heated discussion with Miss Rosa. They were engrossed in a conversation about how seeds developed and turned into plants.

Buddy had waited patiently. Now was the time for him to make his move. He raised his hand, "Miss Rosa," He called out, "there's a word in my book…I can't make it out. Can I show you which one I mean?" Not waiting for an answer, he slid out of his seat, marched around the desk, and stopped alongside where she sat. He placed his book on her desk, while positioning himself so that his side pocket was only a foot from his teacher's face. He slid his hand into his pocket, and slowly pulled the garden snake half way out. The greenish black serpent looked from side to side, and flicked its tongue as it began swaying back and forth.

"Which word are you having trouble with, Buddy?" Rosa asked calmly, as she saw the snake from the corner of her eyes. "Show me. Point to the word, Buddy!" She commanded in a sharp voice.

"Uh, uh, this one, Miss Rosa." He answered as his finger blindly went to the page, and landed on the word 'the'.

"You don't know the word THE!" Rosa asked as she turned toward the snake now eye level to her face. Without a change of expression, she turned to Buddy. "Young man, you aren't being respectful to me, to your classmates, or to yourself. You may go outside, and without hurting it, return that snake to where you found it. After you've released the snake, you will return to class, and after school, you will fill the wood barrel out on the porch. Now GO!"

"Yes ma'am. Right away." He heard himself reply. The children had watched the drama unfold from the very beginning. They began laughing and snickering at Buddy and his miscalculation of Miss Rosa. Surprise and confusion showed on the flustered boy's face. How could this be? A toad had frightened the last teacher; yet all Miss Rosa did was calmly look at the snake…then yell at me! He turned and ran out of the room. Giggles and laughter floated out of the classroom as he crossed the field to release the snake. Miss Rosa had won the first battle.

After Buddy returned, the teacher announced. "Children, tomorrow I want each of you to bring in a plant, flower or an insect. But for now, no snakes, or lizards."

"Miss Rosa!" A small voice called out. "Can we bring worms?"

"Worms are fine. You can bring grasshoppers, lighting bugs, things like that. But, I repeat, no snakes."

The children laughed as Buddy's face flushed red.

After class, the children discussed their new teacher as they walked home. There was a general consensus. She was different from the others they had had. She was more like them, except older and smarter. She always seemed to be one step ahead of their devilment, and pranks. However, if one thing could be singled out as the reason they liked her, they agreed it would be her ability to tell funny stories. Rosa told her first story to the class when Robert, a thirteen year old was asked to read a short story from his reader.

The boy got up and slowly as he made his way to the front of the room. Once there, he yawned, scratched his chest, and with poor posture began to read. His voice was lifeless and he seemed totally disinterested in what he was doing. After he read the story, Rosa said, "Robert, do you know you are acting more dead than alive? In fact, you remind me of a story, a story about the laziest man in town. Have you, or, any of you children ever heard that story?"

The children shook their heads. They had not heard that story.

"Well then, I'll tell you about him." The teacher announced.

Full of anticipation, the children turned their attention to her. She began. "Many years ago, a man by the name of Festus Jones was widowed after forty years of marriage."

"What's widowed?" A student asked.

"When the wife dies, and the husband lives, he's widowed. That's what happened to Festus." Rosa explained. "After his wife had been laid to rest, people noticed Festus wasn't up and about as he usually was; nor was he sitting on his porch as he usually did. Eventually, some church deacons decided to look in on Festus. They went to his house and knocked. They knocked and knocked, but didn't' get an answer. Finally one of the deacons decided to go in. Inside, they found Festus lying in bed, weak and almost dead.

The deacons asked Festus if he was sick. He answered, "Naw, I ain't sick, just don't feel like fix'n ma self food."

The deacons put their heads together, then, went back to Festus. "As Christians, we can't just let you lie here and starve yourself to death, so how about if we get some of our church sisters to bring you a good hot meal every day?" Festus's eyes lit up. He liked that idea just fine.

And, so it began, like clockwork. The ladies took turns preparing and bringing him one hot meal every day for six months. After six months, the ladies began talking among themselves. They agreed, "There really isn't anything wrong with Festus. He's just plum lazy." The ladies felt they were being used. After a long conversation among themselves, they agreed, they wouldn't feed Festus any longer; he would be on his own and fend for himself. Their minds made up, they relayed their decision to the pastor. He wasn't happy with their decision, but he thanked them for what they had done.

In a matter of weeks, Festus returned to his feeble state, more dead than alive. After some time, a few sisters talked among themselves and came to the decision that they had better stop by his house to take a look at him.

The women knocked, waited, then, they knocked again. After getting no answer, the women let themselves in. The shades were drawn, and the house was dark. Moving cautiously they found his room. There on a bed they saw a man lying so still, they could only assume he was dead.

They reported their findings to their preacher who in turn told the congregation, "It is our responsibility to bury Festus in a proper manner." And so a funeral was arranged, a plot was donated, and Festus was laid out on a flatbed wagon to be taken to the cemetery.

A team of mules was hitched to the wagon, and Festus was pulled down Main Street in order that the town folks would have an opportunity to pay their last respects to the old man. As the wagon proceeded slowly through town, some folks placed flowers on it. Near the end of the line of people, the wagon hit a rock; it jarred the wagon so hard Festus let out a loud grunt.

Hearing Festus make a sound, the people cried out, "Festus is alive! He ain't dead after all!"

Hearing Festus, an old farmer walked up to the wagon. "Festus." He began, "I have an offer for you. I have a bin full of corn; I'll give you some; enough to see you through the winter. Are you interested?"

Festus picked up his head, looked at the farmer and asked, "Is the corn shelled?"

"No, Festus, the corn ain't shelled. You'll have to shell it."

Looking the farmer dead in the eyes, he replied, "Well then, tell the driver to drive on."

The children laughed and laughed. After that, when anyone moved slowly, or acted in a lazy manner, they would say, "You're acting just like Festus!"

It wasn't long before the children would get angry at anyone making trouble for Miss Rosa. Their loyalty was one hundred percent with their new teacher. If anyone tried to do something against her, they would rally to her defense. Soon, the foolishness stopped all together, and the class settled down to reading, writing, arithmetic, storytelling and enjoying nature classes.

It had been a particularly hot night, and Rosa had had a difficult time falling asleep. Normally a sound sleeper and able to sleep through anything, this night was the exception. Try as she might, slumber wouldn't come. Becoming more and more frantic as she tossed and turned, trying to find a comfortable position, she heard Uncle Jim's voice. It was a low whisper; he was sweet-talking Aunt Bertha.

She heard several whispered nooo, nooo as Bertha tried to put off his advances, then her acceptance of his passion. It was the first time Rosa had ever heard the sounds of man/woman love making. She smiled as she thought of what lay ahead for her when she and George would one day be united in marriage.

The unforgiving heat and the unexpected activities of her aunt and uncle had kept her awake and added to her inability to fall asleep. Toward morning, she did finally fall into a deep slumber. The lateness of her sleeps arrival made it even harder for her to wake up. Aunt Bertha called her to breakfast three times before she was able to roust herself, and get to the table. After a hurried breakfast, Rosa rushed out the door, up the road and to school.

Once she got to the fence, she stood glaring at if for several minutes. "Fence, fence," She said aloud, "How I hate you, and I don't like to use the word hate. I think it's a sinful word. Lord, forgive my impatience, today." As she looked at the structure, it seemed higher than usual. Maybe it seemed that way because she hadn't slept well and was so tired. She took a deep breath, uttered a soft curse, then, began a hurried climb over the blasted thing. Because she was rushing and not thinking clearly, she started her climb toward the end of the stacked logs, near where the log ends jutted out. She had reached the top and begun her descent when her foot slipped. For a brief moment, she thought she would come crashing down to the ground on the other side. However, her fall was brief. One of the protruding logs caught her dress as it came up and over from the opposite side of the fence.

Now, she dangled in midair, turning like a bug suspended at the end of a spider's web for what seemed an eternity. 'Lord, don't let the children see me like this,' Rosa prayed; realizing she had to do something about her predicament, she began swinging her body back and forth. Finally she was able to grab one of the logs and pull herself back to the fence. Now she worked her way over to the log that had snagged her dress, and unhooked it. Thus far, God had been merciful. None of the children had arrived to see their teacher in a very un-teacher like, undignified position.

Climbing down, she rushed to the school, and managed to mend the tear by the time the children came marching into class. When they entered the room, they found Miss Rosa sitting tall and composed behind her desk with a surprise for them. Weeks ago she had asked Uncle Jim to build a snake cage. He had brought it to the school and covered it with a burlap bag and placed it in a corner. She uncovered the cage and sat it on a corner table.

"Who knows what this is?" Rosa asked as the children gathered around the screened-in framed box. None knew. "Well, it's a snake cage." Squeals of delight, as well as disgust filled the room. Turning to Bruce, Rosa said, "Do you think you can find a Garden snake for the class?"

A big grin spread over this face, "Oh yes ma'am, I can find all the snakes you want!"

"Bruce, we want one about the same size as the one you brought to class before. Do you think you can do that? We will be able to feed it, watch it shed its skin, then, when school is over for the summer, we will release it back into the wild."

Despite the way the day had started, Rosa felt it had turned into a good, productive day. True to his word, in less than a half hour, Bruce returned with a snake that was the right size for the cage. The next day, the children collected insects for the snake to eat, and watched spellbound as it devoured the bugs. In addition, the children were amazed that the teacher had allowed a snake to be part of their classroom. She was unlike any teacher they had ever had before, and they were glad she had become a part of their lives.

As she sat with Aunt Bertha and Uncle Jim at dinner, she told them of her day, beginning with the fence and how she had hung like a bug caught in a spider's web. Her story brought laughter from both Bertha and Jim. Finally she told Uncle Jim what a huge success the snake cage he built had been. She concluded by saying, "I just wish we could find a way to get a gate in that fence."

The next day, Uncle Jim hitched his mules and drove to the general store in Church Hill to pick up some much needed items: feed for his livestock, sugar, flour and other staples for Bertha. While in the store, he remembered they had an anniversary coming up. To honor that occasion, he bought a box of sweets.

Almost home and dog tired, he snapped the harness on the mules' backsides to quicken their pace. The animals responded to his urging for two reasons. They knew they were almost home and nearing the final leg of their hard uphill journey. They also knew they would be given their rations of oats once they made it back to the barn. The wagon rocked from side to side and bounced harshly as the wheels struck rocks and dropped into holes, while Jim urged them on.

The wagon's clatter made it almost impossible to hear any sounds other than the crash, bang and rattle of its wheels, let alone a feeble cry for help. Jim thought he heard something. Maybe it was a voice, but he wasn't sure. His mind was on getting home, seeing Bertha, and having a hot meal. But then, there it was again, something, some kind of sound – he just couldn't put his finger on it. He decided to check further. Something, or someone was making a strange sound. "Whoa there you damn mules. Whoa!" The wagon's noise stopped, and now he could hear better. Jim leaned forward in his seat, cocked his head in order to determine if it was his imagination, or something for real.

"Help…Help me." A voice called.

Now he knew his ears weren't playing tricks on him. Someone was calling for help. Jim yelled. "I hear you, but I don't see you. Where are you?" He asked as he looked all around.

"Here, over here. My legs busted and I can't stand up."

Jim jumped off the wagon and walked in the direction of the voice. "Let me hear you again." Jim called. "I'm over here, on the other side of the fence."

Jim continued on slowly. "Keep talking, I still don't see you."

"Here, Jim, I'm over here. It's me, your neighbor Blair, Blair McMullen."

Continuing a bit further, he stopped near where he thought the voice had come from. "Say something, I still don't see you."

"You could if you looked over on the other side of the fence."

Jim squatted down and, peering through the logs, he saw his neighbor sitting against a tree. "What happened to you, Blair?"

"I busted my leg while I was hunt'n. Slipped off a damn rock and my leg just popped. I tried using my gun fer a walk'n stick, but the stock snapped in two."

"That be'n the case, I gott'a get you to town to Doc Wilson." Jim concluded as he surveyed the situation. "Blair, I can't lift you over, I'm gonn'a have to dig a hole under the logs so I ken pull you through to the other side. Hold on, Let me get the shovel off the wagon."

"Jes do what eva' you got to do." The injured man answered, his face contorted in pain.

Jim returned with the shovel, kneeled down and began digging. After a few minutes of shovel work, he called out. "We're in luck, Blair, there is some rotten logs here in the fence, I may not have to dig, I think I'll be able to yank them out of the way. If I can, I'll be able to get you through, lickity split." After a short while he was able to pull enough logs away to make an opening big enough to crawl through. "I'm coming to get ya', Blair."

Jim got down on his belly and crawled through to the other side. He jumped up and hurried to his neighbor. Squatting next to him he said, "Blair, now, I got to carry you to the fence." Jim picked him up and carried him to the opening he had made, then, gently placed him on his back next to the fence opening. Jim crawled through to the other side. "Now Blair, I'm gonn'a have ta try and pull ya through the opening, so hold my hands as tight as you can. He reached through and grabbed Blair's hands, then gently began pulling him to the other side.

As his body came through the opening, Blair uttered a few choice curses. "Ahh, shit, that hurts!"

"I know it does, but I gott'a get you all the way through, Blair. Then I got to get you up on the wagon."

It took a while, but he was able to pull his neighbor through the opening to the other side. "Now I got to get ya up on the wagon, Blair." A smile spread over Jim's face when he said, "Now Blair, its gonn'a be a bumpy ride to town, but you're in some luck, there's straw on the wagon. That should make your ride a little better." Jim grabbed hands full of the straw and fashioned it into a kind of mattress before he hoisted Blair onto the wagon. Making him as comfortable as he could on the wagon, Jim, with some difficulty managed to turn the wagon around in the narrow lane, then and headed back down to Church Hill.

The bouncing and jousting just about killed Blair, but he sucked it up as best he could until Jim stopped in front of the doctor's office. "Well, we're here, Blair."

"Damn, that was the worst ride I eva' had in my life, but I thank you Jim."

'We're here.' were the most welcome words the injured man had heard all day. Jim carried him into the doctor's office, then, between the two of them, explained in detail what had happened.

Doc Wilson went right to work. He set the leg,s then fashioned a crude crutch for his patient. "You stay off that leg for at least three weeks, ya hear? When you do get up and try to move about, you use this here crutch. I'll come to your place and take a look at you in a week or so."

"Can I settle up with you then, Doc? I ain't got no cash on me."

"I ain't worried about payment. Maybe you got some deer meat hanging around that'll taste better than cash in my book."

"Sure enough Doc. I can do that, be my pleasure." Blair replied with a big grin.

"Jim, I'm gonn'a give you a mattress off my spare bed to get him home more comfortable. You can…"

"Doc, I'll be coming to town in a week, I'll bring it back to you then." Jim offered.

Blair's place was about a quarter of a mile past the school. His gate was the only one ever installed in the meandering fence and was large enough for Jim's mules and wagon to pass through. With Blair's wife's help, the two of them settled him into his favorite rocking chair.

"Jim, I'm mighty obliged to you. If I can ever do you a favor, you jes' ask, you hea' me?" Blair said, grinning and revealing a mouth of missing teeth.

"I must say, today has been a hard day for you, Blair. I just hope you mend real quick. Once you're some better, I'll come and sit with ya fer a spell."

"I'd like that." Blair replied.

Several months passed. Jim and Bertha were having coffee and cake when they were surprised by a knock on their door. "Who in the world would be paying us a visit?" Bertha wondered out loud.

"I ain't got no idea, but I'll go see." Jim got up and went to the door. Blair was standing on the porch, hat in hand. He looked a lot better than the last time he had seen him and had an unmistakable twinkle in his eye. "Can I come in Jim?"

"Sure. Sure. Come in, make yourself at home. Take a seat at the table. We was jes' having some coffee and cake."

Bertha poured him coffee, and cut him a big slice. Blair looked around, then, leaned forward. "Well, I been

do'n me some thinking. And..." He cut his words short as Rosa came out of her bed room and entered the room.

"This here is my niece, Rosa Bradley. She be the new teacher up at the school house, Blair." Jim said with obvious pride.

"I been hear'n 'bout the good job she's been do'n with the children. Anyway, it's a pleasure to meet you, Miss Rosa."

"Yes, and it's a pleasure to meet you, Mr. McMullen." Rosa smiled, then excused herself, and continued out the door.

Once she was out of the room, Blair, in a hushed tone, continued with what he had begun to say to his hosts. a bit earlier.

During the weeks after school had let out for the summer, Rosa was able to spend time at home with her family in Rogersville. It was fun and relaxing for her since she didn't have to pretend to be the prim and proper (older) teacher, something she had learned to do well. But that role didn't allow her to be herself. At home she felt totally free to be the tomboy she was. Summer vacation was a break she needed badly. Unfortunately, it passed too quickly and in what seemed to be a blink of the eye she heard Uncle Jim and his mules outside the house to take her back to Hawkins Mountain and her school.

It took her no time to prepare mentally for the new school year. She looked forward to working with her charges, but as she reviewed what lay ahead, the most worrisome thing she could think of was that cursed fence.

On her first day back, she walked the mile to the school, subconsciously preparing herself for her 'enemy.' For some reason, it had weighed heavily on her mind this morning. As she approached the spot where she would normally climb over, she became momentarily confused. Standing at that spot, she realized things were different.

Instead of facing a six foot stack of logs, there was a hinged gate, with a pegged latch.

A smile bright as the sun spread across her face as she opened, then closed the gate. She began skipping down the path as if she were a child going to school for the first time.

After her day was over, she couldn't wait to tell Uncle Jim and Aunt Bertha, "Guess what?"

"What's got you all fired up young lady?" Jim asked, looking as blank-faced as he could.

"The fence, I mean the gate, I mean there's a gate in the fence!"

"Well, I wonder how that came about?" Jim asked with an innocent face.

"I don't know, but it's such a blessing, I just can't believe it." Rosa exclaimed. "How did it come about? It couldn't have just been a change of Mr. McMullen's heart for no reason," Rosa deducted as she looked at her aunt and uncle with a confused expression.

Aunt Bertha smiled. "Tell her how it all came about, Jim."

"Sit, Rosa, and I'll explain exactly how it happened." Uncle Jim then proceeded to tell Rosa how he came upon Blair, and all that transpired afterwards. "To show his appreciation for what I did, he wanted to repay in some way. Knowing the fence was a big sore spot, he made that gesture of friendship to all of us, especially to you, Rosa."

She was moved to rears, "Oh I'd love to thank him. I really would, if that's possible Uncle Jim."

"He's a shy man, Rosa. That may be a little hard to do. But there's more to show you. Come. Come out back," Uncle Jim urged.

"What do you mean, there's more?"

"You'll see, you'll see." Aunt Bertha said, smiling. She stood and led the way out the side door toward the barn. Jim hurried ahead, opened the barn door, disappeared for few minutes then reappeared, leading a sway-backed dapple gray mare.

"Meet Light'n, Rosa. She's called that because she was born during a thunder storm. Seems a bolt of light'n hit close by when her mama was thinking about givin' birth. Well, accord'n to Blaire, when the lightening hit, she dropped the foal. Oh, by the way, she's all yours, Rosa. Blair wants you to be able to ride to school 'stead of walking."

"Oh, I can't believe it. This is just too much! I've got to send him a thank you, of some sort."

"Don't you worry none. We'll figure out a way for you to do that, honey." Bertha added with confidence.

"Blair said, Light'n is too old to plow, or pull a wagon, but he thought you'd like to have her ta' ride to school. She's just living a life of ease at his place. He said tak'n you to school would be just about right fer her. Makes her feel useful, and it sure beats you walk'n."

Tears came to Rosa's eyes. "I don't know what to say. That's so sweet of him." She rushed to the old horse and began patting her. She seemed to know she would be her new master. As she stroked her, her head bobbed up and down, and she let out a whinny.

Jim had a side saddle that Bertha had used when she was younger. He dusted it off, rubbed and oiled it down and put it on Lightning. Rosa mastered the skill of riding in no time. "I must say, you look pretty fancy sitting up there young lady." Uncle Jim teased.

"It's all like a dream." Rosa said, shaking her head in disbelief at all that had happened to her in such a short period of time.

Her excitement paled compared to the children's when they came to school and saw the dapple gray horse tied under a tree. When apples were in season, she allowed the children to feed her a few. On special occasions, the little children were given rides; the bigger boys were given the responsibility of leading the horse around the field with the little ones on her back. For the next three years, the children, Miss Rosa and Lightning made the mountain a happy place. There was laughter mingled with the songs of the children and the birds and the sounds of the forest animals echoing through the woods.

Strange things had begun to happen around the school ever since the gate was put in. Whenever the wood bin got low, somehow, overnight, it would get full. The swing that needed a new rope got one. Rosa told Uncle Jim about a broken window that needed to be replaced, but before he could get around to fixing it, it was repaired.

Even a leak that developed in the roof was patched before Jim could get around to doing it.

The children would often tell their teacher about seeing an old man off in the distance watching them at play. But, whenever they tried to get close, he would hurry away. They all agreed on one thing. The man walked with a very bad limp

CHAPTER 6

Fulfillment

Lincoln University, located in Chester County, Pennsylvania had been groomed to perfection. The buildings seemed more stately than usual. Nothing was out of place for the graduating class of 1911.

The students who attended Lincoln were proud of the University's unique heritage. It was the first institute in the world to offer higher education in the arts and sciences for youth of African descent. The school was founded in 1854 by Reverend John Miller Dickey a Presbyterian minister and his wife Sara Emlen Cresson, a Quaker. Originally it had been named Ashmun Institute after Jehude Ashmun, a religious leader and social reformer who had strong ties to Africa and youth of African descent. However, in 1866 the school was renamed Lincoln University after the assassination of President Lincoln.

Mary Read had taken a seat as close to the front of the auditorium as she possibly could. If the first two rows hadn't been reserved for school officials, she would have sat there. Thinking ahead, she chose an aisle seat; afraid a tall person might sit in front of her and block her view. She reasoned she would be able to lean out into the isle and not miss any of the proceedings should her fear actually materialize.

She used her fan as the heat began to build and the auditorium filled. Finally the young graduates began to march down the aisle to their seats. "Oh, what a handsome lot they are," she thought, "So proud and dignified

George Isaac Read

looking." She searched for her son, and with a mother's eye spotted him. "Oh yes," she smiled as she and nodded her head, "he's by far the most handsome one there."

As the auditorium filled, the room began to feel as hot as Mrs. Farr's kitchen. She remembered there was a second program on the seat next to her that she could use as a second fan to help her survive the rising heat, but she was too late. A lady had just sat next to her and had made use of it herself.

A hush fell over the room as a tall black man wearing a cap and gown made his way to the podium. After a short welcoming speech, he introduced the University's President.

The president's speech focused on the men in front of him and their responsibility to the Negro race. "You are our future," he began. "You are the hope for a brighter tomorrow, not just for our race, but the nation as a whole. We expect great things from each and every one of you!" His speech concluded, he began reading the names of each graduate. Their names called, each student walked from the middle section of the auditorium to the platform stairs, then to the center of the stage where he was given his diploma by the President.

Mary thought she would faint when she heard, "George Isaac Read." It was the deep, rich voice of the President. A smile spread across Mary's face as she thought back to the day she heard Mrs. Farr tell her son William, he would be attending college. Then she thought of the moment she had asked George to promise he would find out "where this place called college was," and his promise that he would. How proud she was as she thought back, knowing how young he was, yet making that promise with the maturity of a man. She remembered watching her boy study far into the night after spending afternoons working with the doctor and then, after several years, the day he came home with the news, "If I keep my grades up, the doctor will see to it that I go to college." What a happy day that was.

Now her boy's name was being called. Yes, this was the moment she had dreamed of for Lord knows how long. She looked to the left portion of the auditorium to see him just as he stood to begin his journey to the stage.

The President handed George his diploma, then added, "And you are to be commended for graduating Magna Cum Laude, and winning the gold medal for science." He then pinned the medal on George's gown.
This extra attention to her son made Mary even more proud, and she sat even taller in her seat. She leaned toward the lady sitting on her right and whispered, "That's my son. I'm just so proud of him."

The comment caused the woman to smile and to say, "You have every right to be, my dear."

Without warning, Mary began to cry. The sudden flow of tears surprised her. She was happier than she had been in years. Yet, she was feeling an emptiness she couldn't account for. Why was she feeling this tug of sadness now, of all times? It took a while for her to realize a thought she had long suppressed but had now pushed its way to the forefront of her mind.

She had long ago given up thinking about what her life could have been had her husband not been murdered. Yes, she had come to terms with that. But that was then, and this was now, and right now she wished with all her heart that she could share this momentous occasion with him. Her tears were recognition of that deep, unspoken hurt. The extent that both she and her son had been cheated

was now embodied by George receiving these high honors without her husband being present.
With the diploma in hand, George allowed his eyes to search for his mother. Once they found her, his smile lit up the entire stage. Through her tears, she returned his joy with a shy wave and a smile.

With the help of the university, George had placed his name with several employers within the state. Each day, he hurried to the post office to see if his applications had generated any responses. Today there were two letters. He wanted to rip them open on the spot, but for some reason, decided to go back to his room, sit at this desk and calmly read them.

With trembling hands he read the letters. The first one invited him to a teaching position at a small elementary school in Alabama. George shook his head since he had decided after he came to Lincoln and the North, that he would never return to the South to live, or, to work. He threw it away and turned his attention to the second one. His face took on a pleased expression as he read it: a school in nearby York County had a teaching position open in an elementary school. He liked the area the college was in and assumed the school in York would be in an equally pleasant location. Over the next several days, he received more offers, but there was something about the one from York that attracted him. He decided he would apply for the that position there.

His job interview went well; he was hired on the spot. He liked York and decided he would drop his roots in this beautiful old, historic city. He went to the bank and, based on his potential job, was given a loan that enabled him to buy a three story brick home at 531 South Queen Street.

He proved to be an excellent teacher. Administration was pleased with his performance, and George felt this job would provide a secure future for Rosa and a family. Now, all he had to do was go get his bride. On the school's first holiday, George headed for Rogersville to marry Rosa.

George was proud and pleased his new wife liked the house he had purchased. It required much work, but Rosa was no stranger to physical labor. While he went to work, she buckled down to make the home the kind of home both she and her husband would be proud of.

They were married only a few months before she realized she was pregnant. The first child was named George Isaac Read, Jr. To celebrate, they decided to send his mother a train ticket so she could see her first grandson. Mary couldn't believe her good fortune: her boy was a college graduate and now he had provided her with a grandson. After a few weeks of enjoying being a grandmother, she decided to rent out her Tennessee home, and with the permission of her daughter-in-law, to stay on. Rosa was not thrilled at the thought of sharing her home with his mother, but after the next child arrived, she welcomed Mary's presence. The home was a large three story affair with room enough to give George, Rosa and Mary their privacy.

The first born, suffered from colic and cried off and on every evening, keeping Rosa and George up most of the night. One morning, George announced to Rosa, "I'm going to sleep up on the third floor in the back bedroom;

I've got to get my sleep so I can go to work." And so it was that George removed himself (as a regular bed partner) from their bedroom for the duration of their marriage.

The three boys were different as night and day. George was the crying child, but otherwise a good, non-demanding baby. John, the second born, was active and into everything – touching, grabbing, babbling, never sitting still. When he was old enough to play outside in the fenced in back yard, Rosa had to tie him to a tree, otherwise he would 'escape' through the gate and be found on the front sidewalk, usually several houses down the block. Brad, the third was easy in most ways except he was a finicky eater, requiring special food preparation. Mary's presence under these circumstances proved to be a God-send.

The two women were mature enough to respect each other's role and were able to form a bond based on each one's respect for the role the other played in caring for the children and maintaining the running of the home. They would even swap chores to avoid any chance of becoming bored with the assignment each found themselves fulfilling. Rosa was happy and fulfilled. She enjoyed being a mother and felt proud as she pushed her baby carriage down Queen Street. She would have one baby in the carriage and two hanging onto either side it. Because Rosa lived on Queen Street, she didn't see many other people of color. Historically, the 'streets' were where white people lived, whereas the alleys were where most colored, and poor white folks lived. There weren't that many people of color living in York. However, there were some black folks who had roots that dated back to the early 1700's, and they lived in the better homes.

However, most black folks, along with their poor white counter parts were consigned to living in the back alleys scattered throughout the city.

It was a bright sunny day when Rosa spotted another black woman pushing a carriage. The woman had a child in the carriage and one hanging to its side. As if pulled by a magnet, they sped towards each other. "I'm Rosa Read, who are you?"

"I'm Helen Armstead, and honey, you are a sight for sore eyes!" She answered as the two women embraced each other as if they were long lost friends.

Rosa joked, "I was beginning to think there were no folks in town with my complexion."

"Well, there aren't too many of us in this part of town." Helen added with a smile.

The women were starved for information about each other and began cross-examining each other like two skilled attorneys. They didn't stop until each had a complete picture of the other's life and family. After exhausting themselves with this new information, they exchanged addresses and decided that since Helen had one less child, she would visit Rosa first.

Rushing home, Rosa couldn't wait to share her experience and the good news with Mary. And she shared it all in great detail. After she concluded, Mary said, "You let me know a day before she's to come and I'll bake some cookies and make sandwiches so you two ladies can have a good visit, and really get to know each other. It was a small thing, but it was in ways such as this that Mary made herself such a good helpmate to Rosa.

The women took turns cooking and cleaning and taking care of the boys. Breaking up the routine in such a way, neither woman felt worn out if the children had had a bad day or felt bored by doing the same household chores, day after day.

Helen came for a visit and the ladies picked up where they had left off, always trying to get the fullest picture of the other's life. The two women had so much in common that finally Rosa said, "Helen, I have an idea. Aside from being good friends, why don't we become aunts and our husbands uncles to each other's children?"

"I think that's a great idea, Aunt Rose!" Helen said as she got up to embrace her new relative.

The two women held each other tightly for a long, long time. Finally they stepped back and searched each other's face. It was then they both realized they were shedding tears of joy. "Now our children will have cousins." Rosa added

CHAPTER 7

Different Lifestyles

Conowaga Township, York County Pennsylvania

The couple sat at their kitchen table. The smell of scrapple, eggs and coffee permeated the room. The woman was pretty. She was small, less than five feet tall. Her hair was golden, her light blue eyes had a constant twinkle. Sitting at the opposite end of the table, was her husband, a lean, sun burned man of medium build. He wore a bushy mustache under a prominent nose and had the same light blue eyes as his wife.

She spoke first. "Ach Al, it's hard onc't. First, John's son falls through the ice and drowns; then, his Missus grieves herself over the boy to where she just slipped away in her sleep. John said she wouldn't eat noth'n, her eat'n jes' went away. She wouldn't even talk, didn't say noth'n for weeks, just stared into space, then one day she was gone. I guess the poor soul decided she just couldn't go on after her boy died."

"Yah, Sara. He won't be able to keep the farm going with John Junior and his wife both gone. It'll be just too much for him onc't." Al replied in the unique way of the Pennsylvania Dutch.

"We'll miss the boy too, Al. He was our extra hand whenever we needed one, I can't count how many times he helped us hoe, bring in the hay, or to butcher. Same goes for John Senior. We could always count on him when we needed another hand, ain't not? If he leaves, we'll sure miss him." Sara lamented.

"Thank goodness the Fetrows can still be counted on. I tell you Sara, it's hard to get along without good neighbors." Al was referring to the Dutch tradition of neighbors helping their neighbors. During harvest or thrashing time, the other farmers would pitch in and help whoever was in need of another extra hand. No money was involved; payment came in the form of a festive dinner prepared by the wife of the host farmer and the other farmer's wives and daughters. It was hard work, but it was also a fun time, and no matter the chore, the work got done. Those who helped could expect the same kind of repayment when their time of need came.

Breakfast over, Al and Sara, were enjoying their coffee and conversation when their two outside dogs began barking. A car had stopped out front. "Someone's coming Sara." Al announced.

Before he could get outside to see who it was, John Ness appeared at the kitchen door. "Morning, folks." He called through the screen door as the two dogs wagged their tails and sniffed his legs as he peered in. The dogs had recognized him as a familiar visitor.

"Come in." Sara welcomed. "Coffee? Or can I make you breakfast, John?"

"Thanks. I'll take the coffee, but no breakfast."

Al pulled out a chair, "Have a seat, John."

John didn't waste any time, and got straight to the purpose of his visit. "I've come to tell you folks what I've decided to do…and I don't think you'll be surprised. I'm sell'n the place an mov'n to town."

"No, John, we ain't surprised. Fact is, we were just talking about you and how hard it must be fer you try'n to run the place alone."

"Yah, it's too much. I've found me a factory job in town. What I'll do is rent a place in York. No point buy'n till I see how factory work and city life sit with me."

Al poured some of his hot coffee from his cup into his saucer, then sipped it with loud slurps. "It'll be a big change fur ya John, no doubt about that."

"There's more I want to tell ya. I put the place up for sale, and by golly, I sold it in a week."

"John, I'm happy for you and a bit sad, too." Sara lamented.

"Who bought your place, anyone we know?" Al asked.

"No, the man's from Virginia. Man by the name of Sam Chapman. We have a few things to settle before he takes over the place. In fact, he's due out this morning. I'll bring him over so he can meet you folks."

"Sure John, bring him over. But, I can tell you straight out, we'll miss you as a neighbor and friend."

"Yah, I'll miss you folks too, but the buyer, he seems to be an all right man. I'm pretty sure he will work out fer ya as a neighbor," John said between sips of his coffee.

The dogs began barking again. "Someone just stopped out front. I'll go see who it is." Al got up and went out the door.

"I wonder who it might be?" Sara asked.

"Missus, I think Al's coming back with someone." John said. Then added with a smile, "Oh, I recognize the voice; its Chapman, the man who's buy'n my place. Well, I'll be durned."

Al held the door open, then nodded toward Sara. "Come in, Mr. Chapman, Meet my Missus, you already know John?"

Sam Chapman's large body filled the doorway, as he stooped in order not to hit his head when he stepped into the kitchen. "Yup, I sure do, I know that there fella." Then, turning to Sara, he said, "Good to meet you, ma'am." He nodded to John, "I saw your car, that's how I knew you wuz here, jes in case you wuz wunder'n."

"I'm pleased to make your acquaintance, too Mr. Chapman." Sara added with a chuckle.

"When ya' plan'n on move'n in?" Al asked.

"Jes as soon as John gets out." Sam said with a Southern twang. "My woman wants to get settled in. We been move'n every year fer the past four years, sooo, she's fidgety and wants to get hunkered down in one spot."

"Well then, don't sit down. Let's get go'n" John said, as he stood to lead the way out. Remember, Sam, you're the one that said his feet hurt when we started walking the place the other day. We almost covered the whole 76 acres when you got tuckered out. Now, if you're so all fired up and anxious to get moved in to make your little lady happy, then, let's go!" John joked.

"How much more walk'n you reckon we still got to do?" Sam asked seriously.

"We ain't got much more ground to cover. Oh, yeah, my lawyer said you should get your deed today, too. Once we walk the remaining boundaries you'll know where your land ends and Al's begins. You and Al share a lot of common boundaries on the West side of your property. After this walk, you'll be set so you and your Missus can start move'n in. Are you ready?"

"Sure as shit." Sam replied as he followed John out. "Nice meet'n you, folks." Sam called over his shoulder as the two men went out the door and headed for their cars.

Sara turned her eyes skyward as they walked away. "Frankly, I don't get good feelings about that man. And he has a bad mouth, Al."

"You can't tell what a man's like because he has a bad mouth. He was probably not raised proper by his folks. Any way, time will tell, ain't?" Al said as he leaned over his spittoon and let a mouth full of Red Tub tobacco juice plop into the brass container that sat behind the door.

Chapman had moved in and several weeks passed. Al and Sara didn't see or hear from Sam. They decided since he stayed away from them, the best thing would be for them to stay away from him, too. So, they sat back and watched to see how things would work out with their new neighbor.

One morning after breakfast, Al pushed himself away from the table, "Well, I bes' be gett'n to my chores. After, I'm gonn'a take the hounds and walk the woods behind the shed ta' see if I can get a couple of rabbits. I got a taste for some Hasenpfeffer." That said, Al started for the barn.

Before he could get out the door, Sara chided, "Good, those two lazy beagles need to be run so they can start earn'n their keep."

Al stopped, "What did you say?"

I said, "If those hounds are worth their salt, and have any kind of a nose, they should jump at least a dozen rabbits for ya'. Cuz there were sure a bunch around here eat'n outt'a my garden last summer." Sara knew this was a sore spot with Al, and loved to rile him up over his willingness to keep and feed the two useless (as far as she was concerned) hunting dogs.

"Now, never you mind onc't." Al barked. Knowing how unkindly Sara felt about his beagles.

Sara wouldn't let up, "You only run them fer a few days during the year. Otherwise they just lay around, eat'n and sleep'n. That's all they do. Eat, eat, eat! Sleep, sleep, sleep! That's what they do for months and months. Now, Brownie and Spot, they're worth something, they're our eyes and ears. They earn their keep. They bark if anyone or anything comes near the place…because of them I sleep at night."

Sara was referring to the fact that the fenced in area around the house was patrolled and guarded by two large mixed breed dogs. They weren't by nature mean dogs, but could be if Al commanded them to be aggressive. And they were excellent watch dogs, good at sounding the alarm if anyone came near their property.

"Gol dern it Sara, will you stop your yapp'n, woman." She had done a good job of getting under Al's skin and she knew it.

"Al, you wouldn't keep no other animal if it didn't pay its keep, and you know it. If the dumb things would bark when people came around, or would have barked when the fox got into the chicken house and ate half our flock, then, I'd stop my yap'n. An, they were chained right outside the durn house. Brownie and Spot barked, and look how far they were from the chicken house onc't. I tell ya Al, they're useless." With that, Sara went out the other door, leaving Al standing speechless, half in and half out of the opposite doorway.

"Ach, stupid woman. What does she know!" he muttered to no one in particular, then, continued on to the barn. The morning air had been crisp. Now the sun was high and bright, warming the fall breeze to spring like temperatures.

Al had a horse (Prince) and a mule he called 'Mule'. Mule had kicked Al in the forehead, two years ago. Kicking him for no other reason other than he was a mule. The kick knocked Al out cold, almost killing him. He recovered, but as a result of the blow, he had a near perfect U shaped scar on the right side of his forehead and suffered headaches off and on, but, he learned a lesson, he never walked behind Mule again.

After he cleaned the animal's stalls, he put down fresh straw, then, gave them their oats. He left the barn and walked to the rear of his yard where a small keg of apple cider sat on a rough board table. A wooden peg drilled into the table's top held an inverted glass. He carefully placed the glass under the spigot, turned the handle, and let the frost cooled amber apple cider fill his glass. After admiring its clarity, he put the glass to his lips and downed its contents. "Ahhh," He exclaimed, "It's turned hard." He repeated the process two more times. After returning the glass to the peg, he headed for the haymow in the barn. His legs were wobbly as he climbed the ladder to the haymow. He flopped down in the fragrant hay, tipped his hat forward and promptly fell asleep.

"Al! Al! Wake up. It's near dinner time. I've been look'n all over the place fer you. Durn it Al, first you tell me you're go'n hunt'n. When I go outside, I see the hounds are still chained up. I didn't get no work done look'n fer you off and on all day long. I should'a known the cider would be turning hard and you'd be gett'n into it, an' you end'n up in your usual spot, here in the haymow."

Al sat up. "Sara…Sara."

"What! What do you want?" she answered angrily.

"Come. Come sit here next to me." Al said, his eyes twinkling.

"What fer?" Sara feigned exasperation.

"Jes sit with me for a spell." Al patted a spot next to him in the hay.

Sara gave him a stern look, but couldn't hold it for long. A smile came to her lips. "Oh, all right." She said as she sat next to him. The smell of cider was strong on his breath. "Al, why do you get yourself drunk every year?" His eyes sparkled even more "Jes 'cause I wanted to, and jes like I want you now… Sara."

"See, it's your cider talk'n" She said, trying to sound stern.

Al didn't respond. Instead he slipped his arm around her tiny waist, pulled her close, then, kissed her hard on the lips. She remained locked in his embrace for several minutes. Sara was a passionate woman, easily aroused by Al. Suddenly, she pushed him away and stood up. Her hands skillfully removed the hair pins thrust into the large bun at the back of her head, releasing a flow of waist-length golden hair. She lay down next to him and offered her lips.

Sara later awoke with a start. "My God Al, we slept the afternoon most away!" She stood up, then began brushing the hay from her dress and hair.

Al pulled his pocket watch from his pants that were folded up next to them. "It's near 3 O'clock." He said with a contented smile as he reached for his pants, then, slipped them on while lying on his back.

"I best get the food on the stove." Sara said as she straightened her hair. She reached for Al's hand and helped him up.

She went to the house and began cooking, anxious to get the meal on the table. Al decided to go to the hog shed. He reached over the railing and roughly patted the two grunting hogs on their heads. "By golly," He exclaimed as he looked at the two round bodied, contented pigs. "You're go'n to butcher up real good." They knew his presence meant it was treat time, and began pushing their heads through the wooden slats. Their grunts and squeals became more urgent as he walked to one of the many buckets of over-ripe apples he and Sara had picked from their orchard. These otherwise bruised and rotten apples lay under the trees, attracting yellow jackets and honey bees, but were ideal for sweetening the pig's meat. They had several full buckets sitting in the pig shed. "By golly, this will sweeten you up, that's fer durn sure," he repeated as he tipped the bucket. The apples tumbled into the trough, making a rumbling noise as they filled it. The pigs squealed, and grunted louder as they pushed and bumped the other, each one trying to block his mate from the treats.

As Al began walking toward the house, it occurred to him neither John nor his son would be able to help him butcher this year. Maybe he would ask his new neighbor if he could lend him a hand come butchering time. Entering the kitchen, he sat in his rocking chair, (which sat behind the kitchen door,) took out his pouch of tobacco, and carefully plucked out a 'chaws' worth. Ritualistically he stuffed it into the space between his lower jaw and his right cheek. He cleared his throat before he spoke, "I jes' gave the hogs some apples. Their meat should be good and sweet in another two weeks Sara."

"Yah, they should be ready by then." With concern showing on her face she asked, "Al?"

"Yah?"

"With John and his son gone…who will help us butcher?"

"I don't know the man, but I was think'n I'd ask Chapman. I saw him staking some goats in the field between our farms. So, I guess he would know somth'n about butcher'n. Did you see the goats he staked out, Sara?"

"Yah, I saw. But, I don't hold much truck for the animals myself." Sara shook her head as she spoke to emphasize her feelings.

"Me neither, never raised one. I don't know that much about the confounded things. But it means he should know somth'n about butcher'n, ain't not?"

"Al, I don't know about ask'n him. I don't like the man…there's something about him…I…"

"Ach, Sara, how can you say that…we don't hardly know him."

She hadn't had a chance to reply before their dogs started barking. "Al, why are Brownie and Spot barking? They sound really upset."

Al jumped up from his chair and ran out the door. "Ach, De Lieber! Sam's durn goats are on our property! One's in our barn yard eat'n the harness I left on the fence an one is in your garden eat'n your winter kale!" He ran to the nearest goat and kicked it hard in its rear. The big billy goat turned and looked at Al as if he was the intruder, then began munching on the kale again. Al was livid. He grabbed its collar and yanked it away from the plant. He looked around and spotted a rope hanging on the barn yard fence. With a mighty tug he pulled the unwilling beast until he could reach the rope. He tied one end around the collar and the other end to the fence post.

Turning his attention to the second intruder, a nanny, he ran full tilt at the animal, all the while yelling at the top of his lungs. The startled animal looked up at the maniacal man, turned tail and ran out of the still open barn yard gate and back to Sam's yard.

Al walked back to the Billy, and untied the rope. He tried to get the animal to walk with him. Instead, the beast refused to budge. Al had to tug, and pull the reluctant animal all the way back to Chapman's. He was out of breath by the time he found Sam out back, chopping wood. "Gol durn it, Chapman," Al yelled. "Your goats wuz loose and gett'n into mischief over at my place!"

Sam looked up, displaying no concern or showing any reaction to Al's obvious upset. "They were? Well I'll be danged." Sam picked up a log, spit on his hand and returned to splitting the wood he paced on the stump as if Al weren't there.

"Well, will ya take the durn goat off my hands?" Al snapped as he offered the rope to Sam, who continued picking up, stacking, and chopping wood. "Here, take the dang rope!" Al barked once again.

"Jes leave him loose. He ain't go'n nowhere."

"He ain't go'n nowhere! Well, how do you know that? How in Sam Hill did he get over to my place, Chapman? I jes caught him eat'n my good harness. The other fool animal was eat'n my woman's winter kale. Now Sam, you're gonn'a have to do a better job of watch'n your animals."

"Uh, huh." Sam replied as he swung his ax, splitting the log into two pieces.

"Ach the Di Hinger!" Al snapped in frustration. He turned on his heels and stomped home. Sam's large Collie/

Shepard mix that lay between Sam and Al, sniffed at Al's feet as he walked past.

Sara stood at the kitchen door, watching for Al's return. As he entered the yard she asked, "What did he say when you returned his goat?"

"Sara , we got trouble next door. He didn't say noth'n, he didn't care when I told him what his goats had gone and done. He's gonn'a be a terrible neighbor! I'll never ask him for no favor. I'll ask one of the Fetrows, or the Finks to help when butcher'n time comes. I won't ask that skunk fer the time of day."

"I told ya, I got bad feel'ns from that man." Sara reminded Al again.

"Yah, you were right Sara. You were right onc't. I've never had a neighbor I couldn't count on before, ach, it's a shame. A shame when you can't count on your next door neighbor." Al shook his head in disbelief at the thought of such a thing happening.

Several days passed, Al and Sara were still trying to get over the trauma of having Chapman's goats invade their place, when they were awakened from their sleep by the sound of squealing pigs and the barking of Spot and Brownie. "Somethin' is after the pigs, Al!"

"Yah, I hear, I'll get the gun, you light'n the lantern and fetch it along," Al ordered as he hurriedly dressed, then loaded the double barrel 12 gauge. He stuffed a handful of shells into his overall pockets. Sara lit the carry lantern and they hurried out into the darkness. As they approached the hog shed, the pigs' frantic squeals became louder. Something was definitely inside, and doing them harm.

The noises were frightening; the squealing pigs, the frantic barking of Spot and Brownie, and the deep muffled growls, coming from the hog shed. The commotion sent chills up their spines.

"Stay alongside me so I don't make a shadow, then I should be able to see inside." Al whispered. Their hearts were pounding as they opened the shed's door and stepped inside. They could hear the growling more clearly, but they couldn't determine what kind of animal was making the sound. They could hear the frantic scrambling, falling, and squeals as the pig's sought to escape their attacker. But, they couldn't see past the five rows of the 1 X 6 board railing that served as an indoor barrier. The lantern's light was not bright enough to allow them to see clearly through the slats openings to the other side.

"Let's move forward. Hold the lantern higher, higher than the railing. That way I should be able to see." Al said in a hushed voice. They walked forward; Sara raised the lantern. Now the light reached the other side of the railing. One pig was down, lying on its side, its body covered with blood. They could see the scratches caused by the attacking animal's claws, and the puncture wounds from the beast's teeth. It had been mauled from one end of its body to the other. Its side was heaving, and its breath came in rapid bursts. The other pig was still scrambling and falling as what looked like a wolf continued to assail it with snapping jaws. Both pigs and the attacking animal were glistening black from falling and rolling on the wooden floor and the pen's moist muck.

"Gol durn it, I can't get a clear shot without hit'n our pig, Sara!"

Sara spotted something she felt her husband could use, "Al, here's a pitch fork. Can you use that?" She snatched the tool that was leaning against a nearby front wall and offered it. to him.

"Good Sara. Yah, I can use it!" Al leaned the gun against the wall, and without hesitation took the pitch fork. In a matter of seconds he climbed over the barrier. He moved closer to the two struggling animals, planted his feet firmly on the slippery floor, then, he positioned his body so he could make a strong, accurate thrust at the crazed animal. The attacking beast was to intent on its prey it paid no heed to his presence. As he continued attacking, and biting the terrified pig, Al made two rapid thrusts with the pitch fork into the snarling animal's side. Once! Twice! The sharp metal prongs found their mark. The startled animal howled in pain, then tore out of the opening in the back wall; the same opening it had obviously used to find its way in.

Sara handed Al the lantern, then joined him on the other side of the barrier. She took the lantern back as they moved over to the fallen pig. Al knelt to examine it more closely. The pig's breath was irregular, and its tongue was hanging out. The poor animal was in bad shape.

"I don't think this one is going to make it." Al said, shaking his head sadly. "I think it's near to death. It may die of fright." They lifted the light to see where the other pig was. The light revealed it standing in a corner, in a trance like state, shaking violently. It too was badly mauled. The skin was bloodied, ripped and torn from bites and claws. "We best get a towel and a bucket of water so we can clean them up." Al suggested.

They climbed over the barrier, went to the house and returned with a bucket of water and two clean towels and a second lantern.

Daylight found Al and Sara still in the hog pen, exhausted, but feeling better about the outcome of the pig's survival. Both hogs were now cleaned, cooled down, and seemingly feeling better. The fallen pig stood on unsteady legs. His companion was more calm and breathing evenly.

"They might make it back to good health onc't." Sara said with a smile.

"Yah, they both might do good. We'll see in a day or so, Sara."

"Al, what was that animal last night onc't? A wolf? Or wuz it a dog?"

"It could have been either. But, I think it was a dog, Sara. Wolves ain't been seen too often in these parts anymore."

"Al, I'll do my chores, then. I'll get breakfast on the stove."

"Yah, that will give me time to do my chores, too. We can come back and look at the pigs after onc't."

They were glad to have a chance to finally sit down and eat. Both of them were tired and hungry. "I stuck the damn thing pretty durn good. It might die if I hit its heart." Al said between bites.

"If it wasn't a wolf, whose dog could it…"

Al cut her off. "When I took the goat back, Chapman had a dog. He weren't tied fast neither. It could'a been his'n."

"Ach, I hope not."

"Well if it's his'n, he's gonn'a have to know we can't have a pig kill'n dog run'n loose. That's the straight of that."

"What are you gonn'a do, Al?"

"Do?"

"Yah, Are you gonn'a go see him and find out if it was his'n?"

"It wonders me, what I should do, Sara. I guess I should best find out, and get the straight of it."

"Yah, but be careful onc't. If it was his'n he may turn mean on you, Al." Sara's words of caution had no sooner passed her lips, when they heard a booming voice.

"Gross! Al Gross!...I wanna see ya!"

"That's Chapman, Al." Sara said in concern.

His angry voice was upsetting Spot and Brownie. They began barking and jumping up on the fence at Sam, who stood red faced on the other side.

"I'll go see what he wants, but I'm sure now it was his dog. Onc't. That's why he's here."

"Be careful, Al. He sounds ugly and mean."

"I will, I'll be careful." Al took a deep breath, then, went out to face his irate neighbor.

"Al Gross, what did you do to my dog? He came home and dropped dead. An, he's got stab wounds in him. God damn it, what did you do to my dog, Gross?"

"Why do you think it was me what killed your dog, Sam"?

"Because I followed his foot prints, and they lead to your place, that's why. See, there in the sand. You can still see them, plain as the nose on your face." As he spoke, he pointed to the double sets of prints. One coming from his place, another set going back.

Al nodded, "Them prints shows it was your dog that tried to kill my two hogs, now don't it? He chewed em up pretty durn good. He's a pig killer, that's what. It was him or my pigs, Sam."

"The hell you say,. You got no right to kill my dog Al Gross!"

"Your dog got no right to attack my hogs, neither. They wuz sleep'n in their pen. Your gol durn dog wuz in the wrong. I done what I had to do to save them. He had no business be'n here in the first place, Sam."

"The hell you say… I ought'a beat the shit outt'a you, you god damn dumb Dutchman." Sam moved closer, his face dripping sweat, his big hands balled up into fists. He walked menacingly towards, Al who stood behind the gate. Sam reached over and placed his hand on the inside hook to unlatch it.

"I don't reckon that what your think'n on do'n is a good idea, Sam." Al said calmly.

Spot and Brownie had been trained to be passive watch dogs, passive, but watchful. They barked when people passed by, even allowing strangers to enter the yard unmolested, as Sam had once done, a sniff being the extent of their interest in such a person. They had also been trained to be aggressive on command. All Al would have to say was "get em boy!'"And they would have torn into that person or animal.

Then, too, dogs also have basic instincts and an inbred awareness of what they perceive to be threats to their masters. Brownie and Spot were no exceptions. Without any command from Al, the dogs moved to his side. The tone of Sam's voice was enough for them to know he meant their master no good.

They stopped barking. Now their hackles stood erect, and deep growls emanated from their throats. Their quivering lips revealed long white fangs. Together, they represented 180 pounds of potential fury.

Sam stopped in his tracks and removed his hand from the gate hook and stepped back. He knew the animals would tear him up. "God damn it, Gross, you ain't heard the last from me." He bellowed as he stomped back down the road and headed home.

Sara had stood just inside the open front door watching. She was also holding sthe double barrel shotgun in her hands. “Good riddance to bad rubbish is what I say!” She called after the departing figure.

“Yah, I agree. But we will have to keep our eyes open Sara. The man is no good. He’s trouble. An’ he ain’t done with me, not yet least wise.”

Now, they slept lightly, fitfully, with one ear open for any strange noises. When the dogs barked, Al would grab his shotgun, go outside and stand on the porch where he could see the barn, the chicken houses, and the hog shed.

Once he got up and saw a raccoon crossing the yard. He realized that was what had set the dogs off. A few times he heard something walking in the woods, but from his location he wasn’t able to tell if it was an animal, or a person. However, Chapman’s threatening words were now always uppermost in both of their minds.

Not being able to get a good night’s sleep on a regular basis caused Al to experience more headaches than usual, and that put his temper on a short fuse. “Gol durn it Sara, since that man has moved in, I can’t settle my mind down. I know he’s up to no good; it’s just a matter of when he does someth’n. An’ I know it.”

“Al, we will just have to be watchful and wait onc’t”

November was traditionally butchering time. The pigs being injured caused a delay which brought them into early December. And December meant strong winds, and colder temperatures. Butchering would be a harder task now. The crisp fall air had given way to the cold of winter.

“The pigs need more time to get back to their old selves, they’re still off their feed yet.” Al commented as he and Sara leaned over the railing watching their hogs.

“What a shame. It will be a hard winter onc’t before we get to butcher’n, aint’t?”

"Yah. The animals need time after being made scared. Their meat will be tough onc't. We'll have to wait another few weeks."

"Sara, I'm going to go down to the Fetrows and see if Eddie can help us when butcher'n time does come."

"That's what I felt we should'a done in the first place, Al. Ask the Fetrows."

"You're right. I tol' you before Sara, you were right, now gol durn it. So stop yer yapp'n about it!" Sara's womanly instincts were on target, and Al knew it. Al slammed the door, then, hurried across the road to the garage. He backed his Model T out and roared off to the Fetrow farm, a mile down the road.

He pulled into the long driveway, drove past the house and continued on to the huge barn that sat further back on the property. He spotted Eddie, busy working on a broken wagon wheel near the barn yard fence.

"Howdy. Eddie."

"Howdy. Al. What brings you out today?"

"Well, Eddie, I'll tell ya straight out. My hogs got attacked by my new neighbor's dog. They got tore up pretty durn good, so I need to let them mend before I can butcher. I wuz wonder'n if I could ask ya to help me out in a couple of weeks. I know its kinda late to be butcher'n, but could ya?"

Eddie was a man of few words, and spoke in a slow deliberate manner. He looked at Al with bulging eyes that seemed to never blink. He nodded his head, and in a nasal voice asked, "What did he do to make amends for the damage to your pigs, Al?"

"Ach, he's an Outlander. He don't think like us. Anyway, I had to stick his dog with a pitch fork to get him off my pigs, and the critter ran home and died…so, he's put out at me. Fact is, he made ugly talk about what he might do. Now, me, and the Missus ain't sleepn'n good these nights."

Eddie looked away for several moments, then, turned toward Al. "Yah, I can lend you a hand butcher'n time. But, let me tell ya someth'n else, Al. I'd put a Hex on your neighbor if I wuz you. That way you and your missus can get sleep again. The Pow Wow doctor, he could cast a spell on him so he can't hurt you, your animals or your place. I can ring the doctor up an' he can tell ya what to do, Al."

Al looked into Edie's unblinking eyes. He was for the moment speechless, because neither he, nor Sara, believed in pow wowing, and he didn't want to insult Eddie or his beliefs. "Eddie, let me talk to my missus, then I'll let you know." He hedged.

"It's up ta you, Al. But that's what I'd do." Eddie said with conviction.

"Thank ya' fur the advice, Eddie." Al replied sincerely.

"Well, I gott'a get this wheel back on the wagon." Eddie said to signal the conversation was over and he wanted to get back to work.

Al took the hint and climbed back into his vehicle. "I'm much obliged to ya, Eddie." He started his car and headed home.

Sara was out front feeding Brownie and Spot when he returned. "How did it go? Can he give us a hand?" She asked as her husband crossed the road from the garage.

"Yah, he can help us butcher…an, he tol' me how to take care of Chapman, too!" Al said with a twinkle in his eye.

"What do you mean take care of Chapman?" Sara looked puzzled.

"He said he could get the Pow Wow doctor to put a Hex on Chapman; That the Hex'n doctor would keep him from hurt'n us, our animals, or, our property." Al said seriously, knowing what Sara's response would be.

"Ach, Al. I don't put no stock in Pow Wow'n and neither do you. What did you tell him onc't?"

"I tol' him I would talk it over with you. Then I'd let him know if he should contact his Hex man."

"Jes' so long as he don't get put out with us because we don't use his Pow Wow man. I hope he don't hold that against us, and not show up for butcher'n."

"I don't think Eddie is that kind'a man. He won't hold that against us. Leastwise, I don't think so. Oh. I gott'a tell you, just now, when I drove past Chapman's place, he wuz stand'n out in his yard. When he saw who it wuz, he turned his back on me. So, I'd say he's still got hard feeln's against me."

"Well, we won't pay no heed to him, or his foolishness." Sara said defiantly.

Two weeks went by swiftly, and in that time the hogs mended. As expected, the bitter winter weather came, too. Despite the cold, Eddie and Al's past experience allowed them to overcome the disadvantages it presented. They made a good working team since both were careful and methodical in everything they did. There was no lost time or motion once they began.

The water for scalding had been pumped, carried, and poured into the big kettle the night before. Al got up extra early to light the logs to have the water boiling before Eddie arrived. They butchered the hogs swiftly and efficiently. After the hogs were stuck, the blood was collected. After scalding and scraping, the hogs were gutted, hung, sawed in half, then, cut into hams, loins and all of the other standard cuts. The collected blood was used along with the meat from the boiled bone scrapings to make blood pudding. The hog's intestines were flushed and used for sausage casings. The scrapings from the bones was used for scrapple. The head, the brains, the tongue, the snout, the ears, the kidneys, the liver, the heart, the stomach, the knuckles, the feet and even the tail, were all used in one way or another. Or as the saying goes, 'The only thing not used was the pig's squeal.' As darkness settled in, the men finished up.

Sara prepared a hearty meal which the cold and tired men enjoyed and ate with great gusto. When the meal ended, no one moved from the table. A flickering kerosene lamp created deep shadows on their faces, making them look even more weary than they actually were. They were happy, just to be able to sit, relax and have idle conversation and enjoy the kitchen's warmth.

Eddie pulled out his corn cob pipe and a tin of Prince Albert tobacco. After he loaded it, he struck a match and drew several quick puffs. The smoke created a gray/ blue cloud that enveloped his head. His face took on a serious expression as he looked off, belched, then, asked the question Sara and Al knew he would. "Should I ring up the Pow Wow doctor for you folks?" His unblinking eyes locked on Al's face.

Sara looked at Al, expecting him to answer. But he didn't. Instead he returned Eddie's gaze. The reply to his question was in his head. He knew what he wanted to say, but he was still hesitant to voice it. So, he stalled. Finally his brain cleared, and he spoke, "No Eddie, we reckon we'll just let the whole thing lay. Chapman ain't bothered us none, and I jes' as soon not bother about him. But I do thank ya fer the offer. I'm much obliged to ya. The missus and I, well, we reckon he's more talk than anything else. So, we'll just leave it lay." Al concluded.

Eddie had no reaction to Al's reply. For a while they all remained silent, then in his nasal, mechanical way, Eddie said, "Well, suit yourself, Al." His response revealed neither anger, nor disappointment. "Now I bes' be get'n on down the road." When Eddie spoke, the most expressive thing about him was his prominent Adam's apple that moved up and down when he spoke.

"I'm much obliged to you, Eddie fer all your help, and I look forward to return'n the favor onc't."

"Thanks for the meal, Sara. It was good." Eddie stood, put on his coat, then, walked to the door. He hunched his shoulders as he braced for the cold.

"I thank you for your help, too, Eddie." Sara added.

"Happy I could help out…good night." Eddie opened the door and stepped out into the darkness and the frigid night air.

Sara waited until she heard his car start and drive off before she spoke, "Do you think he took offense onc't?"

"I don't think so. He's know'd ever since we wuz kids going to Green Spring school that neither your family nor mine put no stock in hex'n. It was just a few families what did. So, he can't be took by surprise at our answer," Al said with conviction.

"Yah. That's so. But it still makes it hard onc't when you feel one way, know'n he and his folks feel another."

"That's fur sure. But we can't change what we believe to suit him neither." Al said firmly. "I'm gonn'a wash up, then, turn in. I'm tuckered out." He went to the wash stand; poured water from the pitcher into the small basin. Then he unbuttoned the shoulder straps of his overalls and let them fall. He took off his shirt, unbuttoned the top of his long underwear and let it drop as well. He washed his face, body and underarms, took the hanging towel off the stand, and dried himself, then pulled his underwear top back up. When he finished with the towel, he placed it on the nearest chair. Having been scolded by Sara before (for not doing it,) he took the pottery wash basin to the door, opened it and threw the dirty water outside into the night's darkness and returned it to the wash stand. He glanced over at her, expecting an approving look.

"Leave the towel lay; I'll take care of it." Sara offered. "I'll be ta bed as soon as I put everything to rights in the kitchen."

"All right, then. Goodnight." Al said as he went to bed.

It took Sara over an hour to clean up. Afterwards, she felt hot and sticky from the day's activities. She went to the wash stand, and repeated the same ritual that Al had, except she disrobed totally. She washed her body slowly, enjoying the heat from the kitchen stove's dying embers. After drying off, she became annoyed at herself for not remembering to get her night gown first. Now, she realized she would have to run into the cold middle room, and grab her gown from behind the open upstairs door. This was so because the door to the middle room was kept closed winter and summer, so there was no lost heat from the kitchen in that room, or into their upstairs bedroom at all. She took a deep breath, then, made a dash for the garment. After grabbing the gown, she ran back to the kitchen's warmth and slipped it on.

Planning for breakfast and the fire she always made in the morning, Sara took the biggest log from the wood box (which sat behind the shiny black stove) and dropped it into the hot embers of the stove's fire box. The log would smolder all night and burn down to a bed of coals by morning. This would get the morning fire going more easily.

She lit a candle, then carried it to find her way up the steps to their bedroom. She placed it in the holder on side of the bed, blew it out, then crawled quietly under the covers. Al was on his back snoring loudly, ,but his body heat had made the bed warm.

"Al, Al! Turn over." She said in a loud whisper to stop his snoring.

He turned, giving Sara his back. She snuggled up next to him and promptly fell asleep.

They awoke feeling better than they had in weeks. With butchering behind them, they could look forward to the winter months. Their cellar was full of provisions that Sara had put up during the summer. The store room was stocked with hundreds of jars brim full of fruits and vegetables. More than enough to last them until a fresh batch of beans, corn tomatoes and other crops would come in again.

Al would cure the hams in a salt brine for weeks. When they were cured, he would hang them in the smoke house and smoke the meat with hickory wood to add it's unique fragrance to the ham's flavor.

He eliminated attending market on Wednesdays during the winter months, going in only on Saturdays. Despite not having any fresh produce to sell this time of year, he and Sara found ways to provide themselves with a cash income. He would bring in a portion of the scrapple, sausages and some of the ham by the slice. And, he might have a few eggs to sell as long as his hens continued to lay during the cold winter months. They were almost totally self-sufficient, but still needed cash for staples like sugar, flour and other odds and ends they could not produce themselves.

Sara contributed to their income by 'putting up' a variety of items for winter sales. Shoo-fly pie, pickled pigs feet, cookies and chow chow were some of her specialties.

They both enjoyed this time of year. With the hard work of summer behind them, they found preparing for market enjoyable. However, Sara didn't like being out in public, so, the job of tending market fell to Al. At first he was reluctant to do it, but in time learned to enjoy the customers and the routine of tending market. Over the years he developed 'regulars' who shared their lives and gossip with him, and this in turn gave him news and stories to tell to Sara throughout the week.

Sara loved preparing special things. It gave her a chance to show off her kitchen skills and Al would faithfully report to her all of the favorable comments her pies, cookies and chow chow garnered. She would smile with pride and nod as he relayed the praises.

Now all they had to do on a daily basis was feed the dogs and chickens, gather the eggs, milk the cow and keep the stable clean. Al would occasionally take the hounds out for a run, sometimes just to hear them bay when they were on the scent of a rabbit. If they jumped one, (depending on what he had a hankering to eat,) he might shoot the animal. The same could not be said if it was a game bird. If the dogs flushed a pheasant, grouse or quail, he would always try to bag it.

Life was good again. It had settled into a nice routine. They had begun to forget they had Chapman as a neighbor. Sara joked, "Maybe the two of them is related to bears, and they sleep through the winter. Maybe that's why we ain't seen hide, nor hair of either him, or his woman."

Al chuckled at Sara's humor.

Spring came, and with it the first evidence that Sara's bear theory was all wrong. Everyone knows bears and dogs don't like each other. Therefore, if Sam was related to a bear he wouldn't have done what he did. He brought home a big scruffy dog, a mix of who knows what? The animal announced his presence to the Grosses by howling at the moon all night the first evening he was home, and every night thereafter. If there was no moon, a frog's croaking would start him barking. If it wasn't a frog, a hoot owl would set him off. No matter what, something would cause the fool dog to bark, or howl. His voice was big and loud, and despite living in a house with stone walls eighteen inches thick, his voice penetrated through to their bedroom. No matter what they did to muffle the noise, they heard the thing carry on every night.

Al stood in his doorway, looking over at the Chapman's place. "Sara, I can't take much more of that fool man and his dog. They's give'n me headaches most every day."

Sara rubbed her bloodshot, puffy eyes, "It makes me wonder what goes on in his head onc't. Don't he hear the stupid thing when it barks and howls?"

"The man ain't right in the head. He didn't have no proper up bring'n. He's an outlander, that's fer sure."

"Al, someone is toot'n their horn. I think it's the mail man. He must want to see you about something." Al pulled out his pocket watch, "Yah, it's his time. I'll go out onc't an see." He walked quickly to the front yard where Mel Whitmer sat in his car with a newspaper in his hand.

"Al, I could'a put the paper in yer box, but I got somethin' to tell ya in person."

"Well, Mel it's good to see ya anyway. What you got to tell me?"

"From all I been told about Chapman, I think its good news fer ya, Al. Yer neighbor…well, actually his woman came into some money from her kin back home. Since she don't like it up here no how, they's move'n back to Virginia."

"For sure, Mel? Well that's the best durn news I've heard in a spell."

"Yah, pretty sure, Al."

"Did you hear when they's supposed to be skedaddling?"

"From what I was told, it could be any time. I hear he's got the place up for sale, so I guess he want's to get goin' as quick as he can. So I guess he'll be get'n out soon. And which I guess will be good news fer you and your Missus, ain't?"

"Wait till I tell my Missus. I'm much obliged to ya, Mel. Like I said, ya brung me the best news I've heard in months."

"From all I heard about him and his carry'n on, I thought the news would please ya. Well, I'll say good bye, I gotta make my rounds." Mel engaged the clutch, and the car lurched forward, kicking up a cloud of dust as it bounced down the dirt road.

Al ran back toward the kitchen. He couldn't wait to get inside, so he called through the screen door. "Sara! Sara! Ya ain't gonn'a believe what I got to tell ya!"

"What. What is it?"

"Mel said they's move'n…the Chapman's, the Chapman's are head'n back down South!"

"Thank you God, thank you! Oh Al, it's the best news you could'a brung. I wonder onc't why they's leave'n so soon? They ain't been here that long."

"Mel sez, his woman come into some money, an since she don't like it up here, they's pull'n up stakes and head'n back home."

For the next two weeks, Al and his wife tried to tune out the howling dog when they went to bed. They covered their heads, stuffed cotton in their ears, but nothing helped. It didn't matter if the beast howled or barked, the noise penetrated their best defenses and kept them awake most of the night. One evening after dinner, Al said, "Sara, would ya like a glass of my homemade dandelion wine? It might help us sleep better."

"You know I was never much for drink, but maybe jes' this one time, it might help."

Al went to the cellar and returned with a gallon jug of wine. He uncorked it, went to the cupboard and got two water glasses. He filled them both half way. Then raised it, "Here's to a good night's sleep."

"I hope so." Sara said cheerfully, then raised her glass, and in a few gulps, downed the wine.

Al smiled, "Want some more?" he asked as he emptied his glass.

After each had two more drinks, they were easily amused by each other.

"You sure you don't want another?" Al asked with a mischievous smile.

"Noooo" She answered with a giggle. Then added, "Why are you moving back and forth in the chair, Al?"

"I ain't move'n. I'm sitt'n here quiet as a mouse." He said as he snickered at his own words. His snickering made her giggle. Then they both began to laugh uncontrollably.

"Why are you make'n funny faces onc't?" Al asked.

"I ain't make'n no funny faces!" Sara said between giggles.

"You are too!" He insisted between laughter.

"Al Gross." She snickered. "You're tipsy, that's what you are." Sara said, her eyes sparkling.

"Maybe." He agreed. Then, added. "I got an idea. Wann'a go up to bed?"

"Yah, let's." She agreed.

He joined her under the covers, they came together and embraced. "Al…I love you so much." Sara whispered "Forgive me for what I done to make you marry me?"

"Yah, Sara, I do…I love you, too. You're my woman."

`They drifted off into a dreamlike state.

Some hours later, Sara whispered loudly, "Al, Al."

"What?"

"I thought I heard a moaning outside. Listen. Onc't."

His normal faculties were not functioning because of the cider he had drunk. He raised his head to hear. "I don't hear noth'n." He whispered, then promptly dropped his head back on the pillow, and quickly fell back to sleep.

Sara sat up, her ears straining. She was sure she could hear an intermittent sound of some sort. She couldn't identify it, but she was positive she heard something. "Al, Al! I tell ya, I hear something."

"What do you hear?" Al tried to rouse himself, and sat up to hear better.

"I don't know what it was I heard, but I'm tell'n ya' I heard something. But I don't hear it now, now it's stopped."

"Then, let's go back to sleep. I ain't heard noth'n yet." He burrowed his head deep under the covers once again.

Sara sat up another hour listening, but she didn't hear any more sounds. Eventually she gave up her vigil and slipped under the covers and snuggled up against his warm body.

`When the morning sun peeked through their bedroom window, Al sat up fully awake, and alert. He shook his wife awake. "Sara, did you say you heard something last night?" His brain was clear and functioning now.

"Yah, I did. You don't remember that onc't?"

"More like a dream. I don't think my head was too clear, the wine fogged my brain. I remember you said you heard sounds. What kind of sounds?"

"Soft moans. I don't remember ever hearing sounds like that before. I don't know what it was, but I know I heard something. By the time you started listen'n, it stopped. You went back to sleep. I stayed up, but I didn't hear noth'n no more."

Suddenly Al's mind became focused, "I better take a look around onc't." He jumped out of bed, put his clothes on and rushed down the steps and out the door. It took him less than a second to see what Sara had heard. Near the door lay Spot and Brownie, dead. Bits of raw meat were scattered on the ground here and there. "Ach, Du Lieber, Chapman. Chapman was here last night. This is his work." He hurried out back to see his hounds. He could see the dog houses, and two dog chains. Each chain had one end fastened to a stake, the other end, the snap end, was lying on the ground, but no dogs were attached to either end. He walked to the back of the chicken house and saw something that made his blood boil. Both of his hound dogs lay side by side, their throats slit, a short rope tied to each of their collars. He reasoned Chapman must have led them out behind the chicken house, out of ear shot, and methodically slit their throats, slaughtering them like hogs. Al's blood turned cold. He ran back to the house, up the stairs and grabbed his shotgun. Sara was getting dressed.

"Al, what's wrong onc't?"

"Don't go outside till I come back!" He ordered. "Now you mind me! You stay inside!" Al hurried out the door, down the road and the short distance to Chapman's yard. He stood facing the front door, his legs apart, gun at the ready. "Damn you Sam Chapman, come outside!" Al yelled at the top of his lungs, his eyes were slits, his thumb rested on the curved hammer of the shiny double barreled shot gun. But, all he heard was his breathing and the deathly quiet of a deserted house. Nothing was stirring. As his tenseness lessened, he began surveying the property more closely. He saw there was no smoke coming from the chimney and Chapman's dog and dog house were gone. Looking closer he saw the curtains were off the windows and the front door was slightly ajar.

The reality of the situation began to sink in. Chapman had done his devilment in the middle of the night, and just as quietly, slipped away to who knows where. What Sara heard was the moaning of Spot and Brownie as they died of poisoning. His hounds never barked and had obviously been led by Chapman, like lambs to their slaughter.

Al's shoulders slumped, his face ashen, when he returned home and walked into his kitchen.

"Al, what's wrong?"

"That gol durn Chapman, he poisoned Spot an' Brownie, an' he slaughtered my hounds. That's what he done. What you heard was them moan'n from the poison, that's what you heard. I should'a got up, gol durn it. If I had, I would'a caught him in the act. I would'a blown him to kingdom come, that's what I could'a done. I'd put some buck shot up his ass, that's fur sure."

Sara started to run outside, but Al quickly blocked her way. "Al, that man was no good, I knew it the minute I laid eyes on him. I jes' knew it. Let me go outside! I want to see."

"No, it won't do nobody good fer ya to do that. Let me put them away first, you don't need to see them now. I'll dig a hole fer them, then we can give them a proper burial."

CHAPTER 8

Forcing a Decision

York, Pennsylvania 1917

The high ceiling room was dimly lit. The gold in the ornate wallpaper sparkled subtly. The room was beautifully furnished. Flames flickered in the brick fire place. Heavy stuffed chairs, and several elaborately carved straight back chairs, plus a large couch were tastefully arranged. Medallion style framed oil landscapes were placed on three of the walls. The largest wall held a bookcase that ran from floor to ceiling and was filled with a wide spectrum of books. The fragrance from the fresh cut flowers, placed here and there in large vases competed with the strong tobacco smoke that filled the room. The occupants of the room were all colored men enjoying their weekly social gathering. They were part of the emerging black bourgeoisie of York. Most were considered professionals, mainly teachers and ministers. One dentist and a medical doctor were hosts for the evening. However, two men present would not have made the grade in a comparable white social setting.The Pullman Porter gained entry because of his substantial income. The chauffeur brought a kind of prestige because he worked for the Smalls, York's most prominent, and wealthy white family.

Most of the evenings were spent swapping stories and telling jokes. As long as the wives were out of ear shot, many of the jokes were on the smutty side. There was an unspoken rivalry between the men as to who was the best story teller and jokester. The title was given to Bill Felton, a school teacher who had the innate ability to tell story after story. He seemingly, never ran out of material. He could keep the men spellbound for hours with his wit and boundless imagination. The bourbon whiskey they sipped during the evening helped make all of the stories a bit funnier than they actually were.

However, there came a point in the conversation when it became more somber because President Woodrow Wilson had just called for a declaration of war against Germany. His statement was published in the April 2, 1917 edition of the York Gazette, the local daily paper. "We have no selfish ends to serve. We desire no conquest, no dominion. We seek no indemnities... no material compensation." George had brought the article and read it to the group.

Doctor Bowles was the first to respond. "I don't see why we colored people should join in this mess, it's a white man's war. Let him fight it."

Several others echoed the same sentiment until George replied, "I don't agree! President Wilson said later on, "The war is to make the world safe for democracy."

A few of the men laughed. One man complained, "George, that's a naïve view of the world and of America. Look at the lousy treatment the colored man is still receiving after all these years since slavery."

The Pullman Porter spoke up, "Read, the Klan is still lynching us, and no one is doing anything about it. They gets away with it, even when they knows who they is and the actual ones what done it. So where's the justice? Answer me that!"

"What you say is true. But if we are going to live in this country...and we are, we're going to have to look beyond now and look to the future. Look to the time when things will be better, because things will get better, I believe that, and I believe the only way we can lay claim to what is going to be ours as citizens, is to be willing to pay the price of citizenship, now now!." There were murmurs of dissent, but before anyone could speak, George added, "I feel deeply about it. That's why I plan to sign up."

The room fell silent. The men stared at George. Finally, someone spoke, "Read, you make sense to me." It was Bill Felton, the story teller and jokester, Bill was a fellow teacher in York and a Lincoln University class mate of his. They had both graduated in the class of 1911.

George was shocked but pleased that his buddy agreed with him. The two stood, walked to each other and shook hands. The assembled men looked on in stunned silence. A minister said, "Well, I don't know about just jumping into this thing..." Another said, "I think I'll just wait and see..." Most sat in deep personal thought and reflection.

The somber mood was broken when the doctor's wife called, "Foods ready!" As was the custom, the men and their wives had segregated themselves for most of the evening.

It wasn't until those magic words were uttered that they came together to eat and socialize. The men rushed into the room and after a short prayer, ate the offering of fried chicken, ribs, chitterlings, collards and potato salad and joined with the women in polite conversation. Finally someone broke the news to the wives. The room fell silent as each wife looked to her husband for an answer.

Mrs. Bowles asked, "Who, who's signing up for the war?"

"I did, I'm going to sign up." George said firmly.

"And, I am, too." Bill echoed.

One of the women said, "Well, I don't know if those two are fools, or heroes for signing up to get into this war. But, I'm glad it ain't my man!"

Rosa, was stunned. "George, what are you saying? You haven't discussed this with me! How can you do such a thing?" His wife of six years and the mother of his three sons couldn't believe her ears. This had to be some sort of bad joke. They'd been living in their new home, a fine three story brick house with his mother, Mary. They were hitting their stride and just getting their lives in order.

Bill Felton's wife Mary echoed Rosa's sentiment as well. "Bill, are you crazy? You have a family to take care of; you can't just up and go marching off to war!"
Both men wore stern faces when they said they would explain their decisions when they got home. Both wives got the message and didn't pursue the matter further. The room fell silent.

Mrs. Bowles felt the tension as well and saw that the evening was headed in a bad direction. As an experienced hostess, she knew she had to do something to salvage the night. She picked up a fork and tapped a glass to get her guests attention. "All right, it's time to dance!" She tried to sound bright and cheerful. "Let's put the phonograph on and dance, come on folks, follow me." She led the way to an adjoining room, turned on a dim light, then put on a King Oliver record. Everyone was feeling uncomfortable by the verbal exchanges between the Read's and Felton's spouses and gladly followed her into the room. As soon as the music started, the husbands dutifully danced the first dance with their own wives. Then, when the second record began, they sought the wife of one of the other guests.

On June 5, 1917 nearly 10 million men went to their local voting places to register for the draft; George and Bill were among them. Along with dozens of other men, the two found themselves standing in front of an Army doctor. After a preliminary examination of his throat and ears, the doctor asked George to take several deep breaths while he listened intently with a stethoscope. The doctor repeated his request as he looked intently at George. "You're a smoker aren't you young man?"

"Yes, I do smoke," George confessed.

"Do you cough a lot?"

George thought about the question, then, replied, "Now that I think about it, I suppose you could say I cough a lot. Usually at night."

"Does anything come up when you do?" the doctor persisted.

As if on cue, George began coughing, he quickly pulled out a handkerchief and spit into it. "Let me see that." The doctor ordered.

George opened the folded cloth and held it toward the doctor. The doctor looked closely and saw specks of blood mixed in with his sputum. He cleared his throat, "This is the story young man…we would have to conduct more tests to confirm my suspicions, However, just based on what I see, the Army can't use you. I'm sorry, but I must reject you."

George's shoulders sagged. He wasn't prepared for this kind of news. Being rejected had never entered his mind. Bill had gone through the same procedure, and was standing in the far part of the room. Now that his physical was over, he wanted to tell George his good news, but as he moved toward his friend, he saw that George's doctor was still conferring with him.

The doctor said, "Without any further tests, with what I've heard, plus the blood tells me you have serious lung problems. But I will tell you this young man. Stop smoking. Get out of the city, and move to the country so your lungs can get good fresh air into them, and hopefully heal. That's my advice if you want to live. You can forget the Army, it can't use you."

Bill was conflicted. He was happy for himself, but sadness over took him as he listened to the doctor reject his college pal. They left the building together. As soon as they reached the sidewalk, Bill put his arm around his friend's shoulders and tried to comfort him. But he quickly realized nothing he could say would heal the hurt George was feeling at the moment. Bill realized his friend would have to work out his feelings of disappointment on his own. His friend was beyond being consoled.

Mary and Rosa sat in the kitchen trying to understand what a move to the country would mean. They had worked hard to make their house a home. The furniture fit into all of the nooks and crannies, fit as if the pieces had been custom made for each spot. In spite of herself, Rosa had mixed feelings. Of course she wanted to do what was best for her husband's health. However, the thought of uprooting the family, leaving friends, and starting over in some unknown place was frightening. In fact it was an overwhelming thought. Sensing Rosa's sadness, Mary said, "Rosa, the Lord will always help you find a way. He will give you the strength to do this. Just have faith child."

"Mother, I was just feeling sorry for myself. I know the move is for the best. We really don't have a choice in the matter. It will just take me a while to adjust my thinking to a new reality. But thank you for your counsel."

Mary went to Rosa and gave her a tight squeeze. Mary didn't want to pry, but she had a question, "I don't want to be nosey honey, but, what do you all plan to do with this house, and what on earth will you do in the country? I don't see how you can hold on to this place and buy country property, too."

She had been a good mother-in-law; never butting into their personal business at all. In fact, she was a pleasure to have around, helping with the children and the house work. "Well, he and Doc Bowles have been talking about a business partnership. Doc would put up the money if George can find a place where he could run some sort of farm business."

Mary's brow furrowed, "My Lord, that boy doesn't know anything about farming. He wouldn't know a cow from a sheep." Both of the women burst out laughing.

Walking the property boundaries was strenuous for all three men. John Pitts the real estate sales man (between deep breaths) began reviewing the virtues of the farm, "Yes, Mr. Read, you'd be getting this here place at a real good, and fair price; a big farm house, 76 acres, a nice mix of fields and timber land, a barn, several long laying houses and four small brooder houses. The place would be ideal for a poultry business."

Chapman had nothing to say. He stood to the side, smiling as he listened to the salesman explain the virtues of his place. He could add nothing to the sales pitch.

"Well, I have a business partner, I'll need to review the cost with him and then I'll get back to you." The potential buyer explained. “I should be able to give you an answer in a few days.” He offered his hand and the men shook on it.

“I sure do hope your partner will see what a good piece of property you’ll be gett’n. Yes sir, I hope it works out fer ya.” Chapman called out as George walked away and climbed into this Model T. He waited until the car was down the road a piece, then, let out a whoop. “Hot dang! This is the best thing that could’a happened. Sell’n ma place to a nigger. By God that will fix that damn Al Gross. I’d love to see his face when he finds out who his new neighbor’s gonn’a be!” Chapman slapped the agent’s back, as the agent gave him a blank look.

“I don’t know your neighbor…Gross, is it? I’d guess he’s probably not going to be too happy. But money talks as far as I’m concerned. I don’t care if the man’s purple, as long as he’s got the money. Anyway, I’ll be in touch with you as soon as I hear from him, Sam.” The agent walked away from Sam. He wanted to leave as quickly as he could. He really didn’t like the man.

“I’ll be wait’n to hear from ya. This here is too good to be true, so don’t let me down when ya contacts me, ya hear?” Sam yelled at the departing man.

“Well, Sam, I can’t promise you anything, except let’s hope for the best. Well, I’ll see you soon,” He called back over his shoulder. Pitts got in his car and drove off, shaking his head. He felt dirt.

“George, you don’t know the first thing about the poultry business. How can you stake our future on such a notion?” Rosa argued.

"Look, I can take an extension course through the Pennsylvania Department of Agriculture. I know I can learn; I can do it. Anyway, we can't afford the mortgage on the house we're in and buy the farm ,too, and I've got to get out of the city, you know that. Plus, I really don't want to sell this place. This house will be good as a rental, but anyway, we'll have to hang onto it, we may need a place to fall back on if the farm venture fails. I've approached Doc Bowles for financing. I'm sure he'll be interested in some sort of business arrangement."

"With three boys and your mother to feed, I hope we can do it. But you're right; we don't have a choice with your health and all… I guess we should try to do it even if it doesn't work out with Doc. George, I'm sure if we put our minds to it, we can find a way. And as you tell your students, "There's no such word as can't."

George placed his hands on his wife's shoulders, then looked into her eyes, "I know it's a bit scary, but we don't have any other options Rosa."

"What your proposing is, so, so, different. I didn't mean to be negative. I just needed to digest the idea. So, if Doc Bowles is willing to put up the money, I say, let's give it a try. And if he doesn't, we'll find someone else who will. I'm sure we can do it!" She tried to sound positive, knowing full well her pep talk was as much for herself as for her husband. Deep down inside, she wanted to convince herself that what they were attempting to do wasn't totally crazy.

"I'll see Doc tonight. I won't have any numbers for him, but I think I've sold him on the idea that potentially, we can make a lot of money. I know he's got cash sitting around, and he's anxious to do something with it, I'll just appeal to his greed, I think that's probably going to be my best strategy with him."

"Well, I hope you can convince him, George. Good luck."

"Thanks, Rosa. See you later tonight."

CHAPTER 9

Converging Lifestyles

"Al, Al. We got new neighbors. They's Shworts'r. I seen them move'n in whiles't you were at Market yesterday."

"Well, we'll just watch, and wait to see what kind of folks they are, onc't."

George was fortunate that the sale came at the end of the school year. Summer meant he could devote himself full time to getting the buildings in order, and study the material supplied by the Pennsylvania Cooperative Extension Program in the evening. In a matter of weeks, he felt confident that he would be able to get a business going. The property didn't have electricity, although the power lines ran along the public road, ending at his drive way. George decided, based on what he'd read in his poultry books, his priority would be to have the electricity connected to his property. However, he did a strange thing. He decided to connect it to the barn, the brooder houses and the two long laying houses, but not to the house. When Rosa questioned him about that decision, he replied, "It would be too expensive to wire the house. I can't afford to do both now."

The summer was spent sanitizing, fixing roofs, the huge barn and repairing the out buildings that would be utilized for egg production, and raising baby chicks. The work was smelly, hard and seemingly endless. He had no help other than Rosa. Their three boys, ages six, four, and two were too young. His mother tended to the children and did the cooking, cleaning and the house chores while they tried to get the buildings in shape.

Finally, the day arrived when he was ready for his first batch of baby chicks to be delivered. He was as excited as if he was seeing his first born child. The truck from Mount Wolf delivered a thousand 'peepers' in ventilated cardboard boxes. The whole family watched in awe as the tiny yellow fuzz balls were set free to run, scratch and peck in the fresh straw covered floor.

"Well, Rosa, there's our future. Those little creatures will grow and give us a basis to make a living and in time I'll be able to give up teaching and stop running back and forth to York."

"George, I look forward to that day."

"For quick cash, we'll sell off half of these in three months as broilers. The other half we'll keep for egg production since it takes longer to raise egg producers. After the first batch is sold off, we will buy another thousand. Every three months we'll repeat the same process until we have all of the egg producers we can handle. Does that make sense to you, Rosa?"

"Yes, it does."

"You'll have to tend market twice a week to sell the broilers."

"I won't mind that, but I don't know how to drive, George. You'll have to teach me so I can make the trip to market."

"Well, you've seen me drive, haven't you?"

"Yes, yes, I've seen you drive. Why?"

"Well, just get in the car and do the same thing you saw me do."

"I can't do that!"

"How do you know until you try?"

"You're serious, aren't you?"

"Of course I am. You can do it; I know you can. You know I don't have the patience to teach you to drive. I'm a teacher of subjects, not mechanical things like that. Here, I'll sketch out the gear shift pattern, and I want you to remember this. When you shift, push down on the clutch, let off on the gas. When it's in that gear, you let the clutch up, push down on the gas. Keep that in your head, and you'll get the hang of it in no time; in other words, gas down, clutch up. Clutch down, gas up." He sketched out the basic 'H' which was the gear shift pattern, and handed it to his wife. "Of course, you have to steer and stay on the right side of the road. Remember it's a machine. It can't think. It will do only what you make it do. Just learn how to make it obey you. It's just that simple. Remember, you're the boss." Rosa listened with her mouth open, but she knew her husband was dead serious; she was on her own. And so it was that Rosa found herself sitting behind the steering wheel of a Model T Ford….alone.

After a few failed attempts and many reminders to herself, "Down with the clutch, up with the gas, down with the gas, up with the clutch," she allowed herself a smile as she drove out of the driveway and down the road, even though she was weaving from side to side. Rosa reasoned that since the car was moving and she was driving it, she was master of the machine, and she was its boss!

She kept practicing until she felt confident enough to put the car into reverse. She wasn't aware George had stationed himself on the top floor of the barn where he could see most of the road where she was practicing. He watched with pride as she drove back and forth, each time with more confidence until she finally pulled the car into the steep driveway and parked outside the barn door.

George rushed out to the car, bowed deeply, then helped her to the ground. "Well done, my dear, I'm really proud of you." He lifted her up and gave her a big kiss.

"Thanks, George. Well, I guess you were a good driving instructor after all." Rosa said beaming.

"No, you get all the credit for this." He was truly proud of what his wife had accomplished, and all on her own.

The farm house was a far cry from the three story brick Queen street house. The Queen Street building had hardwood floors, two bath rooms and running water. The furniture fit into all of the nooks and crannies of the home as if each piece had been custom made for that exact spot. Now the furniture didn't fit anywhere. In addition, the women felt the furniture looked stupid in such a rough old house. Not only did each room have some glaring problems. The final insult was that she was stuck out in the wilderness and didn't know a single soul. Now, all of her recently acquired friends were more than ten miles away.

The reality of the farm's isolation, the dirty condition it was left in, and the roughness of the house appalled her. She had grown up without electricity as a child in Tennessee. But Queen Street had spoiled her. She had become accustomed to the conveniences of the city and now found it hard to go backward. Now she had no electricity, or running water. In addition, many of the windows were cracked, or knocked out. And, if that wasn't enough, she felt the pressure of helping run a business that neither she, nor her husband, had the foggiest idea how to operate. Despite knowing that this was for the sake of his health, she would on occasion feel quite depressed.

In order to have eggs for the family's use immediately, George followed up on a newspaper ad that offered twelve laying hens and a rooster for sale. They loaded two crates , jumped into the car he had purchased for her travels to and from the market and off they went, with Rosa driving. When they brought the chicken's home, they put them in one of the small brooder houses.

George waved the instruction booklet. "According to this, after two weeks, we can let them roam outside. By then, they will have learned to lay their eggs indoors, in the nests. After they are let out, they will know to come back to their nests after being confined for that period of time."

"What will they eat outside?" Rosa asked.

"They can forage for bugs and worms, plus eat some of the sour grass and clover. It will make for a better-tasting egg according to what I've read. And they'll return to eat the chicken feed in the house from time to time.

John, the second child was about four years old, big enough to go to the outhouse (what they nick named the "White House") by himself. The two holed, frame structure was located about fifty yards from the farm house.

One day as he sat on one of the outhouse seats doing his 'business,' he could watch the big rooster that usually stood on a small knoll just above the structure. He never bothered closing the door because he enjoyed watching the chickens and other animals from his vantage point, and he wasn't old enough to be modest.

John decided to have fun by echoing the big bird's crowing, and he did. Each time the rooster cockadoodledooed. John would, in perfect tone, and pitch, call back, shuuuuuutuuuup! The more the rooster crowed, the more John repeated his shuuuuutuuups! The rooster felt challenged and became angrier with each shuuuutuuuup! Echoed by John.

When the boy emerged from the 'White House' to return to the farm house, his rear fully exposed, his back flap hanging down, showing a little round brown bottom, the rooster half flew and half ran down the incline and charged the unsuspecting boy. The enraged bird leapt high, his legs pulled tightly to his breast. He brought them down in swift slashing motions, catching the boy's rear with both feet and all six claws. Completely surprised by the attack, the child let out a loud scream and ran as swiftly as he could toward the house. However, his speed was no match for the enraged Barred Rock's fury. The rooster made six or seven swipes before the fleeing boy was able to dash up the steps and reach the safety of the porch and his Mom's comforting arms.

The rooster stood below on the ground, his feathers puffed, his head cocked to one side, glaring at the frightened boy. He continued making threatening, clucking sounds as he scratched the ground as if to say, "Now take that you brat, step off the porch and I'll give you more of the same." Mother Mary armed herself with a broom and shooed the bird away from the porch area, and the frightened boy.

"Oh my Lord, your back sides are a mess," his mom sadly remarked. The rooster's claws had made a series of bloody, crisscrossed wounds. She laid him across her lap, and patiently cleaned the deep gashes that covered his rear.

John had to sit on pillows for a week, and walking was painful.

The next day, when John stepped outside and stood on the porch for a breath of air, the rooster spotted him from his lookout on the ridge and charged toward him. The panic- stricken boy screamed and made a hasty retreat back inside the house. His days of being an independent traveler had come to an abrupt end. The rooster would not let the boy out of the house or off the porch without an adult escort. Rosa realized the predicament her son was in came up with a practical solution. "Well, we can't have you not able to walk freely about the place without being attacked, now can we, son?" On the verge of tears, the boy nodded affirmatively.

"Then I think Mr. Bird will have to end up in the pot for Sunday dinner," she announced to a relieved boy. And so it was that the big bad rooster became a stewed chicken and dumpling meal.

The months flew by, however, the back-breaking work seemed endless. But in less than two years, the business began taking shape. The flock of Leghorns had grown to more than two thousand layers, and by raising his chickens by the book, George was able to have high egg production even in the winter, a fact not lost on his neighbors. Twin Cedars, the name the farm was known as because of the two magnificently tall cedar trees that framed the house, became the talk of the Conawaga Hills.

The home took shape, too. The windows were repaired, and the interior walls painted and wall papered. Mother Mary made and hung colorful frilly curtains, making the house warm and homey.

Rosa and her mother-in-law were in sync with each other. They agreed on how strict to be with the children and laid down guidelines for what was permissible and what wasn't. When Rosa had to prepare for market, Mary would help with the killing, picking and dressing of the scores of chickens she took to market twice a week.

One morning as the whole family sat at the kitchen table having breakfast, there was a knock at the door. "I'll see who it is," Mary said, while standing by the stove. She walked the few steps to the door and opened it. On the other side she saw a wiry, medium built, sun-burned man, hat in hand. "Missus, I'm your neighbor, Al Gross. May I come in, onc't?"

"Of course, please do come in. Let me introduce you to our family." Mary said and began the introductions.

Al acknowledged the children and Rosa and Mary with a nod of his head. George stood, and the two men shook hands. "Here, sit down Mr. Gross." George suggested.

"No, not today. I can't stay long. But I do have something I gott'a say ta ya all."

"Well, we'll be anxious to hear what it is that you want to say." George answered, not sure what was on the man's mind.

"It's just this. I want you to know I've watched you people ever since you moved in. Folks around here said you would steal my chickens, and make bad neighbors. Let me tell you, I seen how hard you work, I see you go'n to market. I see how you fixed up the place. No, I say I had niggers before, but now I have white folks as neighbors. I'm glad you folks are here."

Rosa, Mary and George exchanged knowing looks, but made no comment.

"Now," Al continued, "I'd like to invite you folks over for homemade ice cream and cake this Saturday night. Then you can meet my Missus, too."

George and Rosa's eyes met, and they each nodded slightly to the other. George said, "Mr. Gross, we would be delighted to accept your invitation."

Al offered his hand to George, then, walked to the door. Before he left, he turned and said, "It was good to meet you folks. Mr., Missus, You have a fine family, and I look forward to having ya meet'n my Missus." With that, he said goodbye and left.

George waited a few moments then said, "Despite the crude way he put it, the man meant well. I'm sure of that."

Mary spoke up. "I've been around white folks since I was a slave girl in Mississippi, and I'll tell you this. I know white folks, and I like that man. It's in his eyes. He's as honest as the day is long. And he speaks his mind. He would never try to fool you."

"Despite the way he said it, I know what he was trying to say. I think he's a good man, too, Mother Mary." Rosa said.

"I know exactly what he was trying to say. He gets my vote." George added.

The children had been quiet, taught to speak only when spoken to. George, the eldest couldn't contain himself. "What's a nigger, Mom?"

"George Junior, it's a word not allowed in this house. Mr. Gross made a mistake when he used that word and unintentionally brought it in our home."

"But, what does it mean?" The boy pursued.

"The word means a dirty, low down person. Many times it is used against us as Negroes. It's meant to hurt us as a race, because of our color. Do you understand what I'm saying?"

"I think so. But he said we were white. We aren't white."

"No, honey we aren't white. What he was trying to say was he could respect us because we work hard like he does, and he's white. The bad word he used can be anyone who is low down, dirty and lazy. The family that lived here before us were white. They were dirty, low down people, so that's why Mr. Gross said what he did. You see the dirty condition they left this house in. That's what Mr. Gross meant. Now do you understand?"

"Yes, I think so…I know one thing though," the boy said as his face took on a serious expression, "nobody had better ever call me that name." His words were said with conviction and a mature finality.

"That's right. No one should ever call anyone that name. Now you boys go outside and play. Put on your warm clothes."

The boys carried their dishes to the wash stand, then, headed to their upstairs rooms to get dressed.

"Well, how did I do, George?" Rosa looked for approval because she had never had to explain something as complicated to her children before.

"You did very well, and you're quite correct. The dictionary describes the word as, 'a dirty low-down person, usually a Negro.' So in his own way, Mr. Gross was right in describing Chapman as an 'N'. God, I hate that word, I can't bring myself to say it. But I think Mr. Gross is a good man who was trying to give us the highest compliment he knew how to. He meant us no disrespect. And your explanation to the boy was near perfect."

"I agree with that, son." Mary chimed in. Then she continued, "Rosa you did very well in answering the child. The other two boys were all ears. While they didn't comment, I'm sure they'll talk about it among themselves until they have an answer that will satisfy each of them."

Rosa knocked lightly on the door as the rest of her family stood to one side. It was opened quickly by a petite lady, with golden hair piled in a knot on the top of her head. She smiled as she said, "Come in, come in onc't. I'm Sara, Al told me all about you folks, I'm so glad to meet you!"

Rosa introduced herself, her husband and the boys to Mrs. Gross. Sara beamed at each one as she was introduced. "It's so nice to meet you all."

As the door opened wider, the kitchen's warmth washed over them. Al stood, offered his hand to George, then, patted each boy lightly on the head. "I'm glad you folks could come. Mr., why don't we go right outside and start making the ice cream. The boys can come, too. I just put the custard container in the ice bucket, now all we got to do is crank it until it's stiff."

The oak bucket ice-cream maker sat on the edge of the porch. Mr. Gross went down the steps and stood on the ground in order to reach the ice cream bucket's handle without bending over and hurting his back. He began cranking.

"No, no, Mr. Gross. The boys can help. Let them crank it. When it gets stiffer, you and I will finish it up. Is that all right with you?"

Mr. and Mrs. Gross

"You're right, Mr. Let the youngest start. Count onc't. Each one can do twenty turns. Your dad and I will count." Mr. Gross beamed as he watched the excited boy's line up, and take turns cranking. It was enjoyable sharing in their excitement, knowing he was in his way adding to their future memory bank.

And they did crank and crank – first Bill, then John and then George. After each boy had had two chances at turning, the men took over and finished up the hardest turns. Once the custard became stiff, Al tipped the bucket, and let the salt water pour out of the drain hole to the ground. He unlatched the metal crank mechanism, set it aside, then, he carefully pulled the container out of the crushed ice. "Come, let's go inside, onc't?" It's getting dark now.

The women had set out heavy white pottery soup bowls and spoons on the table. Several other plates were piled high with thick, salted, Dutch pretzels, and a red icing black walnut cake sat in the middle of the table. Mrs. Gross opened the container and began scooping out the frozen vanilla custard. "Come on boys. Take a bowl and a handful of pretzels." She sliced the cake and put a generous piece in the bowl along with the ice cream for each child. Then, she served the adults.

"So you want the boys to sit on the wood box behind the stove?" Rosa asked.

"Yes. Missus; I think the boys will enjoy sitting over there by themselves."

"You boys go sit on the wood box." Rosa pointed to the six foot rectangular affair that sat on the back side of the wood stove.

"Yes. Mom." They answered as they took their seats.

The kerosene lamp gave the room a yellowish hue and cast dark shadows on the small kitchen's wall. The coziness and warmth in the room put everyone at ease. The boys sat contentedly as they ate the cold, smooth, sweet ice cream. They alternated eating the ice cream with bites of the crunchy salty pretzels. Once the ice cream was gone, they dove into the cake. Their eyes sparkled with enjoyment as they savored every aspect of this special event.

Afterwards, the boys noticed their bodies made shadows on the wall from the kerosene lamps light. They then held their hands in various positions to make shadow faces and animals on the wall from the light cast by the flickering lamps light. The adults sat around the table enjoying the treats as well. Al spoke first, "Mr. I have a question to ask ya."

"What is it, Mr. Gross?"

"Now, I notice, your Missus took eggs to market all winter. How can that be? My hens slow down, then, stop once the cold weather sets in."

"Mr. Gross, the answer is we have plugged up all the drafts, and fixed all the broken windows, and we get the chickens up and eating early by turning on the lights. If they're kept warm, they'll continue to lay. If they're cold, the feed goes to body fat, not to making eggs. It's just that simple."

"By golly, Mr., that makes lots of sense. I never studied raise'n chickens. I jes' followed what my daddy done when I was a boy."

"Well, I just learned it through my correspondence course. In fact, anything I learn, I'll pass on to you, or if I don't know something you want to know, I'll make it my business to find out for you. How's that, Mr. Gross?"

"I'd be much obliged, Mr."

"Mr. Gross my family wants me to get a dog, but I said with all the chores we have now, we don't need the extra work they make. Anyway, I notice you don't have any either."

"Well, Mister we used to. But that gol durn Chapman, the man you bought the place from poisoned them, poisoned them just before he slipped outt'a here like a skunk in the night. He poisoned two, and slit the throats of two. That's the kind of man he wuz."

"He did? Why on earth would he do a thing like that?"

"Well, he had a dog what got into my pig pen in the middle of the night. The durn animal chewed my pigs up pretty durn good. I stuck the dog with a pitch fork to get him off my pigs. I guess I stuck him pretty good, because he went home and died. Chapman didn't own up to being responsible for what the dog done. Instead, he threatened me…he would'a jumped me, 'cept my two big dogs made him think twice about that. What he done was, he waited until the time was right, then, snuck over with poison meat. He fed it to the two big ones, then slit the throats of my two beagles, that's what he done. He killed all of my dogs, then, slipped away in the night, that's what the scoundrel done."

"I didn't like the man when I first met him, but I tried not to judge him until I had some reason to base those feelings on, but I guess my first impression was right. He really sounds like a really dangerous man. You must be glad he's gone."

"Yes, we sure are. But about me gett'n dogs. Yes, Mr., I plan on gett'n dogs again. It's good to have extra eyes and ears out here."

"Yes, I suppose you're right, but I think I'll wait awhile longer." George added.

The women let the men talk. Then, Sara spoke up. She had always been curious about slavery. She had read about it in school and wondered if any one of them could tell her more.

Mary spoke up, "I was born a slave, Mrs. Gross."

"Were you really? Tell me onc't, did the slave man treat you mean?"

"The slave master was what he was called. No, he never treated me as mean as he treated my mother. He came to notice her because she was so outspoken. She was sold down the river from Virginia to a plantation in Laurel Springs, Mississippi. She was sold off to him because she was so bold. In fact, one day she wouldn't get up and go to the cotton fields. This was on the Smith plantation in Mississippi. The overseer went to her cabin to get her out of bed one morning, but she refused to get up because she was sick. That man didn't want to hear that. So he went back out and got a big tree branch. Well, he beat her bad with it, but she still refused to go to work. Anyway, the overseer went to the master… Master Smith. The master was curious. He had to see with his own eyes who this 'uppity' slave was. He found her beaten so bad, master Smith got upset. So upset that he got after the overseer, and scolded him. Not because he was concerned for her, but because he was afraid he had hurt her so badly she might not be of any more use to him in the fields."

"How can people be so mean? It really wonders me onc't."

The children were all ears, little John asked, "Grandma, did your mama get better?" He asked in concern.

"Yes, child, she did. In fact the master came back to see her a few weeks or so after for that purpose. To see if she was healed." Mary looked over at the children, then back to the assembled adults and said in a soft voice for the adults to hear. "That's when he had his way with her."

Sara was outraged. "Ach. Such people! He was no better than an animal to…"

Al cleared his throat, then gave Sara a hard look, "Shush up woman!" he snapped, then, nodded towards the children.

"It's all right," Rosa said. "They can only understand so much at their ages, and anyway, it's the truth and they need to know it. I don't mind if they hear. So go ahead, Mother Mary, It's all right, Mr. Gross." She gave Mr. Gross an understanding look. Rosa knew Mother Mary would be discreet, and the children would not grasp the full meaning of what she described.

"I didn't rightly know how you would feel Missus, that's why I, well you understand…" Al said in explanation of his rebuke of Sara.

"I do, I do understand, Mr. Gross."

Mary continued. "Well, that's how I was begotten. He gave me the name of Mary Catherine Smith, although my mother's given name was Fitz. Well, him being white, and all, that's why I look the way I do." Mary was referring to her keen nose, straight hair and light complexion. "I wasn't put in the fields; in fact, I lived in the big house instead of with my mother in her cabin. He put me in the care of a woman servant and had her raise me. Master Smith sent my mama back to the field right after she birthed me. In fact, he didn't let her have too much to do with me after that. On Sundays, that's when I was allowed to see her…I could see her at church. That's why church was always so special to me, because we could sit together. I liked that because I could sit real close to her, and we could sing together and hold hands. That's what made me feel like I had a mama again."

George was proud of his mother, and suggested, "Tell the folks how you learned to read, Mother. It's an interesting story."

"All right, I will son. The head servant gave me the task of polishing utensils, setting the table and keeping the dining room clean. Then, they let me work in the kitchen, cutting vegetables and such. We had it lots better than the field hands up in the big house. Anyway, the master had a daughter about my age. She would come down to the dining area and play with me. One day she came with a book, and she started reading to me. She wanted to teach me to read. Anyway, while we were sitting together reading, her mother saw what we were doing. She became furious, and scolded her daughter. She screamed, 'You can't teach her to read…slaves aren't allowed to read!' Then she dragged her daughter off. She was so put out."

"How can that be; why shouldn't you learn to read?" Sara asked. The concept of slavery was something she couldn't fully grasp. Hearing stories of such brutality was perplexing to her.

"The slave master had it all figured out. They wanted to keep the slaves ignorant. They knew we would be less of a threat to them if we were kept dumb. Well, her daughter was strong willed. What she did was, she hid some books in a kitchen closet, and whenever she could, she would come and take me off. We would hide for hours and she would school me. The head servant lady knew what we were doing, but she just looked the other way and pretended she didn't know what was going on. She could have gotten into a lot of trouble if Mrs. Smith suspected she knew what was going on."

"What a shame. To have ta hide to get book learn'n." Sara said, her voice full of indignation.

Al shook his head, "It's not right that people are so mean to other folks. For myself? I judge a man by the way he treats me. If he's honest and hard working, that's what counts in my book."

George smiled, "Mr. Gross, I couldn't agree with you more." He stood, looked at the boys, his mother and Rosa, then, announced, "I think we better get home now. We have quite a few chores to do tomorrow." His family stood and then moved toward the door.

"Mrs. Gross, Mr. Gross, I can't thank you enough for such a wonderful evening, and I must say, it has been a pleasure to meet you both." Rosa said as she walked over to Sara and hugged her tightly.

Mary followed Rosa's lead and hugged Sara, too. Then, said, "You're good people, I look forward to getting to know you better."

"Why don't we do this again come Saturday?" Sara suggested.

"We will if I can bring the custard and the ice the next time." Rosa answered.

"All right; if that's what you want, we'll do just that." Sara said smiling.

Once outside, the boys raced down the moonlit road. They had been quiet for several hours. Now they felt free to whoop and holler their lungs out.

That first night started a tradition that lasted for years during spring, summer and early fall. Only sickness, or a farm emergency interrupted what became their Saturday night ritual.

The children attended Green Springs School, a one room building where one teacher taught eight grades, tended the fire and kept the place swept and cleaned. The Dutch children were openly curious about the new arrivals, honestly so because most of them had never seen a black person before. They marveled at the boy's curly tight hair, and wondered if their color would come off, and tested that theory by asking to rub their new classmate's skin to find out. Once their curiosity was satisfied, each of the Read boys made friends based on their personalities, or, whatever else the ingredients are that form the basis of friendship.

`Six years slipped by. The business had grown and prospered. Twin Cedars was becoming known as one of the leading egg-producing farms in the area.

The saying, 'When it rains, it pours,' became a truism for George and Rosa. Their storm began when George came home early from school one day.

"Mother Mary, I think I heard George…I wonder what happened to bring him home now?" Rosa asked with concern.

The answer came quickly. When George opened the door, it was obvious he was a man in shock. "That damn Doc Bowles!" He growled.

"George, what on earth is wrong?" Rosa asked.

"Doc was happy when I bought him out a few years ago. He was happy because he didn't think we would make it. He was positive the business would fail. So, he was happy when I paid him back his start up loan. He knows we're doing well, so now he's angry that he's out of the picture. Now, he's used his influence on the school board to get me fired. He's a jealous, spiteful man, that's what this is all about." George was furious, hurt and confused. "The superintendent called me in and told me my classes were not on a par with the others. Rosa, I know for a fact, my classes are scoring as high, or even higher, than the others. It's an out and out lie. I see the hand of Doc Bowles. It's the only possible explanation for what they did to me."

Rosa was in shock, "Oh, no; just when we were getting on our feet financially." Rosa lamented. "But I'm sure you're right, George. In fact, I meant to tell you this before. When I was at market, one of my customers said Doc Bowles told her we cheated him out of a lot of money. But she said she spoke up for us, right to his face. The lady said she told him, she didn't believe we would cheat anybody based on her dealing with me at market. She wanted us to know what kind of poison he was spreading around town about us."

"Nothing surprises me about that man. Well, I'll just have to look for another teaching position somewhere else." His voice was flat, and he looked defeated.

But George wasted no time looking for work. He sent his resume to various schools in nearby towns, as well as to ones out of state. Finally he heard from a school in Wilmington, Delaware, some eighty miles away. He waited to hear from others, but the Wilmington offer was the only one that came. He interviewed for the job and was hired on the spot. Reluctantly, he accepted. The long distance made the offer a mixed blessing, but he realized he had no other choice.

"Rosa, it means I'll have to stay in Wilmington during the week and come home Friday night, then leave on Sunday. Unfortunately, it will be more work for you and George Junior. He's going to have to take my place so far as the work I did during the week is concerned."

"I'm sure he'll be able to do it, but what a shame. Another two years in York, and you could have quit your job. But, I suppose if you're willing to travel that far, then we should be grateful that you were able to find work so quickly." Rosa was trying to make their new reality less harsh than it actually was. A positive outlook is what she knew was needed to bolster her husband's morale, as well as her own. She knew she needed all of her faith in order to get through the uncertain days that lay ahead.

He held his wife's hand, "It's going to be hard all around. But we have no choice; we'll do whatever it takes to make a go of it."

"Son, that's a long drive for you," Mary said in concern, "Are you sure you will be able to do it?"

"Mother, I've learned to adjust to many obstacles. This will be just one more adjustment. I'll manage and you all will, too." George said with confidence.

"Where are the boys?" Rosa asked.

"I haven't seen them in quite a spell." Mary answered.

"I think they're outside playing." George said. "I'll go see."

The boys had just finished a game of mumbly-peg, and darkness was starting to settle in. The three children were standing on the ground just below the porch. They were intently looking at a bright glow on the hill across the valley. "I'd better go tell Dad there's a fire on the hill," John said as he dashed up the steps. As he did, he almost collided with his father, who was coming out. "Dad, something is burning across the valley." As he pointed, the flames began leaping high into the sky. Within minutes, it grew less bright and began to take on the shape of a cross.

"I see it, son." George knew instantly what it was, and his heart sank.

"What's going on?" Rosa asked as she and Mary came outside to see what the commotion was.

Mary looked over Rosa's shoulder. "Oh, Mother of God, it's the Klan, and they're burning a cross. It's intended for us, Rosa." Mary concluded.

"Why are they burning a cross for us?" George Junior asked.

"Boys listen, that cross is meant as a warning to us. The people who lit it are members of the Klu Klux Klan, and they don't want us here." George said bitterly.

"Why don't they want us here?" George Junior asked.

"Because of our color. They don't want to see a colored man get ahead, and I guess we've ruffled a few feathers doing as well as we have."

"But, we don't want to leave here. We want to stay!" John cried.

"Did I say anything about leaving?" George snapped.

"No sir, you didn't." John replied, relief in his voice.

"I said, they wanted us to leave. But we aren't going anywhere. This is our home!"

George walked over to George Junior and placed a hand on his shoulder. "Boys, I want you all to hear and understand what I am about to say to your big brother. George, you are the eldest, and as such, when I'm away, you will be in charge of your bothers when they're not directly under your mother's, or grandma's care. You are to make decision that will be best for the whole family when I am not here. You are to look after your mother, grandmother and your brothers." Turning to John and Bill he continued, "Do you boys understand what I have just said? George will be in charge of you when I'm away, and you will listen to him. Is that understood?"

"Yes sir," they answered as their eyes grew large from alarm.

"From now on, things will be done differently around here. George Junior, I'm going to teach you to shoot the pistol and the shot-gun. Once you've learned, I want you to fire the pistol off every day. Fire a few rounds in the morning one day, then in the afternoon on the other days. I'll fire some rounds off at night when I come home on the weekends. Which reminds me, I have something else to tell you boys. I won't be home during the week. I've had to accept a job in Delaware which is some distance away. Another thing. Listen, and listen to me closely. No one is to know that I'm working in another state. We don't want people to know I won't be home during the week. This is a family secret. Is that understood?"

"Yes sir." They all answered.

George Junior wasn't quite twelve years old when he became a man. The weight of the business and the protection of the whole family had suddenly been placed on his young shoulders.

Rosa was busy at the stove when she heard a knock, and Sara calling through the door. "Missus, I made some chow chow."

Rosa opened the door. "Oh, Mrs. Gross, how good to see you. Come in, come in."

"Missus, I hope you like it." Sara stepped in with the two jars.

"I know I will, because I've tasted it at your house." Rosa answered smiling.

Sara set two jars on the table and then, looked up at Rosa, "Missus, I don't mean to be nosy, but we don't hear your Mr. leave'n in the morning. Is he all right?

"Sit down Sara; I didn't want to burden you with our problems. But George lost his job in York. He's teaching down in Wilmington, Delaware. So he's going to be gone all week now. And, just as bad, the Klan burned a cross last week over on that far hill." Rosa pointed to the East. "Needless to say, we're keeping George's absence a secret, we..."

Sara was furious. She couldn't hold her anger back, "Ach! Those no good people. Trouble makers, that's what they are. Al said a man asked him to join a group that would keep the white race pure. My Mister said he would punch him in the nose if he didn't get out of his sight. The man said he was from Virginia and things were different down there. I bet he's part of that same bunch of no goods."

"A lot of Southerners are moving into the area, bringing their hateful ways with them," Rosa added ruefully.

Sara went to Rosa and put her arms around her. "Missus, don't worry none. Everything will be just fine, you'll see." She touched Rosa's face, then, hurriedly excused herself to rush home and tell Al the news.

It was early Friday when George pulled into the driveway. He had just said hello to his family, when there was a knock on the door. George went to the door; Al and Sara were standing on the other side. His face was serious, "Come in, come in, Mr. Gross, Mrs. Gross."

"Mr, Missus, my woman here told me what happened last week, I want you to know, we will stand with you. And don't you worry none; I don't think they have any nerve, all bluster and talk. But, I do have a few ideas."

"I'm anxious to hear what they are." George replied.

"Now, I got me two beagles for hunt'n and two good watch dogs again, I'll move one of the watch dogs over here, closer to you folks. I'll put one dog on the far side of your house, and the other one between the two of our houses. That way they'll bark if they hear something funny going on at night. That is if it's all right with you?"

"Yes, Mr. Gross, I'd appreciate that very much. Like I said, the boys and my wife have been after me for years to get a dog. Well, I think I'd better get one, maybe two, and the sooner the better from the looks of things."

"Yah, Mr. I think you should do just that. But until you do, we'll put my dogs in place."

"Yes, yes. By all means. Let me help you move the dog houses when you're ready to do it."

"All right, we can do it tomorrow, but Mr. I think, it might be good to sit up tonight and Saturday night. That's when they go to the bars and get nervy…after they've downed a few. And I wouldn't let it be known you ain't home during the week."

Sara sat quietly, listening and nodding her head.
"Mr. Gross, you're right. Even our youngest boy understands the need to be secretive about my being gone. You folks are the only ones who know about my new job. How can I thank you for…?"

Al cut him off. "Mr. as far as I'm concerned, your family is my family, and I'll look after them just that way when you're away. It wondered me why your boy was firing a gun every onc't and awhile. Now I understand. That's a good idea, too. I'll be back around ten tonight."

"Thanks. I'll be ready." George offered his hand.

As soon as Al and Sara left, John spoke up. "I thought no one was to know our family secret. Now they know, too."

"Well, our family has just grown. The Grosses are like new members. We can consider them like an Aunt and an Uncle, Rosa answered.

"Can we call him Uncle Al, and Mrs. Gross, Aunt Sara?" Bill asked quickly.

"When they come over next time, we'll ask them if that would be all right with them. What do you think of that?" Rosa replied with a broad smile.

The boys went to bed happy with the thought that they would have an aunt and uncle, and best of all, they would be right next door, not in some faraway place called Rogersville, Tennessee.

Bill was asleep, but George and John were still wide awake when they heard Mr. Gross knock shortly before ten o'clock. They jumped out of their beds and went to the window. They could see their father and Mr. Gross clearly in the moon light as they crossed the road, then, watched them disappear in the shadows of the nearby woods. They saw that each man carried a gun on his shoulder.

"I wonder if they will shoot a Klan man tonight?" John whispered.

"I don't know. But I guess they will if the Klan tries anything funny around here…like burn our house down." The eldest boy said seriously.

"Do you think they will…you know, burn our house down? Do you think they would try to do that?" John asked, wide eyed.

"If they do try, Dad and Mr. Gross will give them a surprise…BOOM, BOOM!" George's imitation of a shotgun made John laugh.

"Shhh! The window is open. They'll hear us and Dad will yell. Anyway, we better get to sleep," George advised his younger brother.

Both boys climbed back into bed feeling safe, and promptly fell asleep.

Across the road, the men found tree stumps and made themselves comfortable.

"Mr. Gross, I can't tell you how much your friendship and that of your wife has meant to my family and me." The darkness made it easier for George to speak from his heart to Al. "It has relieved my mind beyond anything you can imagine, especially now that I'm not going to be home during the week."

"Mr., Let me tell you onc't. Since I lost my friend, and neighbor, John Ness, I never knew how important a good neighbor was. Just like a family member, that's how he was, too. Once he was gone and I had Chapman, it was like a bad dream. I can't tell you how bad it was. But now, with you folks, I feel blessed to have you and yours here. By golly, it's just like my family got bigger. Mr. I mean that. As far as I'm concerned, you're all my family."

"Mr. Gross, that's very kind of you, but I must tell you this. My boys want to call you and your missus, Aunt and Uncle. So the feeling is mutual on our part, too."

"I'm might happy and proud to hear that they do, Mr." Al said, pleased to have heard how his neighbors and their children felt about them, too.

"I don't know if I was supposed to mention this, Mr. Gross, or, if Rosa was going to discuss the matter with your wife and they were going to surprise you. But, under the circumstances, I had to let you know how my family felt about you and your Missus."

"I won't say anything to my Missus. When she mentions it to me, I'll act surprised. I'll put up a good show," Al said with a chuckle. "Mr. Listen…I hear a motor. It's a car coming!"

The men got up and moved further back into the shadows. The car was coming from the south, from the direction of the Fetrow farm. Soon the headlights pierced the darkness, moving slowly towards them like gleaming cat eyes.

"We'll see if they are up to no good soon enough." Al whispered.

They tensed as they raised their weapons to the ready and placed their fingers lightly on the hammers of their guns.

The engine strained as the car slowed to climb the incline that led past Twin Cedars. It came to a near halt as it reached the hill's top directly in front of the house and the two men standing in the shadows. But, the car slowed because of the weakness of the motor, not because its occupants had any bad intentions. Once it reached the level stretch, the engine revved up, gained power, then continued on down the bumpy road. Al and George stepped from the woods and watched the car continue on its way.

"I don't know who they wuz, but they weren't out to make mischief." Al mused, then, added, "Other than ol' Ike Folk a mile down the road, there ain't no other houses, so a car driving down this road at night seems out of place."

"From what I hear, other than his wife and his three little girls, ol' Ike doesn't have any living kin, and he's too mean to have any friends. So, I doubt if they were going to visit him." George added.

"No, Ike don't bother with no one. He's a loner. Maybe they're go'n up and over the mountain the hard way. There's a small settlement on 'tother side. By the sound of that motor, they's gonn'a have a devil of a time clim'n that there big hill." Al said jokingly.

"Maybe they won't make it all the way to the top." George laughed as he pictured the car chug, chugging up the steep hill.

"You're right Mr. They might get half way up and start rolling backwards. In fact they may come rolling past here backwards before the night's over." Al and George both laughed at that vivid picture.

George had taken up smoking a pipe a year ago, and was quick to point out to anyone who commented about his smoking that he didn't inhale. "Mr. Gross, I think I'm going to have a pipe."

"Then I think I'll have a chaw, by golly."

The two men returned to their positions on the tree stumps, and enjoyed each other's company, the night air, the evening sounds, the hooting of the Great Horned Owl, the rustling branches and the haunting call of the whippoorwill. They sat quietly and contentedly for another hour.

"Mr., I think we can call it a night. Its past one in the morning. What do you think?"

"Yeah, that's a good idea. I think you're right. Let's call it a night."

"Wann'a do it again tomorrow night Mr.?"

"That might be a good idea. Another night out can't hurt. You know, if it weren't for the fact we're here on serious business, I could learn to enjoy doing this…just sitting outside and listening to the night sounds," George added in a nostalgic way.

The men shook hands, and went home their separate ways. Saturday night, the men met again to stand vigil. The night was almost a repeat of Friday night, with one difference. It was even less eventful than the previous evening. Not one car came down the road during their three hour watch.

Sunday, George helped move the dog houses and stake the animals in the places Al felt they would do the most good for both families. The dogs Al had purchased were magnificent specimens: two pure bred Black and Tan Coonhounds. The dogs were known for their keen noses and big voices. Al put the female between his home and Twin Cedars because the bitch was more alert and quicker to bark at anything or anyone strange.

As soon as Al and he had finished positioning the dogs, George summoned George Junior and Rosa. He had made up a list of chores to be done, then, sat them down to give them instructions as to what to look for in terms of the flock's health. He reviewed the list with Rosa and George Junior until he was comfortable that they both understood what he felt were the most important things to be on the lookout for.

"I'll do the inspection when I come back next Friday. Now, don't let me down boy, I'm counting on you," George said as he patted his son on the shoulders.

The days flew by, and Friday rolled around quickly. During the week Sara had made apple butter, which she wanted to share with Rosa and her family. She also brought a jar of blueberry jam that she had made at the end of summer. That morning, Al had asked George Junior to go hunting with him and his two new beagle hounds, Sleepy and Leapy.

As soon as Al left, Sara headed for Twin Cedars to visit with the ladies. She carried her 'goodies' wearing a smile. She loved sharing with her neighbors. When she arrived, Mary greeted her at the door. As soon as Sara came in, Mother Mary went to the kitchen cabinet and pulled out an apple pie she had made, then, quickly put on a pot of coffee.

Sara presented her gifts to Rosa. "Oh. Sara. How sweet of you, The boys will love you for it. They enjoy anything you make, Mrs. Gross."

"I'm glad they do onc't."

"I made an apple pie, how about a slice to go with the coffee, Mrs. Gross, Rosa?" Mother Mary asked.

"Sure, why not." They answered with big smiles.

The coffee made, the pie sliced and put on plates, the women sat down at the big kitchen table.

"Mrs. Gross, I have a question for you. The boys want to call you Aunt Sara and Mr. Gross, Uncle Al. Would that be all right with you and your Mr.?" Rosa asked hopefully.

"Oh. Missus. I would be so glad. Yes, yes, please tell them I would be honored to be their Aunt. And I can speak for Al too. He will be so happy, too."

"Thank you Sara, the boys will be delighted."
Mary poured the coffee, then, put the sugar and cream on the table. After she took a seat, she turned to Sara. "Now, Mrs. Gross I told you about my childhood. What was yours like? You never told us."

"I guess I don't never talk about it too much. But since you asked, I will tell you. I grew up on a farm not far from here. Hard work was all I ever knew. I had no brothers, or sisters, so, I was expected to do the work of a man. I always felt my mama and daddy didn't love me too good. I felt they would have liked it better had I been born a boy, because they could'a got more work out of a boy."

"Well, that's terrible." Mary replied.

"Do you ever see your parents now?" Rosa asked.

"No, they has both passed on. Other than Al, I ain't got no live kin. Lest wise, none that I know of. That's why what you tol' me about the boys wanting to call me Aunt… well it means so much to me…and it will mean the same to Al, too, cause he ain't got no live'n kin neither."

"Well, Mrs. Gross, now you both have family…you have us, and I want you to remember that, Sara." Rosa said firmly.

"Yah, Missus and it makes me feel good onc't too. You have no idea." Rosa didn't know that Sara wasn't able to bear children, that she would have given anything to have been able to give Al the child she knew he wanted. But something was wrong with her, and she felt awful about it. Now, she would have children who will call her Aunt Sara. This made her happy beyond words.

Sara's hands were resting on the table. Rosa and Mary took them into theirs and held them tightly. They sat that way in silence for several minutes.

"You're such a good, kind woman, Mrs. Gross. And we love you. Don't you forget that." Mary said, breaking the silence.

"No, No I will never forget that and I thank you for saying it." Sara dabbed at her eyes with her apron, she was so moved by the loving words.

"But go on, we want to hear more about your childhood," Rosa urged as she fought back tears, too.

"Well, when I was young I liked school a lot. I enjoyed going to the little one room school because I could learn, be with other children...and have a chance to play. In those days Cora, Mable and Minnie Fetrow were my best friends. They were just like sisters to me. We played together, walked home together and once a week Marble and I took violin lessons from Mrs. Meckley, the doctor's mother."

"Do you still play?" Mary asked.

"We would love to hear you." Rosa added.

"No, my fingers are too stiff and thick from work. No, I ain't had no chance to keep up with such as that."

"That's too bad." Mary added.

"I'm sorry we keep interrupting, please go on." Rosa urged.

"Now, you folks may not know about such things as pow wowing. It's like believing in witch craft. Some among us believe in it, but my parents, they didn't...Al and I never put no stock in such either, but the Fetrows did. Once I was visiting at their place when they had a pow wow doctor come visit. He came to keep the evil off their place, keep the curse off their farm, as well as from themselves. When the doctor came, they asked me to leave because they knew I didn't believe. In fact it was Mom Fetrow who told me to leave."

"Since they live just down the hill, are you and the Mr. still friendly with them?" Rosa asked.

"Their brother Eddie helps Al butcher. And I go down to buy ducks, and if need be, to use their phone, but the sisters and I, well, we speak when we see each other, but we don't visit. I guess you could say we just ain't close no more."

"That's too bad, too bad that you girls have drifted apart." Mary said.

"Listen, I think I hear George's car." Rosa said.

The women fell silent waiting to hear footsteps on the porch. "It's George, he's home." Rosa said with a smile as she jumped up to open the door to greet her husband.

George Junior had an inward sense of pride as he walked the woods. It was an honor to have been asked to hunt with a grown man, especially a man so knowledgeable of the woods as Mr. Gross.

The two tramped behind the hounds as they crisscrossed the stubble in the corn field, noses to the ground, searching for a scent. Sleepy let out a howl and broke for the fence row brush; Leapy followed closely on his heels. As the dogs entered one side of the thicket, the rabbit took off from the other side. A smile formed on Al's lips. He knew the chase was on. He pointed, "Move over there about thirty steps, George, that way when the dogs bring him back, one of us will get a good shot."

Without hesitation, George did as he was instructed. "Awooo, Awooo," the dog's rich voices echoed off the hillside. The brush row blocked their view, but they could tell by the excitement of their voices they were hot on the rabbit's trail. For a while, the dog's voices went away from them, then, the rabbit must have turned and headed back towards them because their howls were now getting much louder, closer. "Get ready George, they's com'n back!"

The rabbit burst out of the brush row, not far from where the dogs had first entered. "It's your shot, George!" Mr. Gross yelled.

George raised his gun, followed the rabbit for a brief second, then gave it a slight lead and fired. The 20 gauge roared. The rabbit tumbled in a heap. "Good shot, boy!"

Sleepy ran to the dead rabbit, picked it up and began trotting away as if it was his prize. A sharp whistle from Mr. Gross caused him to change his mind. The dog turned and brought the dead animal to Al. "Drop it, boy. Drop it!" He commanded. Sleepy reluctantly obliged.

Al reached into his hunting jacket and gave both dogs a piece of beef jerky as a reward for their good work.

"Good shot!" He said as he patted George on the back.

"Thanks Uncle Al, just lucky, I guess." The boy said modestly.

Mr. Gross smiled and winked knowingly. "Well boy, let's see if your luck will hold up for the rest of the day."

They hunted until darkness began to settle in. By sundown, they both had full pouches. The two tired hunters headed home very happy. Now they would skin and gut their days kill.

Mary got up extra early the next day to make breakfast for George Junior. He had mentioned he wanted to go hunting again at day break the next morning, and she wanted him to have a good breakfast before heading out to the woods. She knew Rosa, (who would relieve her of her breakfast chores occasionally) wouldn't be up to making breakfast since she and George liked to stay in bed a little later on Saturday. Mary would feed the other boys when they straggled into the kitchen an hour or so later. Then she would shoo them outside to play.

Finally George and Rosa came down for breakfast. Mary served them coffee, ham, eggs, home fries and biscuits, along with the blueberry jam Sara had given them. Mary announced, "I fed George Junior earlier, he took his gun and went off into the woods. Now I'm taking a walk. I need some fresh air."

"Have a pleasant walk, Mother." George said between bites of the hot buttered biscuit. He turned to his wife, "Rosa, I noticed last week George Junior acted like he's carrying the weight of the world on his shoulders.

Why is he so serious all the time?"

"Well, George, think about it. The boy is under a lot of pressure. He tries so hard to please you. He attempts to do everything you ask of him, and he doesn't want to let you down, and he's anxious about not having you feel disappointed in him. He has a lot of responsibility and it's wearing him down. Remember, the boy is only twelve. Why don't you do something with him? Did you know Mr. Gross took him hunting yesterday?"

"No, no I didn't know that."

"Why don't you join him? He's out in the woods somewhere right now. It would be good for both of you." Rosa urged.

"That's a good idea. As soon as I finish my breakfast I'll see if I can find him."

After he took his last bite, he excused himself and went outside. He found John and Bill sitting in a big apple tree. "John, do you know which way your brother went?"

"Not really, He got up early this morning. He was gone by the time Bill and I got up. Last night he said he was going hunting."

"Do you know which way he would have gone?"

"No sir, I don't. He didn't say which way he was going."

"All right son, thanks."

George walked to the back of the barn and looked over the field in hopes he might spot his son from that vantage point. Finally he yelled, "George! George!" but, there was no reply. He thought, 'Well, since I can't find him I'll do a few chores in the barn before the farm group gets here this afternoon.'

Being out in the woods gave George Junior a feeling of peace. It soothed and freed his soul. Hunting with Mr. Gross had been a special treat and he had enjoyed the day out with him, but he realized he needed time alone. There were so many things going through his head, he couldn't keep them straight any more. He walked until he found 'his' rock and took a seat on the huge boulder.

He thought back to the day he had gone exploring and discovered this big solitary boulder deep in the woods. It was a magnificent stone, large as an automobile, covered with thick green moss on its north side, and flat as a table on top. When he came upon it, he wondered how and when it got there. It puzzled him, since it was the one and only boulder in the whole area. Was it God's hand that placed it there? Or did it fall from the sky millions of years ago? In any event, he enjoyed speculating as to how it did get there.

He never tired of trying to solve the mystery of 'his' boulder.

The woods were quiet, yet alive with the sounds of birds and the sight of scurrying animals; two squirrels jumped from branch to branch on a nearby tree. A lone buck with a huge rack walked quietly down a well worn path some hundred yards, away giving George a glimpse of his majesty. A peace-fulness began to envelope him. Soon the pressure he felt inside his chest began to melt away. The simple act of sitting, watching and listening to nature did that for him every time.

The boy smiled as he thought back to yesterday and his day of hunting with Uncle Al. He was such a nice man, – calm, deliberate and fun to be with. George had told his brothers he was going hunting. He also said he was getting up extra early to discourage them from asking to come along because he wanted to be alone. He knew they would want to sleep late since it wasn't a school day. His day of hunting with Mr. Gross, plus the skinning and gutting of the six rabbits was enough hunting to last him for a good long while. He had put the rabbits in salt water to soak overnight to get the blood and any wild taste out of the meat. He knew either Mom, or Grandma would fry them up in an egg batter for dinner. He felt proud that he had been able to provide such a good meal for his family.

He had no control over the moods that seeped into his being. But every now and then, feelings of sadness would overcome him. At first he was puzzled. He didn't understand why he had these black moods. Then one day he realized it was because of the pressure his father put on him to run things during his absence. Yes. That was what bothered him. That was what made him tense. He felt he couldn't please the man no matter how hard he tried. He knew he did everything as perfectly as was humanly possible. But his father never made him feel he was doing a good, or satisfactory job. Suddenly he felt tired. He lay back on the rock, closed his eyes and let his mind drift. Finally he dozed off and fell into a deep sleep.

He awoke with a start, confused and disoriented. His stomach was growling, and he realized he was hungry. Suddenly panic set in. He had planned to be out in the woods no more than two hours. He had no idea as to the time of day, and his father was home and worst of all, he hadn't done his weekly walk through the chicken houses with him. With his gun tucked under his arm, he headed for home at a fast trot.

After a few minutes he was out of the woods. Now he entered the corn field behind the barn where the dogs had jumped the first rabbit yesterday. From his vantage point he could see the main road. What he saw caused a wave of panic to run through him. He saw one, two, three, four cars parked a hundred yards down the road from the house. Each car had two or more white men sitting in them.

His gut tightened. The burning cross flashed through his mind. His father's words about the Klan not wanting them there burned in his brain. He remembered his father's admonition, 'Watch for anyone or anything strange.' His trot became an out and out dash to the house. As he turned the corner of the barn he saw his father entering the upper level door. "Dad! Dad! They're here, get your gun! It's the Klan, the Klan, they're down the road – a whole bunch of them in cars!"

"All right son…just calm down."

"But Dad, there's a lot of them. Get your gun! I just saw them." George Junior's normally large round eyes were bigger and rounder. And despite the crisp fall air, beads of perspiration had formed on this forehead. But more bewildering to him was his father's seeming calm at this clear and present danger.

"Son, I should have told you when I got in yesterday…I'm expecting a group of local farmers who want to visit our place and learn about our egg production methods. It slipped my mind. I'm truly sorry to have caused you this needless worry."

George Junior stared at his father with a look of disbelief and anger. "You should have told me." He was furious, but he didn't dare say more. He wanted to scream at his father. He wanted to say, "I work like a man, but you don't respect me as a man. I have the responsibilities of a man, but you don't acknowledge what I do. Otherwise, you would have told me about today's visitors. It wouldn't have just slipped your mind." But he didn't. He turned and walked away.

At that moment, cars began pulling up into the driveway. "Don't leave, son. Unload your gun, put it inside the barn, then come back and stand with me." His father turned toward the arriving visitors and pointed to the area where he wanted them to park. George Junior did as he was told, then returned to his father's side. Once the automobiles were parked, the men exited their cars and walked toward George and his son. "Mr. Read?" The tall man called.

"Yes. Sir. That's me. And this is my son George Junior, my right-hand man."

George Junior was shocked and pleased by his father's complementary words. And, he was further pleased that as the men introduced themselves, they shook his hand, too.

The men formed a semi-circle around the two Georges. Arthur Beck, the leader of the Farmer's Association said, "Mr. Read, we were waiting down the road for Bill Clark here. He had a last minute emergency, so we apologize for being a little late. We're still missing one more bunch, but we didn't want to hold you up any longer."

"No problem, Mr. Beck. Well, shall we get started?" George asked.

"We're ready. And by the way, most of us have heard a lot about Twin Cedars, and if ya' don't mind, we want to learn how you keep your egg production up during the cold months. If you could answer that question that would be a big help, I'll tell ya'."

"I think I can help you out on that." George said confidently. For the first time, George Junior saw his father in action. Immediately, he noticed his demeanor changed to that of a teacher who knew his subject inside and out, and lesson one was about to begin. As they walked from building to building George began his monologue.

"Most importantly, you should get your chickens up and eating early. That's why you should have electricity and light in your houses. Now, we turn the lights on with a winged back clock that turns when the alarm goes off."

George Junior, went to the clock, sitting on a shelf against the wall, and reset it so the alarm would go off. Once the clock alarm sounded, the turning wing hit the switch, turning the lights on. The demonstration was done as if it had been rehearsed a dozen times. The men stood with open mouths.

"So, in a way, you're fooling the chickens by starting their day earlier. They think the sun is shining even if it's raining." The men laughed.

"When do you get them up?" A voice called out.

"Five in the morning. They have to eat in order to make eggs. The next thing is to keep your flock free of disease. You must disinfect the roosts, the feed hoppers, and the drinking cans on a regular basis. And, you must change the litter on the floors as soon as it gets dirty from droppings. Disease can wipe a flock out in no time."

"Can you tell if a chicken is a layer or not?" Another voice called out.

"That's a good question. The short answer is yes. Let me explain. First, you look at the color of its legs and feet."

The men laughed. One farmer commented, "I never thought I'd be look'n at a chicken's legs."

"Well, you better start looking." George replied with a smile, I'll tell you why. If the legs are bright yellow, it means the bird is using the food for itself. The legs should be a pale yellow, and the toe nails should be short.

Now, do you know why?" George asked.

The men looked at each other, but no one ventured an answer.

"If she's got long nails, it means she isn't scratching, pecking and searching for food. It means she's fat and lazy, just using the food for herself. Also, look at her wattle and comb; they should be pale, not a bright red. If she looks too pretty, she's using the food to make herself look good to the rooster, or to make fat, not eggs." The men laughed again.

"Is it true chickens catch colds?" Arthur Beck asked.

"Yes, they can. That's why you must plug up all the drafty spots, and insulate your buildings. If they're cold, they make fat to keep warm, not eggs for market. And that's the secret to hauling eggs in the winter. Insulate, stop the drafts and keep them warm." There was a brief murmur among the men. "Now, when they act droopy, you know what I mean, drop their wings and stand around; with their eyes half closed, that's a clue the bird has a cold, or is sick in some way. What you should do when you see one like that is catch it, get the bird away from your flock as soon as you can. I suggest you have a burn pit, or barrel. Burn all the sickly ones to destroy any diseases they might be carrying.

"Can you tell if a chicken is laying?" A farmer asked.

"Yes, you can." George said.

Without a word, George Junior walked toward a cluster of chickens, bent over and in a quick motion grabbed a chicken by its legs and handed it to this father.

George placed the chicken under his arm, the chicken's rear end facing forward, then, he placed two of his fingers over the chicken's vent. The men pushed closer.

"A good layer has space for two or more of my fingers; that means she's a good producer. If, the vent space is tight, and has space for only one finger, well then, she's not a layer."

George led the men through his two long laying houses, the upper part of the barn and his three brooder houses.

The farmers were fascinated. They had been following out-dated tradition handed down to them by their fathers and grandfathers and had no idea of the complexities of modern egg production.

As they headed back to their parked cars, George added, "Feed is expensive, carrying non-producers over the winter months cuts into your profits. So get rid of them. Does anyone have any questions?"

"No, I don't think so," Arthur answered, then, turned to his group, "Any questions?" There was a murmured, "No" from the men.

Arthur continued, "As I said, there was one more car load, but they must have broken down, or gotten lost. But on behalf of our Farmers Association, we want to thank you, and your boy." There was a group "Thank you" offered by the men as well.

"It was our pleasure." George said. One by one the men filed past them and shook their hands, then climbed into their cars and drove off.

George turned to his son, "Thanks for your help, son. You were very good."

"You're welcome, Dad." The boy had been annoyed at first because his father hadn't said it was he and his mother who actually did the work and ran the place. Then he remembered there was a very good reason for his dad not to go into too much detail, not to mention his being absent during the week. He also remembered how his father had referred to him as, 'My right hand man.' And he had just complemented him by saying he had been 'Very good.' That made him feel a lot better. George Junior felt appreciated by his father for the very first time.

Whether it was the tension of being away, his needless financial insecurities, or the lingering suspicions that the Klan might reemerge, George tended to run on a short fuse.

One day he grabbed John for a minor infraction, pulled his belt off and put the shocked boy across his knee and whacked his bottom with the strap several times.

Rosa witnessed the entire episode in horror. She was upset at her husband's behavior, but said nothing. A week later, the same thing happened. This time she spoke up and scolded him for not having patience, then cried louder than Bill who was the recipient on this occasion.

After a few more such episodes with the children, and Rosa's outbursts, George finally got the message. He fumed and fussed at her because of the way she was reacting to his version of discipline. Finally he declared, "All right, if you think I'm too hard on the boys, I won't touch them. But, if they grow up to be bums, it'll be your fault." True to his word, from that day on, he turned the job of administering punishment over to his wife.

CHAPTER 10

Sticks and Stones

A Read boy attended the one room Green Spring School ever since they had moved to the country eight years ago. Now all three boys attended school. They walked the country mile to be taught by Miss Penn, an attractive woman in her early thirties. She taught kindergarten through the eighth grade. The boys, twelve, ten, and eight, had the usual school problems, but nothing untoward based solely on their color.

Rosa was hanging clothes on the line in the back yard, enjoying for the moment the crisp, afternoon fall air. Life was good and she was happy, lost in her own thoughts. As she hummed a tune, her bliss was shattered when she heard one of her children screaming.

"Mama! Mama!" It was John. "Mama, they beat us up!"

Rosa looked down the road and saw all three boys running towards the house, she was sure, even from the distance she was from them. She saw blood on their faces. They charged up the hill to their mother. As they came closer, she could see them more clearly. She was shocked and horrified at what she saw. "Boys, what happened?" Each one had an assortment of cuts and bruises; George had a bloody nose, John's lip was split, and Bill had a huge lump on his forehead.

Mary heard the commotion and scurried outside, "What happened to the boys?"

"Someone beat them up."

Rosa was beside herself, but she realized she would have to maintain tight control of her emotions. She could not give in to being a hysterical mother. In a calm firm voice she said, “Now, one at a time, tell us what happened. George. You first.”

It took him several moments to stop the sobs that kept erupting deep from his chest. Finally, he managed to say, “Ma…Ma, the Bailey boys, they beat us up!”

Rosa knew all of the local names, but that one didn’t click. “Bailey, I don’t remember that name. Why did they beat you up?”

“They said they won’t go to school with no nigger.” John pursued.

“They just moved up from Virginia,” George added. “They’re our ages.”

“How many of them are there? Did they fight you fair?”

“There are three of them, but they’re way bigger than we are,” Bill added.

“Now boys, if they fight you again, you will have to stand up and protect yourselves and each other. You must fight back. Is that understood?”

The boys all nodded.

Rosa filled a wash pan and wiped the blood off their faces. Her heart was breaking, but she never let on to the boys. It took all of her self control no to show her sorrow for the beating they had taken.

Mary said, “I do declare, if it isn’t one thing, it’s another. Now Rosa you can’t let those boys go back to school until you speak to the teacher.”

“No, I don’t think I’ll do that just yet. I want the boys to solve this problem themselves.”

"How can you say that? Look at them, they're all beat up. I don't think that's right to expect them to solve this problem!" Mary shouted at her daughter-in-law. This was the first time the two women had had a serious disagreement. Having had her say, Mary stomped back inside the house before Rosa could respond.

The boys went off to school the next day, and returned home in the same condition. Only this time John had a bloody nose, Bill had a split lip and George a variety of bumps and bruises. Rosa was more upset than the day before. "Did you fight back?" She asked.

"No, when they started beating us, we ran away. We ran, Mama, because they're bigger than we are…all three of them." John protested.

"Well, if you won't fight back, then I'll have to, and do you know what they will do to me? They'll put your mama in jail because I'm a grown up, fighting children."

"No, no… we don't want our Mama to go to jail," The boys cried, afraid that they would be responsible for their mother being in trouble with the law. The fright they were experiencing from their beatings at school felt all consuming. It was real and painful. But this was a different kind of pain, one they could not allow to happen.

"Well, then, you must fight back!"

Bill, who had remained quiet, finally spoke up, "Mama, they have knives. They said next time they see us after school, they're gonn'a cut our ears off."

"You say they have knives?" Rosa asked in disbelief.

The boys all nodded, "Yeah, they even showed them to us during recess," John concurred.

George added, "They said, if we kept coming back to school, they would use them next time."

John asked, "Can we have knives?"

"No boys, you can't, I won't allow you to fight with knives. But, we will find a way for you to be safe, I promise." She realized this was a really serious problem, and one she had no idea as to how to solve.

Mary tried hard to keep her opinions to herself. But now she felt she had to confront her daughter-in-law. This was just out and out wrong. "Rosa, you see what I mean? You must speak to the teacher. It's the only way to handle something like this. They can't keep going back, they may get killed."

"No Mother, there are a least five ways to solve every problem; we just have to think of those other ways. I've been a teacher and I know it won't end until the boys show they can take care of themselves. Miss Penn can't protect them from those boys, they have to do it themselves." Rosa was firm, but at the moment, had no idea as to how she would be able to live up to the promise she had made to them. How in the world was she going to keep them safe at school?

"Well, Rosa, I just don't agree with you on this." Mary walked away, quite upset.

The next day was Friday, and while she understood the dynamics of the situation, she had no plan of action for her boys. She thought. "I've got to think of something. I need to come up with a plan. Mary is right. I can't send the children back to school with things the way they are.

But what can I do?" She was frightened and frustrated.

When she was sixteen, Rosa had taught in a one room school in the mountains of Tennessee; teaching children (some of whom) were older than she. So, she understood children, and the mentality of bullies. But she knew she was right about one thing: her boys would have to settle the matter with the Bailey brother themselves. But how could they do that? That was the question.

Rosa had a restless night. She tossed and turned for hours. Finally sleep overtook her and she slept almost through the night. Then, out of the blue an idea came to her which woke her from a sound sleep. She smiled as she reviewed the concept that had come to her. It would work, she was convinced it would. Now she could hardly wait for morning to come.

When the sun peeked over the hills, it found Mary busy at the stove preparing breakfast. The boys straggled in and took their seats at the table. Rosa entered the kitchen and in her most cheerful voice said, "Good morning everyone."

The children didn't bother to look up as they mumbled "Good morning" in return. Their faces bore the look of impending disaster -- a disaster they knew awaited them at school. Mary's "Good morning" was barely audible. She was still so angry she didn't know if she could be civil toward her daughter-in-law. To further make her point, she kept her back turned when she returned Rosa's greeting.

"Children I have something to tell you. You won't be going to school today."

Mary whirled around, "Are you crazy! You can't keep the children home! What's that going to solve? Why don't you walk them to school and speak to the teacher and tell her what's going on? That's what you have to do." She shouted.

Rosa ignored her outburst.

The children cheered. "Oh. Good! No more school!"

"I said, today you won't be going to school. Monday you will be going as usual."

The children moaned. "Then we'll get beat up again."

"No, you won't. I can almost guarantee that. I have a plan, but we won't put it into action until Sunday, so enjoy the day off."

"Now, what are you up to?" Mother Mary asked in a gruff voice.

"Mother Mary, I do have an idea. I want to share it with George when he comes home tonight. If he agrees, then I'll explain it to you. Just trust me on this."

"Humph. I still don't see why you're being so stubborn about this, Rosa. It's just common sense to go and talk to the teacher." She groused.

"As I said, you will have to trust me for a while longer. Just let me see how George feels about it. Then, I'll be more than happy to tell you what I have in mind."

Mary made no further comment as she scurried about the kitchen, keeping her back to Rosa most of the time.

The children enjoyed the day off. George Junior did his chores early and, after firing the gun, acted like a boy his age should and played with his brothers.

The day passed quickly. Towards evening George pulled in from Wilmington. He had a bouquet of wild flowers that he had picked from the road side. With mock solemnity, he presented them to his wife.

She played along, and accepted the flowers with a curtsy. His gesture made her forget for the moment that she had been worried sick for the past few days. Rosa was never so glad to see anyone in her whole life. After he greeted his mother and the children, she asked him to step outside. She quickly explained the problem with the Bailey boys. Afterwards, she shared her idea of what she thought might solve the problem.

After listening, George said, "Rosa, what's why I married you. No matter what the problem, you always seem to find a solution. You're really one in a million." He put a bear hug on her and kissed her. "I needed to hear that you think it's a workable plan. I just hope and pray it is.

"It will work. I'm positive of that. So, stop worrying."

"Well, I truly believe it's the best way to get the problem solved." Rosa sighed.

Sunday came quickly, and George followed his usual routine and did his weekly check of the car. Feeling satisfied, he walked over to Rosa, put his arms around her and looked into her eyes, "Good luck. I know your idea will work, so don't worry. I have every confidence in you and the boys." He gave her a quick kiss and headed back to Delaware.

As soon as he left, Rosa called the boys together. "Now children, we have some work to do. George Junior, get a saw. John, get an ax. And Bill, tear up this red rag into small strips and bring them along."

Mary watched as Rosa ordered the boys about. She tried hard not to ask, but curiosity got the better of her.

"Now, what on earth are you doing, Rosa? You did say you would tell me what you had in mind."

"Let us do what we have to do first. Then, I promise I'll explain everything to your when we get back, Mother Mary."

Mary shook her head and walked away, still quite upset.

Rosa led the boys down the deserted road to within fifty yards of the school.

"Now here is what we are going to do. From here clear back to the farm, I want you to gather throwing size stones. You will stack them off the road, in the brush; far enough in so no one will see them." The boys looked puzzled, but said nothing. "Also, I want you to cut sticks, good stout sticks about this long, and this thick." She indicated with her hands the sizes she meant. "Cut them in threes, so there is a stick for each one of you. Hide them further down the road past the second stack of stones. Bill, you tie a red rag at each location so you boys can spot each location easily. Here's the plan. If they attack you after school, run to the first pile of stones. Then I want you to throw them as hard, and straight as you can at those boys. Then run away. Those boys will think you're out of stones and running away from them. But you'll fool them. Stop at the next stack of stones and let them have it again. If they keep coming, run to the stack of sticks. Then charge those boys. This will surprise them. If you catch up to them, whack them as hard as you can. Use two hands, and hold tight to your sticks, don't drop them and don't let them take the sticks away from you. You don't want them to be able to use them on you. Now, this is important, too. Each time you throw your stones, or use your sticks, go for the same boy each time. Pick the boy nearest your size. Is that clear?"

The boys stood around their mother as she spoke. Little by little, smiles began to spread over their faces. They could visualize the coming battle, and for the first time felt they had a good chance at winning.

If they come after you, run to the next stack of stones and let them have it again! That's the plan. We will stack stones and sticks all the way back to the house. I don't want you to run out of ammunition. How do you feel now, boys? Do you think you can do that?"

"Oh, yes, Mama. We can do that." The boys were happy for the first time in days.

"Once we get home, let's practice throwing some stones, just to get your arms warmed up. What do you think?"

And they did, they worked their way back to the farm, stacking stones and sticks and marking each location with a small red rag as they went. Once they got home, they threw stones at an old bucket. After ten minutes, Rosa said, "That's enough. Save your strength for tomorrow." The boys laughed and patted each other's backs.

"Rosa, now you have to tell me what on earth you are doing."

"Make me a cup of coffee and I will, Mother Mary." And she did. She explained in detail her plan for the boys. The more she spoke, the more Mary smiled and nodded approvingly.

Despite George's and Mary's reassurance that her idea seemed like a sound one, Monday seemed to be the longest day Rosa ever remembered. Now that they were out of sight and on their own, doubts and fear overcame her. Would her children be able to defend themselves? 'Maybe I sent them off to be slaughtered. Oh God, what have I done?" She was so worried, she couldn't focus on anything except the clock. If she wasn't looking at the time, she was staring down the road in hopes of seeing her boys heading home. When Mary glanced at Rosa and saw how distraught she was, and went to her daughter-in-law then put her arms around her. "Child, I know what you're going through. Don't worry. What you did was right, and I want you to know that I agree with you. They must learn to stand up for themselves."

"Thanks, Mother Mary, I appreciate you saying that. I really do." But despite Mary's comforting words, in a few minutes, Rosa jumped up, reached for her sweater and started out the door. "Mary, I can't take it any longer…. I'm going down that road to see what happened."

Just as she opened the door, she could hear the boys calling; "Mom! Mom!" And there they were, her three boys, running down the road toward the house. But she couldn't see them clearly enough to determine if they were injured. "Dear God, let them be all right. I won't be able to take it if I sent them off to be hurt." Rosa whispered.

"Mama, we did it!" It was John's voice.

"We fought back. We made them run." George said with a broad smile covering his face, as they ran toward their mother.

"We chased them. We chased them, and they ran." It was Bill.

"Oh, boys, I am so proud of you…you are my three little men." Rosa said, her arms opened wide waiting to smother them with hugs and kisses.

Mother Mary stood alongside Rosa. She, too, offered her comforting arms to their three warriors. "You are really wonderful young men. You boys should be proud of yourselves." Then turning to Rosa she said, "You too, Rosa, it took a lot of nerve to do what you did. I learned something from you today, I mean that."

CHAPTER 11

A Light in the Window

For the past months, Rosa felt she had been walking under a huge cloud of trouble, a cloud that had poured so much rain on her, she felt she was slowly drowning.

Now she lay in bed feeling restless, not able to find a comfortable position no matter how she tried. It had been a hard and busy day, but despite her weariness, she was unable to find a relaxing way to position her body; or to slow her mind. Her brain jumped from one thought to another. She was powerless to stop it. A tug of war was raging inside her. Her physical being was demanding sleep, but another part of her was remembering the traumatic events she had recently experienced, events her brain hadn't had time to sort through or digest. Despite her overwhelming desire for slumber, her restless mind won the battle and began reviewing the past few months.

Her first thoughts were of her boys and the trouble they had had with the Bailey brothers. She remembered the day she had sent her sons off to fight, and how they had received two bad beatings as a result. Then she relived the fright and confusion she felt when she tried desperately to hide her panic from her children and Mother Mary and finally the relief she felt when she was able to develop a plan that worked and provided safety for her sons.

What she had hoped and prayed for happened. Her boys and the Baileys eventually became friends. Her council had been sound, and everything had worked out for the best. "Thank you, Lord." She murmured.

Then her thoughts turned to the business. The farm was on a sound financial footing, and things were running smoothly. The work was hard, but the rewards were great, too. The boys were happy and George had been promoted to a position of principal in the Delaware school system. They were financially secure. Yet, despite all of that, she felt empty.

Then she focused on herself, and began counting the weeks since her last period. It occurred to her that she could be pregnant. Her periods had been irregular for years...she had gone two, but never three full months like now. Over the years she had had abortions and thought she would not be capable of becoming pregnant again. That belief had held true ever since the birth of her third son, six years ago. Now she realized she might have just been lucky all of that time, or maybe her body had changed in some way. In any event, she knew for a fact she was three months late now.

Rosa viewed the possibility of being pregnant with mixed emotion. Secretly, she had always wanted a girl. Could this pregnancy be that blessing? On the other hand, she remembered George had said, "We can't afford any more children." If she was pregnant and he found out, he would pressure her to get rid of it. She quickly dismissed that thought and returned to the glorious possibility that if she was, this pregnancy might produce a girl. That thought gave her an anchor to drop, a reason to think, 'I want something for myself, and it's a baby.'

Rosa had never lied to George and didn't intend to start now. "I wouldn't say anything to anyone; not even to Mother Mary. I'll keep this to myself, or, until I have to explain the bulge in my belly. By then, it'll be too late for an abortion." With that thought in mind, she fell asleep with a smile.

Despite not having a full night's sleep, she awakened refreshed. She had made up her mind, 'I will have this baby!' That decision made, she approached her day differently. There was a purpose in being alive, a reason beyond working like a man, living in a house without electricity, or running water. She laughed aloud at the thought that the chickens had all of the modern conveniences, and she didn't. But George wouldn't budge: he steadfastly held to the worn out line that, "We can't afford to wire the house and bring in running water."

She looked forward to the first movement of the baby inside her. It would reaffirm her womanhood. It had been six years since that glorious, warm feeling flooded and filled her body.

A few weeks later Mary commented as Rosa entered the kitchen, "Rosa, I do declare, there is something different about you… I just can't put my finger on it."

"Is that so." Rosa answered with a smile. "Well, for the life of me, I can't imagine what would make you say something like that." However, as she spoke, she turned her face away from Mother Mary's prying eyes.

After having coffee, the two women went to the slaughter shed. They stood side by side, gutting and cutting chickens into parts at the counter. As they worked, Rosa began to daydream. The thought of a cuddly little girl sent a shiver of joy through her body. Hiding her pregnancy was not something she wanted to do…but she rationalized, George had thrown her on her own when it was to his liking. She remembered the time he made her learn to drive on her own. Well, she was going to make this decision on her own, too. Her cold wet hands gently slid down to her stomach, unseen by Mary, she gently patted her belly, and it felt comforting.

For the first time in a long time, she realized there were things she felt were missing in her life. She did have wants, important ones, too, and they were not being met. All she had time to think about was running the farm and taking care of the boys and the chickens. "Those darn chickens," she thought. "They live better than I do."

The idea of having the baby gave her strength. Despite her hard days outside and in the chicken houses, she found time to get into the kitchen, peel some apples and make a cobbler.

Later in the day, Mary announced, "All right everyone, dinner is ready."

Rosa and the boys came in from the outside, washed up, and took seats at the kitchen table. After a short prayer, Mother Mary served smoked ham, mashed potatoes and green beans with biscuits. The boys washed it all down with fresh milk from the cow Rosa had purchased from a neighbor. John asked, "When are you going to tell us a story, Mom? You haven't told one in a long time."

"John, you're right. I'll tell you what. After dinner, you boys wash and put away the dishes, and then I'll tell you a story. First let's have some apple cobbler. Would you like that?"

Rosa heated the dessert, skimmed some cream from the milk crock that sat in the cellar way, and put it in a pitcher. The boys loved to pour the cream over the cobbler and mush it into the apples and crust. She served the golden brown apple dish in generous squares, then, called the family to the table. The fragrance of apple, cinnamon, and nutmeg, filled the room. Everyone dug into the oven warmed dessert with gusto. After polishing off the first slice, the boys asked for seconds. She went to the cellar way and filled the pitcher again. Once they finished their second helpings, she reminded them of their obligation, "All right boys, you can do the dishes now."

They washed, dried and put the dishes away. Bill asked, "Mom, will you tell us the watermelon story?"

"Is that the one you want me to tell?"

"Yeah, Mom, tell us the watermelon story," his brothers echoed.

Rosa took a seat in the corner rocker. "All right, I will. I just hope I can remember it. It's been some time since I tried to recite it."

John blew out one lamp and George turned the table lamp down. The boys then sat on the floor in a semi circle, facing their mother.

"Now, let's see." Rosa frowned, "Oh yes, I think I remember it." She cleared her throat, then, began.

As she narrated the story in rhyme without missing a beat, the room resounded with laughter. John fell over and bumped his head on the kitchen floor. His misfortune caused his brothers to laugh even more.

"Did you hurt yourself, boy?" Mother Mary asked as she reached over to comfort him. She too had a smile on her lips as she asked and rubbed his head gently.

"No Grandma, I'm not hurt," he lied, too embarrassed to admit his head really did hurt.

To get the focus off of John, Rosa said, "All right, all right. It's almost time to turn in. You boys can stay up another hour and play some games; then, I want you to go to bed. John why don't you get your wash-cloth. Pour some cold water on it and hold it against your head. I think it'll make you feel better."

Still embarrassed, John went to the basin and pressed a wet cloth against his head.

Smirking at their bothers' mishap, George and Bill set the checkers on the kitchen table. George turned the lamp back up and the two became engrossed in their game. John got a book, and lit the lantern he had extinguished earlier, then took a seat away from his siblings on the wood box and began reading. He wasn't feeling too kindly toward them anyway.

After an hour Grandma reminded the boys it was time to go to bed. Each of the brothers, (starting with the youngest) poured water into the wash basin located in the corner of the kitchen and followed their usual routine. Each boy threw out his dirty water, then, poured fresh water for this sibling. The washing done, they lined up to take turns kissing their mom and grandma before they went upstairs to bed.

With the boys in bed, Mother Mary felt free to ask the question that had been on her mind for some time. "Rosa, are you sure you don't want to tell me something?" Her dark brown eyes locked in on Rosa's face.

"No, I don't think so, Mother Mary."

"Rosa, I wasn't born yesterday!" Mary said, exasperated. "You're keeping something from me…and I think I know what it is."

Rosa had never lied in her life, and she found it impossible to dodge such a direct question, especially from this astute woman, "Mother Mary, I do have something I was going to share with you and the whole family for that matter. It's just that I wanted to be positive of what I was going to say. In fact, I wanted to wait until it would be too late for George to try and pressure me into doing something about it."

A smile spread across Mary's face. "I thought so. You're pregnant! That's what it is. I've been thinking that for some time now." She nodded knowingly.

"Mother Mary, I want this baby more than anything. I want, and need this baby. I'm just afraid George will get angry and start lecturing in his factual way that we can't afford it along through here. You know how he can go on and on."

"Yes, child, I do know."

"Well, I wanted to keep it quiet until I was so far along there wouldn't be anything he, or anyone could do about it."

"You could have trusted me, honey." Mary said comfortingly, "I think you should have another one. I only wish God would have given me a life where I could have had a whole house full, but…" Her voice trailed off as she thought about her murdered husband – killed in the prime of his life, killed for no other reason than he was a black man serving on an otherwise all white jury, doing what free people are supposed to do. She tried not to be bitter, but she was. She had been robbed of a chance to have a full life with a husband who was a good man in every way. Her eleven month old boy grew up never having a single memory of his father. Yes, she had every right to be bitter. But now she had to focus on a new life that was about to be brought into this world.

"What month do you think you're in?" she asked.

"I'm going into my fifth; I should be due in January."

"I thought I saw a glow about you, Rosa. I've notice it for some time now. Well honey, your secret is safe with me. If people had babies based on afford, there wouldn't be any babies born, now would there?"

"No. I guess not. Anyway, I feel better now that you know. I hated hiding such a joyous thing from you. I'll tell George soon…when I catch him in an extra good mood." Rosa said smiling.

The two laughed, as Mary said, "Well, when we ladies get together we will have to tell Sara."

"Oh yes, I can't wait to tell her," Rosa beamed.

Sara jumped up from the kitchen table so quickly, her chair tipped over and crashed to the floor when she heard the news. Ignoring the fallen chair, she rushed to embrace Rosa. "Missus, I'm so happy! When are you due?"

"In January." Rosa smiled.

Sara put her arms around her waist. Her gray-green eyes sparkled as she looked up into Rosa's face. "Such good news. Won't we have fun raising a new baby?"

"Yes, we will. Poor thing will get spoiled to death between all of us hens." Mother Mary added laughing.

"How has the Mr. taken the news?" Sara asked.

"I haven't told him yet. I will in a few weeks. I'm really not looking forward to telling him." Rosa confessed.

"Oh, I think I understand what you're saying, Missus." Sara replied.

From that day on, the ladies spent every spare minute knitting blankets, baby socks, caps and other necessities. Rosa was so certain she was going to have a girl, she convinced the women to knit and crochet with only pink yarn and thread. Every time they got together, they laughed, joked and made predictions about what day in January the 'little girl' would be born. When they got together on Fridays, they stopped well before George was due home.

The ladies were knitting and sewing, having a glorious time. They were laughing and joking, so much so, they didn't hear the car pull into the driveway, or the footsteps on the porch. They were startled when the door opened and George walked in.

"Hello. Everyone!" He called out.

The flustered women looked at one another, feeling foolish that they had been caught, knowing there was no way they could hide their activities.

George began to shed his coat, then, explained, "We were given the day off because the school's roof developed a bad leak. Delaware has been having heavy winds and rains over the past few days."

Rosa sprang to her feet to greet him, hoping she could deflect his attention from what was strewn about on the table and chairs.

While they hugged, George's eyes surveyed the room and he saw instantly what they were doing.

He backed away from her embrace. His face took on a hard look. "What are all of the baby clothes for? Why are you all making baby clothes?" He asked gruffly.

There was a momentary silence, then, a power larger than herself took over, and Rosa became a woman possessed. She put her face within inches of his. "I'm pregnant, George. I'm five months along and there isn't anything you, or anyone can do about it! I want this baby, do you hear me! I'm going to have it, and I don't care what you say! And, I don't want to hear that 'we can't afford a baby' line. The chickens get everything they need. Well, I need this baby!" She realized it had come out all wrong; this was not what she had wanted. She had planned to control the time and place to tell him. She wanted to wait until they were both totally relaxed and had reacquainted themselves after his week away. ‘Too late now,’ She thought. Having had her say, she backed away from him.

“You’re what?” He roared. “You’re five months pregnant! Rosa, I don’t understand. How could you have let this happen? You know we can’t…”

She cut him off. “I…I work like a dog, George. I feel like a man, I want and I need this baby. We can’t afford this baby? Well, who can? Babies are born every day, and somehow they get raised, fed and cared for…”

He interrupted, “Rosa, our children are going to go to college, and it takes money to educate a child. Our boys aren’t going to stop schooling when they finish Green Springs like the Dutch do! Anyway, we will discuss this later!” He turned and in an instant was out the door, his coat half on, half off.

Rosa’s first thought was Sara, and she went to her, “Mrs. Gross, he didn’t mean anything by what he said. He’s upset, and I apologize for his lack of manners. I hope he didn’t hurt your feelings.”

“Missus, don’t you worry none. I understand what he meant onc’t. You folks are ed’decated, you’se have book learning. And he wants that for his children, too. Oh yes, I understand onc’t?”

“I feel badly about what he said, and the way he said it, Mrs. Gross.”

“No,. No, don’t you feel bad. What he said is true. We don’t put that much stock in book learn’n.” Sara stood. “Anyway, I best be gett’n home and start Al’s dinner.”

“Do you have to leave now?” Rosa asked, feeling terrible because of George’s lack of tact.

"Yes, I'm sure, Missus. Anyway, you folks need time alone."

The three ladies hugged, then, said their good-byes.

As soon as Sara left Mother Mary counseled, "Mrs. Gross isn't offended, Rosa." She understands what George was saying and his upset at the situation. She's all right."

The women exchanged glances, "I hope you're right. That woman is too sweet and good to be insulted or hurt in any way." Rosa was angry with her husband for a number of reasons now.

"Trust me, Rosa. She understands men."

"I hope so." Rosa walked to the door. "Well, I might just as well get this over with now."

"Yes, honey, you might just as well." Mary went to Rosa and gave her a comforting hug and an encouraging pat on the shoulder. She knew the dread her daughter-in-law felt as she prepared to confront her husband.

George had slipped on a pair of overalls he kept hanging on a nail in the shed. His back was to the door as he loaded one hundred pound bags of chicken feed into a wheel barrow. Rosa stood in the doorway until he finally turned around. His anger had not subsided. When he finally acknowledged her, he started his tirade where he had left off in the house, "How could you do this to me? You know how I feel about having another child; it's just bad timing Rosa."

"Now, hold on George! You keep telling me how you feel. Have you thought about me, or how I might feel? Have you? Do you realize I have wants and needs, too? All you seem to really care about are these damn chickens and what they need."

"Now Rosa, that's not true. I do care about how you feel and..."

She didn't allow him to finish, "George, why don't you ask me how I feel. Ask me what I want, what I may need? Why don't you, George?"

Rosa had never spoken to her husband this way; and he was taken aback by the firmness in her voice. "Well then, why don't you tell me what's on your mind…what you do want." His voice was softer, calmer now. She had finally gotten his attention.

"First of all, I don't mind the work, but I do miss some of the things we had in town. Do you have any idea of how hard your mother, the boys and I work around here? Do you realize I'm getting up in years, and I want another baby, especially I want a girl…if I don't have it now, I'll soon be too old. You don't have to worry about the finances of having another baby. We couldn't starve even if we tried. Maybe we don't have all the money you want, but we are comfortable. No, more than comfortable, we are more secure than most folks."

"Rosa, I'm planning ahead. It's not just about now. College is going to cost us plenty when the time comes, and to send four children off to school is going to be hard."

"So, it'll be hard. This is hard. Running this place is very hard. But since when is hard a reason not to do something if you really want to do it. I'm surprised at you, George. I really am."

"I don't think you understand the reality of the situation." He wasn't used to being challenged this way.

"Of course, I understand the reality of this situation. Don't you sell me short, George! If there's a will, there's a way, and you know that as well as I do."

"Well, I think you should have an abortion, that's what I really think!"

"Oh, you do, do you! Then you haven't heard a word I said! Forget that, George, forget it! I'm too far along. Can't you get that through your head? You know what I think? I think you better get used to the idea of being a father again!" Rosa had had enough of his stubbornness for one day; she knew his mind was closed. She had a sudden impulse and acted on it. She went to him and gave her startled husband a peck on the cheek. Walking away, she added, "And you owe Mrs. Gross an apology for your remark about the Dutch not going to college!" Her head was held high as she went back to the house.

He stood staring after her with his mouth open. She had never behaved or talked to him like that during their whole marriage.

It took them a while to think things through. By the second day, he had come to terms with his new reality, and had managed to digest what he had not ever expected to deal with again in his life. When he awoke, the sun hadn't yet come up, but his wife wasn't in bed either. He threw off the covers, jumped out of the four poster bed and hurriedly dressed. Then he set out to find her.

As he walked through the house he caught a glimpse of her form through a side window as she stood alone in the yard. He went out and joined her. For a moment he just stood next to his wife. Then he said softly, "Rosa, I've been thinking…I do realize how hard you, Mother, and the boys work. And I do understand, maybe not as much as you want me to, but I do know that things are not easy for you as a woman. Rosa, I'm going to try and make things up to you…make things easier somehow. Go ahead Rosa, let's have the baby. I'm sure we'll manage." She turned to him and offered her lips.

The ladies later picked up where they left off and plunged into their ritual of knitting, storytelling, snacking, drinking coffee and in general, having a glorious time. George's acceptance of Rosa's condition made life fun again for them all.

As time passed, they began to fuss more and more over Rosa as she grew in girth, and weight. "Don't reach for that, it's too high for you. Wait, I'll get it for you." "Rosa, don't you dare stand on that chair! You might fall." "Here, give me that. It's too heavy for you to carry." The chorus of do's and don'ts didn't come only from the ladies, but from her children as well. The boys learned quickly that their mother was to be pampered, and joined the 'watch patrol.' They felt they had a vested interest in the new arrival, too. After all, they would have a new brother or sister to play with.

"Will you all stop watching my every move? I'm not an invalid; this is not my first baby," she protested, but to no avail. Her every move was monitored by five sets of eyes.

Winter arrived, and both Sara and Al knew how hard and unpredictable the weather could be during January. That was when they decided to work out a plan in the event Rosa went into labor during the night, and the Mr. was away.

When the ladies got together the next time, Sara said, "Missus, Al and I have been thinking, onc't. When your time nears, and if you start labor in the middle of the night, set a lamp in the window. My Mr. and me, we both get up during the night, that way one of us would see the light. Then, Al would know to go to the Fetrows, and ring up the doctor. We thought that would be the best way to fetch him if the Mr. ain't home at that time.

"Sara, you're one sweet, thoughtful lady." Rosa exclaimed.

"Bless your heart, Mrs. Gross. You're a wonderful woman." Mary added.

"Ach, that's what neighbors are for." She said modestly.

Rosa added, "I think the baby will hold off until George gets home for the weekend. I would like him here when I come due, and he'll be a part of the birth."

CHAPTER 12

New Arrival

The month started as a typical January: strong winds, bitter cold, and snow. Then as the weeks passed, the weather became mild – a January thaw had set in. But, as the month neared its end, flurries began, and the temperature tumbled, and the weather turned bitter cold. During the night and into the morning of January 29th, 1925 snow began falling heavily -- first as light flakes, but as the day progressed, the snow fell harder and harder;. Soon, it began to accumulate. The flakes blew and swirled about from the strong westerly winds. By early evening the snow had stopped, but not until eighteen inches had fallen and formidable drifts had developed in random patterns in the road.

As sleep enveloped the occupants of Twin Cedars, the winds began to make Wooooo, woooo, sounds and blew the fallen snow into high drifts, blocking parts of the road here and there in a random way.

Rosa tried to ignore the first pain, but by 3:30AM, January 30th, she woke Mary, and had her light a lamp and placed it in the window facing the Gross house. "I hope one of them gets up tonight and sees the light." Rosa said with concern.

"Al, Al, get up! The Missus…her times come. The lamp is on in the window." Sara had slept lightly. She had a feeling about her neighbor coming due that night.

Al jumped out of bed, fully awake. Instinct had told him as well that the event would probably happen in the middle of the night while the Mr. was away. He had promised George. that he would look after his family as if it were his own, and by golly, that's exactly what he was going to do. He pulled his heavy pants on over his long underwear which he'd worn to bed. Because he felt the baby would come soon, Al had carefully laid out his warm clothes each night for the past week. He did this to insure that he would be able to get out of the house quickly. As he buttoned his shirt, he said, "I'll hitch Prince to the sleigh and go on down to the Fetrows and ring up Doc Meckley, you can go and stay with the Missus."

Sara looked out of the window as she dressed. "Al, the snow looks too high for me to walk. After you hitch up Prince, stop out front. I'll ride with you to their house, onc't, and Al..."

"What?"

"I can see by the moonlight, there's high drifts in the road."

"Well, we'll see when we go outside. Now, you just get dressed and wait out front. But you hurry, onc't. I want ta get down the road so I can ring up the Doc."

"Al, I think he'll have trouble getting out here from Zion's View because of the drifts." Sara cautioned.

"Well, if we have ta' we'll get the neighbors to clear the way. That's what we'll do onc't."

"Oh, Al. I hope everything is going to work out."

"Ach, don't fret none, everything's going to be just fine." He said, as he hurriedly left the bedroom and ran down the steps and to the barn. He trudged through knee-high snow that had formed into gentle mounds and peaks from the once strong winds. The moon's brightness made the snow sparkle like a million diamonds, and the trees cast dark patterns on the fluffy carpet of white. Al realized Sara might be more right than she knew. The drifts would be a problem for the doctor.

Entering the horse's stall, he patted Prince on the rump and walked toward his head in order to unhitch him from the stanchion. "Whoa there, boy, steady now, I got ta get ya harnessed up. Not used ta be'n botherd this time of night are ya, boy?" Prince tossed his head and whinnied. Once the harness was on, Al led the horse to the sleigh which sat alongside the barn yard fence and hitched him up. In one sweeping notion, Al brushed the snow off the sleigh's leather seat with his gloved hand, then climbed up and sat down on the frigid seat.

With a 'click' of his tongue, Prince began a gentle trot around the barn to the road and towards the house. As the sleigh approached, Sara stepped off the porch and walked to gate. Their dogs ran to the front to watch their masters and barked at the unusual activity occurring at such an early hour. Sara rushed out the gate and to the sleigh as Al leaned over, extended his hand, and pulled her into the seat beside him.

"That didn't take too long did it, Sara?"

"No. No, it didn't. But Al, I'm so nervous, I just hope she is holding on."

"Now, Sara. You just stop be'n a worry wart," he scolded gently. Within a minute they reached Twin Cedars.

"You run in, and just yell out to me what's go'n on, no point in me go'n in, too. Just be a waste of time for me to do that."

Sara scrambled off the sled and waded through the snow to the front door. She knocked, but didn't wait for an answer, instead she pushed the door open and stepped in.

Mary walked towards her with open arms, "I'm glad you're here, Mrs. Gross. She seems to be in hard labor already."

"I'll tell Al." Sara turned and yelled. "Al! Al! She's in hard labor…she's due anytime now."

Al didn't answer. Instead, he yelled, "Giddy-up-boy!" The jet black horse broke into a fast trot. The horse made steady progress as it went through the accumulated snow, it wasn't until he encountered the first drift that Al urged him to go faster, hoping he would be able to plow through it by his raw strength. Al shook his head in concern. He knew the drifts shouldn't be too bad at this end because of the thick forest that bordered the road. But even if the drifts were no worse than the one he had just encountered, no horse could do this for five miles.

He also knew the drifts would be worse where there were open fields. And he could picture them on the flats by Doc Meckley's place. He reasoned it would be impossible for the Doc to get through to Twin Cedars without the drifts being opened up. Instinct was telling him he would have to call on the neighboring farmers to help out. Al also noticed where the woods grew on both sides of the road there was hardly any drifting at all. He reasoned the snow drifts would probably be bad in some spots at this end and get worse near the Doc's place because of the open fields. He turned into the Fetrow's lane and stopped by the kitchen door, knowing ahead of time what had to be done.

He jumped out of the sleigh, hurried up the steps, then banged on the door. "It's me...Al, Al Gross," he yelled. "I gott'a use your phone to ring up Doc Meckley! The lady up at Twin Cedars, the Read lady is gonn'a have a baby any time now! Eddie…Mom! Do you hear me?"

The upstairs window opened. Eddie Senior stuck his head out. “Yah, we heard ya.’ Hold on Al, Mom and me will be right down.” Shortly there were footsteps, then, the door opened. “Come in onc’t.” the short square built man offered. “You know where the phone is, Al, see if you can rouse the operator.”

“I’ll talk to the Doc, but I’d rather you ring up the operator, Eddie. I ain’t used the phone that many times.”

“Mom Fetrow had gotten up too, having heard their conversation. She acknowledged her guest with a curt, “Morn’n Al” and went directly to the wall phone to begin cranking the handle vigorously. Mrs. Fetrow knew the operator would be sound asleep at this early hour. Eventually, a sleepy voice answered.

“Yes?”

“This here is Mom Fetrow. Hold on, Martha, I’m gonn’a put Al Gross on.” Mom handed the ear piece to Al, as he stepped close to the wall and spoke uncomfortably into the phone’s mouth piece.

“Hello, Martha. Sorry to get ya’ outt’a bed, but we got a baby coming up here on the hill. The lady from Twin Cedars, she’s expect’n any time now. So ring up Doc Meckley for us, onc’t.”

Al could hear the phone ringing and a tired voice answered, “Hello, this is Doctor Meckley.”

“Doc, we got a baby coming up at Twin Cedars. The Read lady, she seems to be due any time now.”

The words came out in a rush. “I know where Twin Cedars is. But I got a problem…the roads are blown shut in spots up here in Zions View. You’re going to have to get some folks to clear the main road and my lane so I can get through. I barely got home yesterday afternoon from my last house call. The drifts were that bad then.”

“Well Doc, I figured as much. Eddie and his son and me, will start gett’n help from the farmers along the way. You get ready and we'll be there afore you knows it.”

“All right Al, I’ll be looking for you. I’ll get dressed and get my horse hitched up.”

Al handed the phone to Mom Fetrow to hang up. Then, he turned to Eddie, “Eddie, doc Meckley said the roads is blown shut up his way, so we gonn’a have to roust the neighbors to clear some of the drifts so he can get through.”

Eddie turned to his wife, “Get Eddie Junior outt’a bed. Tell him to hitch up the horse and sleigh, an’ bring his self and a shovel to the Fink farm. I’ll ride with Al.”

Al realized he left so hurriedly he hadn’t brought a shovel. Eddie found shovels for the two of them, then, jumped into the sleigh. Al snapped the reigns and headed to the Fink farm located up the road and around the bend.

Al banged on Joe Fink’s door. A head popped out of an upstairs window. “Now, who the hell is knocking at this gol durn time of the morning!”

“Joe…Joe Fink! This here is Al Gross, and Eddie Fetrow. We got a baby coming up at Twin Cedars. It’s the Read lady. She’s ready to drop her baby most any time now and Doc Meckley says the drifts are bad in Zions View. Sez he can’t get out. We need your help to open up the drifts.”

“Al. You go on to the Whitmer farm. I’ll get my boys up, and we’ll go on past to the Dorsey place and get them up.”

“Me and Eddie will go on to the Bailey place if we can get that far and ask them to help out. We’ll probably start hitting the bad drifts once we get up that far, the woods end and the fields start opening up around there.”

Seeming to sense the urgency, Prince's pace quickened without any urging out of Fink's lane, and up to the main road. The road was passable because the woods had trapped the snow and reduced the amount that reached the road.

Luckily, Prince had been able to barrel through the few drifts he encountered without trouble, now, as they neared the Whitmer farm, the drifts began to get higher. Finally they reached the horse's chest. Prince could go no further. Al and Eddie jumped out and began shoveling. The snow was light and fluffy, and in no time they had made an opening large enough for the horse to pass through. As soon as they did, Joe Fink and his boys came up the road and went through the cleared opening, heading for the Dorsey place. Al and Eddie got back in the sleigh to continue on to the Bailey place.

Al and Eddie both went to the kitchen door and banged on the side of the house with their fists. An upstairs window opened, a man stuck his head out the window.

"Who the hell is thair'!" The voice bore a strong Southern twang.

"I'm Al Gross, and this here is Eddie Fetrow. We got a baby coming up at Twin Cedars, it's the Read lady... and the Doc can't get through, we're need'n help to shovel the drifts to get him through."

The irate man's head leaned further out of the window. "Let me tell ya' all someth'n. I ain't leav'n my warm bed to bring some gol damn nigger baby inta this world, an I ain't send'n my boy neither. So you both can jes' get!"

Eddie and Al looked at each other. "No good trash!" Eddie exclaimed as he grabbed Al's arm to lead him back to the sleigh.

"Ach, Du Lieber, let's go." Al hissed, "The man's no good." They heard Bailey slam his window shut as they walked away. "You should rot in hell!" Al yelled as he walked away.

"He ain't noth'n but trash." Eddie snarled.

The two men got in their sleigh and joined the other men who were working feverishly. The Finks, the Whitmers, and the Dorseys, plus their sons and hired hands were making great progress opening the drifts. The men yelled encouragement to each other when weariness set in on one of their number. When they came to a farm, Al or Eddie would go to the house, pound on the door and ask the farmer to join in. Altogether, eighteen Dutch farmers joined the band of volunteers.

The last two miles of open fields proved to be the hardest. However, by then they had devised a method to efficiently break through the high drifts. First they made a narrow opening through the drift. While it was narrow, it was wide enough to allow a man to pass through. The opening made, several men would go through the drift, and start shoveling from that side. With men working from both sides of the drift, they could widen it enough so a horse and sleigh could pass through in no time at all. It was near day break by the time they reached Doc Meckley's lane.

Doc saw the men in his lane and knew it was time for him to leave. He charged out of his house, threw his black bag into the sleigh and climbed aboard now that he saw the men turn into his lane and work on what looked like the last drift blocking his way. The farmers had an adrenaline rush once they reached his lane, and flew through the remaining drift that blocked the Doc's way.

Sitting in his sleigh, the doctor watched until they broke through, and he snapped the horse's reins. His dapple gray responded with a whinny, and a burst of speed. The men stood on either side of the opened path, waving and cheering as he tore past them. The Doc called out, "Good job, boys. See you later!" As he disappeared down the road, the men's cheers and whistles filled his ears.

Once the Doc had received the phone call, his wife became busy in the kitchen. She was ready for the cold, exhausted farmers. Mrs. Meckley went to the door, "You boys come in and warm yourselves. I got some hot coffee, jam and biscuits for you. Come on, now, come in help yourselves!"

The chilled farmers stomped their feet to shake off the snow on the closed-in porch, then, piled in the warm kitchen. Some took seats, but most stood around the kitchen's wood stove and soaked up its welcomed warmth. She poured coffee from two big pots, as the men helped themselves to the jam, butter and the mounds of biscuits piled at each end of the table. The men were careful not to step on the collie pups that sniffed their feet.

Rosa lay on a bed in a downstairs room, Mother Mary at her side holding her hand. She got up and wrung out a wash cloth, then placed it on Rosa's forehead. "Oh, this baby is going to be the death of me yet…ahhhh, ahhhhh!" the pain was so sharp. "Where is the doctor, Mother?"

"Now, Rosa, you just calm yourself. He'll be getting here soon, I'm sure." Mary tried her best to sound calm. Inwardly she was as worried, and just as frantic as Rosa was becoming. But she tried to be calm for the expectant mothers sake.

Sara was in the kitchen busy stirring the pancake batter, preparing breakfast for the still sleeping boys. She heard the ladies and called out. "Al and the others must have got through, and I bet ol' Doc is on his way right now." She wanted to help calm Rosa, too.

"Oh, I hope and pray he is." Rosa moaned.

Later, Sara glanced out the kitchen window, and saw a horse-drawn sleigh tearing down the road. "Here he comes, here comes Doc Meckley!" Sara clapped her hands for joy, then, ran to tell Rosa the good news.

"Thank God." The expectant mother sighed when she heard the news.

Mary went to the front door and held it wide open. The doctor rushed past her. "Where is she?" He demanded.

"Over in that room, doctor." Mary pointed to the open door, then, led him to the small bed room.

As he walked towards the door he began removing his outer garments. He paused by a nearby chair and dropped his hat and coat on it. He entered the bedroom and asked in a calm, friendly way, "Well, Mrs. Read. How are we doing? How far apart are your pains?"

"I think they're just minutes apart now, doctor… Ahhhhhh, I've got one now…Oh God! Oh God! I believe the baby's coming now, doctor."

Turning to Mary he barked, "Get me clean sheets, a pan of warm water and a towel." He threw the covers back. Then turned around impatiently, looking for the requested items. As soon as they were delivered, he slipped the clean sheet under Rosa. Just as he did ,the baby's head appeared "Well, here it comes, Mrs. Read. Now push! Push hard, Mrs. PUSH! PUSH HARD!" He ordered.

Rosa pushed, then, let out a piercing scream. In an instant, the baby was out. The doctor caught it in his big hands, held it by its heels, then, he slapped its bottom. The newborn let out a cry, and then gulped its first breath of air. Instantly, a smile crossed the doctor's distinguished face. Doctor Meckley had over his career, delivered hundreds of babies. Yet he found each birth to be a new miracle; each birth made him feel humble and in awe of this great mystery. The doctor wasn't a regular church attendee, but he knew there had to be some greater power to design such a perfect phenomenon. He rejoiced within himself, rejoiced because he still experienced the same thrill today that he did when he delivered his first baby some twenty years earlier. He knew that bringing a new life into the world was the main reason he loved being a doctor. After he wiped the infant clean, he took care of the umbilical cord. As he did, he glanced over at the new mother and then wrapped the baby in a pink blanket. "Mrs. You gave birth to a fine healthy baby boy."

"A boy? Oh. No. It was supposed to be a girl." The mother cried out.

The doctor wasn't caught totally off guard because the blanket he was given provided an obvious clue as to what her thought process was. "Well Mrs., God had other plans and gave you a boy. And if I do say so, he is a fine, healthy one. Here, he's all yours now." He leaned over and handed her the baby.

She looked down at the baby with mixed feelings. She was pleased it had arrived healthy, but her heart was set on a girl.

Upstairs, the boys began to stir, "George, Bill! Wake up. I heard a baby crying." John sat up in bed, his head cocked to one side, straining to hear. "There, hear that?" A faint cry floated up through the floor into their bed room, "Let's go down and see the baby." He urged.

The boys hurriedly threw on their clothes and ran down the steps. They stopped short of their mother's bedroom when they saw a big man standing by her bed. Slowly they edged their way to the open door and stood quietly outside the room. The doctor heard the boys and turned around.

Once he made eye contact with the doctor, George Junior asked, "Can we come in and see the baby?"

"Sure, you can come in and see your Mom, and meet the baby, too." The boys were full of anticipation as they crowded into the room. "Let's see what the baby looks like…what is it, a boy or a girl?" John asked.

"It's a boy." Rosa answered.

"Oh. Great! We have another brother to play with." Bill exclaimed.

"He's got lots of hair." John remarked.

"Why are his eyes closed?" Bill asked.

"They were open a little while ago, boys, he's just resting them right now." The doctor said with a chuckle.

"What's his name going to be, Mom?" George Junior asked.

Well boys, I've got to be frank with you. I was so sure I was going to have a girl, I didn't pick any boy names."

"Oh Mom, let us name him!" John was ecstatic.

A look of concern crossed her face, "Now, wait a minute."

"No. Really Mom. We can do it. We'll find a good name for him, can't we?" John turned to his siblings, as they nodded vigorously.

"All right boys, I'll let you give it a try. But be serious about it. No funny names now. Now you understand I still reserve the right to say no if I don't think the name is appropriate."

"Don't worry about that, we'll give him a good name." George Junior said solemnly as the boys bolted for the door, stumbling over each other to get out of the room in order to get started on this special assignment.

Sara and Mary smiled as they listened and watched the boys' excitement over their new baby brother.

The doctor shook his head in amusement. "Well, Mrs., This should be interesting. I must say, the boys seem to be mighty happy to have another brother."

"Oh doctor. I should be ashamed of myself. It's just that I did have my heart set on a girl. I'll love him all right. But I just have to get over my disappointment that I will never in this life give birth to a girl."

Mary said, "Rosa, as the doctor said, God made that decision for you. And you know the old saying: 'Man makes plans, but God makes the decisions.' This is a good example of that, and a lesson for all of us."

"I understand how you feel, Mrs. Time will heal this disappointment. You're a strong, practical woman. You'll get over this and be just fine, I'm sure." The doctor added.

"Doctor, I never thanked you for coming out here in the middle of the night. The baby wasn't exactly considerate was he? I mean, getting you out of your bed and all. Thank goodness you did get here when you did." Rosa said with relief.

"Actually, Mrs., You can thank Al Gross, and all the farmers who did the hard work. They had to shovel drifts for several miles to get me through. Did you know that?"

"No, I didn't know…oh my, I certainly will. I had no idea that…"

The boys burst into the room, "Mom! Mom! We have a name." John announced.

"So soon, what is it?" Rosa asked.

"Mom. How about this name? Charles Richard Read? Charles after your favorite cousin, Charles, and Richard, so we can have a brother we can call Dick. What do you think? Do you like those names?" The boys stood wide eyed, hoping for their mother's approval.

Rosa thought for a minute, then, repeated the name. "Actually, I do, boys. It has a nice ring to it, I think you all did just fine. All right, your brother is officially Charles Richard Read, or, just plain Dick." Rosa gave them a big smile.

"Yeah! " The boys cheered. They cheered so loud, they woke their brother. His screams affirmed he had a healthy set of lungs.

Mary, Sara and the doctor all exchanged smiles as they watched and listened to the drama of name selection unfold. It was a happy scene to witness.

"What's that noise? I think I hear men's voices outside." Rosa asked. Mary and Sara went to the front door, and looked down the road.

Mary came back to the bed room, "Rosa, I do declare, there must be a dozen or more men coming up the road with Al. Some of them are walking, some are on horseback and some are riding in sleighs."

"Those are the farmers that got me through the drifts, Mrs." The doctor announced.

The men came into the yard, one yelled. "Where's that there baby that got me outt'a my bed?" Another added,

"Yeah, where's that young'n that woke me from a sound sleep."

Doctor Meckley took charge and went out to the front porch. "Now boys, I can't let you in, but I'll tell you what. Since you all worked so hard to bring this little fella into the world, I'll hold him up to the front door window so you can all get a peek...how's that?"

"That's fine, we just wann'a peek." Eddie Fetrow yelled as the men crowded around the front door

Doctor Meckley went to Rosa and explained what was going on, and what he had promised the men, and asked if it was all right with her.

"Oh. Certainly. Please tell the men I'll be eternally grateful for what they did. Tell them I thank them, and my whole family thanks them for the bottom of our hearts."

"I will, Mrs., I'll tell them what you said." With that, the doctor scooped the baby up, and went to the glass front door. Mother Mary pulled the lace curtain to the side while doctor Meckley held the baby up to the door's window so the men could see the results of their labor. A loud cheer went up when they saw the small, brown face peering out from his blanketed cocoon. The doctor turned to Sara and handed the baby to her, then stepped outside.

"Boys, she gave birth to a healthy boy. His name is Charles Richard Read. Now, Mrs. Read said to tell you all thanks, and she will be eternally grateful for what you all did. She thanks you and her whole family thanks you for what you did for them. And I say the baby says thanks, too," The doctor added with a smile.

A farmer yelled, "You know what? That there baby's a Dutchman, a Shworts'r Dutchman!" Another voice concurred, "Tell Missus we were glad to oblige, Doc. But tell her next time to have her baby in the summer." The men laughed. Another farmer added, "Yeah, and in the daytime, too." That made the men laugh even more.

"Hey Doc," A farmer called out, "How come that there boy was in a pink blanket?"

The doctor laughed, "Well boys let me put it this way. The mother expected a girl, but God had other ideas, and gave her a boy."

"I'll ask my Missus to send her up some blue ones. We don't want that there boy in no damn pink blanket. Do we boys?" There was a chorus of "no's."

"Jake, I think the Missus will take care of that in time, but I'll tell her about your offer." The doctor answered.

"Tell her good health, and good luck." Another voice called out.

"I'll be sure and tell her everything you said, boys. She'll get a good laugh out of your recommendations for the next baby." Doc Meckley said as he turned to go back inside he added, "Thanks, boys, see all you around."

The farmers slapped each other on the back, and shook hands all around before they dispersed and headed home.

The doctor returned to Rosa's room "Well Mrs. Read, I've got several messages for you from the farmers."

Rosa smiled, "I'm anxious to hear what the men had to say."

"Well, first off Mrs., your son is considered a Dutchman, a black Dutchman by the farmers. And…"

"Oh. How nice. That's quite an honor."

"Also, the boys asked that your next baby be born in the summer, and during the day time. So you be sure and keep that in mind, if you know what I mean." The doctor joked.

She smiled, "Yes, I get the meaning…doctor."

Now, I have two more messages. Jake Knaub asked me why the boy was wrapped in a pink blanket. I explained why, but he said he would have his Missus send up some blue ones if you want, because they don't want their Dutch boy in no pink blanket."

Rosa sucked in her breath, "I guess I will have to remedy that, won't I?"

"Yes, Mrs. I think you will. Now, if I remember right, the last thing was to tell you and your family, 'Good health and good luck'."

"Oh. How nice. I can't tell you how overwhelmed I feel by the kindness of those men. I'll never be able to thank them enough." First the tears came, then, she began to sob.

Mary stood by the door, smiling as she listened to what the men had said. Then she walked away.

The doctor took another look at the baby, and reviewed a few do's and don'ts with Rosa in terms of the baby's care.

Rosa asked, "How much do I owe you for your services doctor?"

The doctor smiled, "Well, Mrs., I have a dairy farm, so we have lots of milk, but my Mrs. is always running out of eggs. How about a month's worth? Does that sound fair?"

"That sounds more than fair. Suppose we add a few broilers for you and your wife each week too. You and your Mrs. like to eat chicken, don't you?"

"You bet, and I thank you. I will say this has been quite an experience. Well, I'm going to go now. By the way, fetch the baby when you come to bring the eggs. I'll want to take another look at him, too. Anyway, I still have a few chores to do myself when I get home. So, I'll say goodbye to you folks." With that he left.

Sara pulled Mother Mary into the kitchen and whispered, "Did you see the Missus hair, onc't?"

"Yes, yes I did. Shall we tell her?"

"Yah, before she sees herself in a mirror. It might shock her too much if she ain't warned." Sara replied. The two ladies went back to Rosa's room and sat down on the bed,. Her eyes were closed. They looked at each other to see who would speak first. Sara nodded to Mary, indicating she should be the one to speak.

"Rosa, are you asleep?" Mary began cautiously.

"No, I'm just resting my eyes." Rosa replied sleepily.

"Now Rosa, I have something to tell you, and I don't want you to get upset when you look in the mirror. But you're going to see something different about yourself."

"What are you trying to say, Mother Mary?" She sat up in her bed, suddenly concerned.

"What I'm trying to say is, you have a white streak in your hair. It must have come from the anxious feelings you were having worrying about the doctor getting here and all. I think it's quite becoming." Mary added, trying to make her feel that it didn't detract from her looks.

"I do? I have a gray streak? Get me a mirror. I want to see."

Sara went to the dresser and picked up an oval shaped hand mirror and gave it to her. Even with the advance warning Rosa was totally shocked at what she saw. In the exact middle of her head was a two inch wide white streak in her hair. "Well, if that doesn't take the cake. I went to bed to have a baby with a head of black hair, and now I have a great big streak of white. Now isn't that something? Does it look bad?" She asked the ladies.

"No, Missus. It makes you look…" Sara searched for the right word, "Spiffy, yah, that's it, spiffy, Missus. It looks good on you."

"And I agree with Mrs. Gross. Rosa it makes you look, as Sara said, Spiffy." Mary said smiling.

The women laughed, then gave her a hug.

The days went by, and the family quickly developed a routine around the new arrival. The boys loved to fuss over him whenever they could. And Mother Mary and Sara vied for the chance to hold him when he cried. Rosa breast fed him, and he responded by gaining weight and sleeping for long stretches of time.

The baby was wrapped in a blue blanket shortly after the doctor left because Mother Mary hadn't bought into Rosa's certainty that the baby would be a girl. At night, when everyone slept, she had secretly made several blue baby outfits and blankets, some even edged with blue crochet yarn. When Rosa saw her baby wrapped in blue, she looked at Mother Mary, "Now when did you do that?" She asked, pleased that Mary had more common sense than she had.

"Oh, I found the time at night. I didn't want to intrude on your dream of a girl, but I know these things can go either way, so…"

"Well, I thank you for having the wisdom that you do." Rosa smiled as she went to her and gave her a great big hug.

Rosa sat in the kitchen rocker as her husband walked in. "Hello, George, you missed all of the excitement. I'll fill you in later. But first, come here and meet your new son."

He leaned over and kissed his wife on the forehead, as she offered him his son. "Well, well. He sure has a lot of hair." He said admiringly. George took the baby in his arms and looked at it with love and amazement. "You didn't get the girl you wanted, how do you feel about that?" He asked, knowing how badly she had wanted a girl.

"Oh, I got over the initial disappointment real fast. He's a fine healthy baby, and I'm really grateful, grateful in so many ways to have another son."

"Are you sure you're going to be content with four sons?" George asked, half kidding, half serious. He was anxious to know whether or not he would be ambushed by another surprise pregnancy.

"No, George. I'll be happy and content with this one. You can relax now. No more surprises, I promise." Rosa smiled. "But, there is one thing,' she added.

"Oh. Oh. Now here it comes." He answered as his eyes narrowed.

"I think I'd like Dick to have a puppy to grow up with. The watch dog you got is good for outdoors, but he's too rough to be around the baby."

"Phew. You had me a little concerned for a minute. Actually, I think that's a good idea."

"So, how do you feel? Being a new dad and all?"

"Good, it feels good to have a little one around again. You were right in holding out for what you wanted." At that moment he got a whiff, "Oh, oh. I think our son just left you a present." He made a face as he handed the baby back to its mother.

“I’ll take care of that.” Rosa said with a smile.

Mary, busy at the stove, heard her son’s comment. She went to Rosa and without a word, took the baby and tended to its needs.

George was not a hands-on father. On occasion, if he was in the right frame of mind, he would pick the baby up, walk in circles for a short while, then, hand the infant to any of the women who might be present, usually to the nearest one when he decided his fatherly chores had been fulfilled. Starting with their first born, on the nights the baby was cranky and cried, he would seek the quiet of the room furthest away. His reasoning to Rosa was his usual refrain, “I need my sleep.”

The sun was peeking over the far hills when Rosa began serving the bacon and eggs she had prepared for her family’s breakfast. She hadn’t turned around when she was about to ask Mary if she wanted one or two eggs. When she did look, she realized the noise she heard behind her was John coming into the room. Mary wasn’t up and about. “It isn’t like her to sleep late.” Rosa said to no one in particular. “Good morning son. Do your mother a favor, go knock on your grandmother’s door. She must have stayed up late knitting last night. I’m sure she would want to join us for breakfast.”

“All right Mom.” He went to her door and knocked, lightly at first, then a little harder. “She isn’t answering, Mom.”

“Well, go in and shake her gently. She’s probably in a deep sleep, or having a dream.” Rosa joked.

John opened the door and got a glimpse of his grandmother. He knew instantly she was no longer with them. He ran from the room, tears flowing. “Mama, Mama, Grandma is dead!”

It was two weeks to the day that Dick was born when Grandma passed.

"When I go to the great beyond," Mary had begun, "Don't you bury me in that colored cemetery in North York. I'll never rest in peace if you do." Rosa was in bed remembering the conversation they had had some six months ago, and the dilemma it presented to honor her request.

"Oh, you stop that nonsense, Mother." Rosa had life in her body. She didn't want to discuss death at that time. "You're healthy as anything, so I don't want to hear that kind of talk… you hear me?" Her voice was sharp.

Mary responded with equal intensity, "That may be, but one thing is for sure. I will die someday, and when I do, I don't want to be buried in that place! I'm quite serious. You find me a place near to home, so I can feel close to you all when I'm gone. I swear, I'll never have peace in that place."

"Mother Mary, you know I don't like talking about such things. We have lots of chickens to pluck, and apple pies to bake before we start worrying about your passing."

"Will you listen to me? I'm serious, and I want you to take me serious!" Mary insisted.

The earnestness of her request overcame Rosa's reluctance to talk about death, and dying. She took Mary's hands, "I'm sorry. I really am. I've been putting my feelings ahead of your honest desires. I understand what you're saying, and why you're saying it. I wouldn't want to be buried there either," Rosa replied sympathetically.

"You've seen the place. It's on a steep hill, it's unkempt, and my Lord, I'd be lying on my side for eternity, I'd never be able to rest in peace that way. Lord knows, with a heavy rain, my casket could slide down that hill, and I'd end up in the street below." A smile crossed her lips as she laughed at her own wit.

Rosa laughed as she answered, "All right, I promise, I'll find a place closer to home, a place where you'll be able to rest in peace." She patted her hand, then gave her a hug.

That night as she lay in bed Rosa wracked her brain, trying to think of a starting place to what seemed an impossible mission. Since they moved to the country seven years ago, they had lost contact with the two black churches they had attended in town. All of the nearby churches were white, and as a family, had never considered setting foot inside their doors. She knew they had burial plots, but also assumed they were for white folks only. "Lord, Lord, where do I begin?' She thought. As she wrestled with her problem, Doctor Meckley came to mind. Although he was white, he seemed to be a fair minded man. He had taken care of the boys, and Mother Mary whenever they were sick, and he was her doctor now that she was pregnant.

With that thought in mind, she went to Mary the next morning. "I've got to run to Zion's View. I'll be back in an hour or so." She didn't reveal the true purpose of her trip. She would wait until she had something positive to tell her.

"All right, Rosa, you take care when you drive these roads," she cautioned.

"I will. See you soon," she replied as she went out of the door. Rosa drove to Doctor Meckley's farm, and pulled into his long tree-lined lane and parked by the door that displayed a, 'Patient Entrance' sigh and went in.

Before she could sit down, another door opened and the doctor appeared. "Well, hello Mrs. Read. Don't tell me it's your time already," he said with a chuckle.

"No, doctor. I've come to ask you a question, and it doesn't pertain to medicine."

"Then I may not be able to help you." He replied with a broad grin. "Well, why don't you come into my office and we can talk. I must say I'm curious to know what's on your mind since it's a non-medical question." He held his office door open and ushered her in. Pointing to a chair, he took the seat next to it. "Now, what is this non-medical question you have for me?"

"Doctor, my mother-in-law raised a question and I can't help her. She can't rest, and neither can I at this point. The other day she asked me to find a burial place for her out here near the farm. She doesn't want to be buried in the colored cemetery in North York. As you know it's situated on a very steep hill, and she's afraid she would always be tilted to one side, instead of lying on her back. She's afraid she wouldn't be able to rest in peace." Her words were coming out awkwardly and in a jumble.

Doctor Meckley smiled, "Well, we can't have that can we?" He was amused, but realized it was a serious problem. He walked to the wall mounted phone, then, turned to this visitor. "I just might be able to help you. I'll call Reverend James, the minister at the Zion's View Lutheran Church. He should be able to give us some guidance." He cranked the phone, then, waited for the operator to come on. When she did, he asked her to ring up Reverend James. "Reverend James… This is Doctor Meckley…I'm fine, thank you, I'm calling because Mrs.

Read, from Twin Cedars is in my office, and she has a question that's more in your domain than mine…No, I'd rather she discuss it with you in person if you have some time." The doctor glanced at Rosa and smile. "You can see her now? That's marvelous." The doctor covered the mouth piece. "Can you go and see him now?"

"Oh, yes, yes of course." Rosa answered eagerly.

"Yes, she will be right over. Thank you for your willingness to hear her out, Reverend." He hung up the ear piece, then, walked over to Rosa. "Well, it looks like you may be able to get an answer fairly quickly."

"Thank you so much. I can't tell you how much I appreciate this."

"Don't thank me just yet; let's see what happens after you meet with Reverend James. If he can't help you, you be sure and let me know."

Rosa left the doctor's office and drove on to Zion's View; another mile or so further down the road. It took her no time to reach the Reverend's parsonage. She had passed by the stone parsonage house and church numerous times, but had paid scant attention to it. As she slowed the car, she assumed the man sitting on the front porch was Reverend James. The man stood as he saw the car slow. He unfolded his tall frame from the rocking chair and walked out to the road toward the parked car. As he approached he extended a long slender hand in greeting.

"Mrs. Read?" He asked.

"Yes. And you're Reverend James?"

"That's correct. I'm so pleased to meet you Mrs. Read." He held her hand as she stepped down from the car's running board. The Reverend was well over six feet, and wore thick glasses low on his small hawkish nose; the lenses in his glasses enlarged his blue eyes. "I've heard so much about you folks, and your farm. And, I must apologize for never finding the time to pay you all a visit."

"You're more than welcome to come and pay us a visit anytime." Rosa replied sincerely.

"Your place sounds fascinating. Some of my members have been to your place, and have told me about their visits."

"We would be pleased and honored should you decide to come and see us, too."

"Thank you, and I will take you up on that invitation one of these days. Now, what is the question you asked the good doctor that he deferred to me?"

Rosa recounted Mother Mary's worry about the North York cemetery, and the fact that it sits on such a steep hill, and why she felt she couldn't rest there. She also relayed her mother-in-laws concern that her casket, on a heavy rainy day, could slide down that hill. And that she wants to be buried closer to the farm. As she concluded her narration, Revered James chuckled.

"Mrs. Read, I'm not laughing at you, or the situation your mother-in-law worries about; however, the picture of her casket sliding down that hill… well, I 'm sorry." He held his hands to his face and shook his head.

"Don't apologize, Reverend. She has laughed at that prospect herself." Rosa confessed to the amused man.

Then, his face became serious, "Now, I don't take stock in this separate burial business anyway. God made us all, and I think to separate dead folks, or the living, is just plain foolishness. The ones that think that way must think heaven is going to be separated, too. Colored folks here, white folks over there. Humph!" His face began to redden.

Rosa added, "Reverend, I hate to say it, but there are people who do think that way."

"Mrs. Read, you're right. In fact, there may be a few of my members who feel that way too…may not agree with me, and actually do believe that nonsense. But to set your mind at ease, let me say right off, we do have lots of space in our cemetery and I think your mother-in-law will find the ground nice and level." He couldn't suppress the smile that crossed his lips as he spoke.

"Now, Reverend, we don't want to cause you any problems with your members."

"Mrs. Read, I usually don't mention this to folks, but some years ago, my grandfather's house that sat just outside of York, was an underground station for runaway slaves, so your request is pretty tame stuff, don't you think?" His eyes twinkled with pride.

"Well, Reverend, on behalf of any unknown ancestors of mine who may have come this way, I want to say thanks to your Grandpa." Rosa joked. She felt totally at ease with him. He was really a genuinely nice man.

"I think my Grandpa would more than approve of my helping you with your request. There's lots of space in our cemetery. In fact, let's walk over there now and you can pick out a plot." The more the Reverend spoke, the taller he grew in Rosa's eyes. "Unless it's part of a family plot already taken, you can select any place in the cemetery you like."

"Reverend James, I don't know how I can thank you. You will have made Mother Mary a very happy lady. Now, may I impose on you and make a further request?"

"I don't see why not?" He replied smiling. "And, you're not imposing. That's why I'm here. I'm here to help folks. It's really my pleasure." He said sincerely.

"May I...I mean, I would like to reserve a plot large enough for my husband and myself too. Would that be possible?"

"Pick the spot, and we'll work out the details, and the cost. How does that sound?"

"I wish to thank you so ever much, Reverend. This has been a most rewarding visit."

The Reverend escorted Rosa back to her car. Once she was settled in her seat, he said, "By the way, you and your family are most welcome to attend our service on Sunday. We would be pleased and honored to have you folks, remember that now."

"Oh, I will. I will. Thank you again, Reverend James."

CHAPTER 13

Coping with Loss

Mother Mary's funeral and burial was a simple affair, attended by family members: Al and Sara, the Fetrows and the Finks. Rosa asked Reverend James to conduct the grave side service. Mary Catherine Read was the first person of color to be buried in Quickles Cemetery, February 13, 1925.

The house seemed empty with Mother Mary gone. Rosa missed her companionship, her insights and her day to day wisdom; she also had to admit from a selfish stand point, she missed her help with the new baby, and the unending chores. The business was growing, and she found herself working harder and harder to keep pace with the demands of the growing farm.

The boys felt her loss, too. "Things don't seem the same with Grandma gone, I miss hearing her sing." Bill complained one day.

Then too, their youthful emotions had been subjected to two extremes in a short period of time; The joyous high they felt from the birth of their brother, then, the heart break of Grandma's death. The two events coming so close to each other raised questions they couldn't resolve. John articulated their feelings best. "It isn't right, Mom. She won't even get to see us grow up, and she only got to see Dick for a few days, it just isn't fair."

Rosa took the question seriously. “Boys, the Lord giveth, and the Lord taketh away. He is the decision maker, don’t ever forget that.”

“But why would He do that?” It doesn’t make sense.” George Junior persisted.

“Children, there are things in life that don’t seem to have answers. But if you believe in the Lord, you know He is the Creator, and has a master plan for all of us. One day it will be clear to us as to why He did what He did. But for now, we just have to believe she is in a better place. Can you understand that?”

The boys looked at their mother, trying hard to digest what she had just told them. Finally John said, “As long as she is in a better place, then I guess it’s all right that she isn’t here with us.” His brothers all nodded in solemn agreement.

Discussions like that allowed Rosa to breathe a sigh of relief. She felt they could now get on with their lives without the presence of Mother Mary. Now that they all knew she was in a better place, they could all move on.

On a visit, Sara lamented, “It ain’t the same without her Missus.”

“No, it isn’t Mrs. Gross.”

“Did the doctor say what took her?” Sara inquired.

“Well, no. He said he felt her heart just gave out.”

The door opened and George walked in. “Hello. How is everyone?” He said in a lifeless voice.

“Hello, Mr. It’s good to see you.” Sara responded.

Turning to Sara he said, “Thank you. It’s good to see you, too Mrs. Gross. Is your Mr. well?” Without waiting for her to reply, he continued, “I guess I’ll take a walk through the long laying houses.” He stood for a moment, looking confused, then, went back out the door.

"Missus, He don't look right, he don't sound like himself. He's different."

"I expected him to take his mother's loss hard, but he's just a shell of his former self, and I don't know what to do about it." Rosa's brow furrowed. "He's become withdrawn, even his eyes look dull, and he doesn't have any interest in anything anymore. Not even in the business."

"Oh, he just needs time Missus. He'll get better with time."

"I sure hope so. He always goes over the books, and he's missed things that I know he should catch. Normally he's quick to spot an error. Now, he's just going through the motions. His heart and mind aren't really in anything he does. He and his mother were very close. They only had each other his whole life, so I understand why it's hard on him, but, I've got to get him to overcome his loss somehow."

"Yah, it's such a shame, such a shame." Sara lamented.

She went to Rosa and gave her a hug, "He'll get better, Missus. Just give him time. Time will heal him, I'm sure," she counseled.

Rosa was setting the table when George walked in after making his rounds. "Good, "she thought. "The boys are outside; this is a good time to have a serious talk with him.' Acting on that feeling, she went to her husband, "How did it go?" she asked, to open a discussion. "Did George Junior have everything done the way you had instructed him?"

George had taken a seat on the wood box and was looking out the window. He didn't respond. It was obvious he was in deep thought.

"George, I'm speaking to you!"

He turned dull eyes toward her. "Oh, I was just thinking about something," he countered in a monotone voice.

"George you're going to have to pull yourself together. Your mother is gone. We all miss her, but life goes on." She knew she had to snap him out of his black mood.

"I know, but…"

"You have a family, a new baby, a growing business, you have your job and you have me!" She pleaded.

George looked at her for a brief while before he responded. "Rosa, I must confess something. You know I'm a practical man. For whatever reason, I never prepared myself for my mother's death. I just didn't give her mortality a moment's thought. Now, I have to find a way to handle her not being here. She's been in my life ever since I remember. She inspired me to go to college, to be a man…I guess I thought I'd have her around forever." Without warning, his body shook, and deep sobs erupted from him.

Rosa knelt down and held him close, "Shhhh… shhhh, it's all right George, everything's going to be all right." She assured him.

The kitchen door opened, "Hi Mom." John led the parade of brothers into the room. "What's for dinner?"

Rosa regained her composure quickly as George pulled away from her embrace. "How does ham, mashed potatoes and collard greens sound?" she answered in a calm voice.

"Oh. Good!" the boys answered with enthusiasm.

George didn't acknowledge the boys. He stood up quickly and walked past them and out the door.

"I'll set the table." John volunteered.

"What can Bill and I do Mom?" George asked.

"Everything is about ready to be served. So, you two can just take your seats."

After George wiped his tear-stained face, he returned to the kitchen and took his place at the head of the table, then offered a brief prayer. Once the food was served, everyone began eating. The room was quiet except for the sound of clanking silverware, and an occasional appreciative groan from one of the boys as they ate.

The meal's quiet mood was broken by the loud cry of their baby brother in the next room. "I'll get him." Bill offered as he stood.

"All right, bring him in and put him in his basket." Bill returned, all the while trying to sooth his baby brother. "Come on now Dick, you don't want to wake the dead." His words seemed to freeze in the air. Everyone's eyes went to him. He realized instantly what he had said. "Mom, I didn't mean anything…I, I just..I meant…"

"Shut up, you dope!" John hissed at his stricken brother.

"John, you be quiet!" Turning to Bill she said, "It's all right son. I know you didn't mean it the way it sounded." Then looking at John, "And, you young man will not call anyone a dope, and certainly not your brother. We don't use disparaging words in this house, is that clear?"

John dropped his head and muttered, "Yes, Mom."

"Now tell your brother you're sorry."

It was hard, but he managed to mumble, "I'm sorry, Bill."

Even though he still felt wounded by his brother's words, he replied, "That's all right, forget it."

George sat in a trance, not involving himself.

The baby had become quiet once he had been placed in his basket. Now he started crying again.

"He probably needs a change." Rosa observed.

"I'll do it Mom." George Junior volunteered.

Bill and John cleared off the table, and began washing and drying the dishes. Both were still upset with each other, but didn't dare verbalize their feeling. However, they glared at each other whenever their eyes met.

George Junior handed the cleaned baby to his mother as she settled in the rocking chair. She offered the baby a breast, then, softly sang the story of Jessie James. The baby's feeding complete, she burped him, then wrapped him in several blankets. Rosa discovered her new son loved the cold. So, she set him outside in the closed in, but unheated porch, where he would sleet deeply for hours.

George Junior always began his day early. He did so because his chores were many, and varied, and he liked to get a jump on some of them before breakfast. As he started, his father walked in. "Good morning Dad. After you look around, let me know if everything is all right in here. There are a few things I haven't had a chance to do yet, but I'll get to them soon."

George hardly returned the boy's greetings and seemed disinterested in what he had just said. "Umm, yes, yes." He replied in an absent-minded way.

The boy wanted to please his father and was anxious to hear him voice approval of the job he was doing. His brothers were responsible for the upper laying house; his mother took care of the layers in the barn and the peepers in the four brooder houses. As the eldest, he was responsible to see that his younger brothers did their jobs in their father's absence. And while they took their responsibility seriously, he knew he was the one his father would reprimand if they had lapses in their performance.

His father took a few steps in, his eyes hardly focused on anything before he turned back to leave, "Yes son, everything seems fine. The windows you fixed are nice and tight and…uhh…well, everything seems fine." He opened the door, and vanished outside.

He looked at his departing father in bewilderment. The roosts needed cleaning, there were still windows that needed replacing, and the watering cans were filthy. As he pondered what had just transpired, John walked in. "Did you see dad this morning?" he asked his brother.

"Yeah, when I got there he was already inside. He said everything looked fine. But some of the light bulbs were out, and the roosts were dirty. I guess he didn't see that."

"What's wrong with Dad?" George Junior pursued. "Since Grandma died, he's changed…he doesn't act like himself anymore."

George Junior walked closer to his brother, "I know one thing. Since Dick was born and Grandma died, it's been harder on Mom. She has all of the usual stuff to do outside, plus the cooking, the house and Dick to take care of. She got that gray streak when he was born but now, she's getting grayer all over. She doesn't look well, and she seems tired all the time," he said quietly.

John nodded. "Yeah, I have noticed. If the house had running water and electricity, it wouldn't be so hard for her. She wouldn't have to pump and carry water like she does. I don't know why he's so cheap!" he said angrily.

"Tell you what. Let's try and do some of her outside work before we go to school, and help her more in the house," George Junior suggested.

John grinned, "Let's shake on it. We can tell Bill when we see him, all right?"

George Junior helped John finish up, then, they headed back to the house. Rosa had started breakfast and was ready to serve. As they entered the kitchen John asked his usual question, "What's for breakfast Mom?"

"We are having pancakes and sausage. How does that sound?"

"That sounds good to me, Mom." Both boys noticed the table wasn't fully set. Wthout a word, they finished setting it.

George Junior looked around. "Where's Dad?"

"He had to run into town on business," she answered.

Bill walked in and took a seat next to John. As Rosa flipped the pancakes on the stove, John leaned over and whispered into this ear, "We're gonn'a start helping Mom more, inside and outside. She's looking tired. Are you with us?"

Bill nodded and took his brother's extended hand, then they both exchanged smiles. George Junior watched and gave them both a wink. The pact was complete.

As they ate, there was a knock at the front door. "I'll get it," Bill offered.

"If it's a salesman, tell him we don't need anything." Rosa was in no mood to waste time. She knew it had to be a stranger, because the local people and all of their friends came to the kitchen door in the back. "All right. Mom, I'll get it," Bill called as he ran through the house to the front door. He returned quickly, "It's a man; he said he went to college with Dad!"

"Go back and invite him in."

Bill retraced his steps, then returned leading a broad shouldered, athletic looking man into the kitchen.

"Hello; everyone," the stranger said in a deep, melodic voice. "I'm Bill Felton." Looking at Rosa, he smiled, "And you must be Mrs. Read."

"That's correct." She answered, returning his smile.

"Your husband and I went to Lincoln. In fact, we graduated together, the class of 1911," he said with pride.

"Well, I'm so pleased to meet you. My husband has mentioned you often."

"That's good to hear."

"Now, let me introduce you to my family. This is our eldest, George Junior." Pointing, she added," That's John and next to him is Bill. Oh yes, asleep over there is our newest addition, Dick, and I'm Rosa."

Bill Felton acknowledged Rosa with a nod of his head, then walked to each boy and offered his hand. He tip-toed over, and looked at the sleeping baby. "Mrs. Read, you have a mighty fine family," he whispered.

"Well, thank you. But, you don't have to whisper. He sleeps through everything."

"Is Piggy, uhh, I mean, George around?" The man's voice had a jovial ring to it. His nose was sharp, his eyes were small, black, deep set, and sparkled like lit coals. They were framed by a pair of thick bushy brows. When he smiled, deep dimples appeared in both cheeks. He was a very handsome man.

"George went into town. He'll be back shortly," Rosa explained. "Can I offer you some breakfast Mr. Felton?"

"Well, Mrs. Reeeeed. I don't mind if I doooo." His voice had a sing song quality, and he stretched out his vowels. Often, he punctuated his comments with a, ha, ha, ha, ha, sounding all the world like machine gun bursts. His odd mannerisms brought smiles to everyone's face. "You might be wondering why it took me so long to look up your husband after so many years. Well, I can explain."

"Oh. No. You don't owe us any explanation, Mr. Felton. I'm sure George will be ever so glad to see you, especially along through here." Rosa didn't explain the feeling she had that this man from his past might be just what the doctor ordered for her depressed husband.

"Well, I do have a reason to explain, because you folks may know my wife."

"Is that so Mr. Felton? How's that possible?" Rosa asked, as she served him breakfast.

"You see, I went to Ohio after graduating Lincoln and found work as a teacher out there. My first wife passed, and in time I remarried. The lady I married, a fellow teacher, had taught in Smallwood School in York. We were talking one day and she mentioned a teacher she had worked with, a George Isaac Read. When I described him, I knew it was Piggy…I mean George."

The boys were all ears and realized he had used the name, Piggy earlier when describing their father. John spoke up, "Who's Piggy Mr. Felton?"

"Ha, ha, ha, ha! You caught me, didn't you? Well, that was your dad's nick name when he was a boy. Not too many people know that. I found out when he was telling a story about his childhood to a group of his classmates in college."

"Was he fat? Was that why they called him that name?" Bill asked, trying to picture his lean father as a fat boy.

"Nooo," He replied with a twinkle in his eyes. "Do you want me to tell you why he was called that?"

They answered with a chorus of "Yeeeeeesssss" Echoing a new found speech pattern.

"Well, it seems, he could out eat all of the guys he hung…uhh, I mean, that he knew."

The sound of a car door slamming broke through the chatter and laughter. "That should be your father boys. Go see if he needs help. He may have things to unload."

The boys jumped up from the table, and scrambled out the door. "Hello, Dad." They yelled. "We have company, someone from your college," George Junior announced.

"His name is Bill Felton." John added.

George's face lit up. "Well, I'll be!"

Bill Felton walked out onto the porch. As soon as he saw George, he exclaimed, "Weeeelllll, you old son of a gun….maaaannnn, you're a sight for sore eyes." He jumped off the porch, and ran to embrace his pal of years gone by.

"You're a sight for sore eyes, even if you're still ugly as ever," George kidded. Each man put a bear hug on the other, then backed away, and began throwing playful punches at each other.

"You know Piggy, uhh, excuse me, I should say professor, I had to do some detective work to find you, you know. Not many people in town knew anything about you, or your whereabouts."

"Yeah, that would make sense. Only a few colored families would know where we are, or what happened to us," George explained. "Once we moved out here, we lost contact with most of our friends in town. We've been busy trying to run a poultry business, and needless to say, that didn't give us time to do anything except work hard and try to make it a success."

"You're right there. Most of the colored folks I asked said, 'Oh, the Reads. They moved out to the sticks somewhere. We don't see them anymore…they just dropped out of sight,' " Mr. Felton explained.

"So, how did you find us?" George asked.

"My wife had to go see Doctor Kimbrough. While she was there, she figured you all would still be using him since he's the only colored dentist in town, so she asked him. And, she was right. He had your address. Another coincidence is; you know my wife from your days at Smallwood Elementary School and the Presbyterian Church you used to attend."

"Really?" George was really shocked. "What's her name?"

"You would know her as Mary Ann Chester."

"If my memory serves me right, she was a good looking high yellar lady," George said, smiling.

"Your memory serves you right." Bill replied. "That's my lady"

Rosa came outside and yelled, "All right, everyone. Come back in and finish your breakfast. George, I can put some pancakes on for you if you want me to."

"I'd like that. Bill, after we eat, I'll show you around the place," George said.

For the first time in weeks, Rosa heard life and enthusiasm in her husband's voice.

After eating, the two men disappeared outside and didn't return for several hours. When they did, they found their way to the seldom-used living room. Soon the whole house reverberated with laughter, the likes of which it had never heard before. George came alive. His laughter erupted from his belly, and Bill's came from an equally deep place. The two swapped stories about college and anything else that came to mind. At times their voices dropped to a whisper, then, there would be an explosion of laughter.

Rosa smiled; she couldn't remember when she had last heard her husband so happy. In fact, she realized, she had never heard him laugh that way, ever!. The hours seemed to slip by quickly, and she was delighted, grateful that Mr. Felton had dropped in out of the blue. She stuck her head into the living room, "Excuse me. Mr. Felton, I hope you're planning on staying the day and for dinner, I'm going to make fried chicken with fix'ns."

"Well, Mrs. Read…I don't mind if I doooo."

"Good, I'm so glad you can join us." She went to the kitchen and began preparing the food: chicken, gravy, biscuits, mashed potatoes, succotash and beet greens. The boys set the table, peeled the potatoes and washed the pots and pans as she prepared the meal. When the meal was prepared, she had John call the men to dinner. Then he passed one of the two platters of crispy golden brown chicken to his guest.

After everyone had piled their plates high with food, he continued his reminiscenses with Mr. Felton. George said between bites, "I remember this boy, we called him 'The Beast,' and he played opposite me when we had scrimmage. Now, I was playing center, well, every time I snapped the ball, he would bring his knee up and slam it right into my face. If he didn't knee me, he would throw a hand full of dirt into my eyes. Each time I'd say 'Stop playing dirty!' he would put on his innocent look and say, 'I don't know what you're talking about, boy.' I never did understand why, but, he was harder on me than anyone I ever played against in a real game. I'll tell you one thing. Every time I left the field I'd have a bad headache from those knee shots he landed to my head."

"Mr. Felton, did you play football?" John asked.

"Yes, yes I did John. In fact…"

"Mr. Felton, would you like some more chicken?" Rosa interrupted.

"Well, Mrs. Reeeed, I don't mind if I doooooo."

His response brought smiles to everyone's face.

She filled another platter and handed it to her guest. After helping himself, he exclaimed, "Mmmmmmmmm, Mrs. Reeeeed, this is some mighty fine chickeeeennn!"

Rosa smiled, "I'm glad you're enjoying it Mr. Felton." She thought he was a delightful man, and was thrilled that he had managed to reach her husband in ways she hadn't been able to. She savored every outburst of laughter she heard. "I'm sorry, Mr. Felton, I interrupted your answer to John."

"Oh, that's all right; but to answer your question, John. Yes, I played in the backfield. I knew your dad was taking a beating on the line, so, I decided that wasn't for me. I was a running back. If you were fast, and I was pretty fast…I could get away from big guys like the beast most of the time. Anyway, I had another reason. As far as I was concerned, nobody appreciated what the line guys were doing. They looked like a pile of men beating up on each other. I felt there was no glory in that." He looked at George and laughed. "All of the eyes in the stands would be on the guy running with the ball, and that was for me. I got the glory while your dad got a beating. You see, in life we have choices. That was mine, and that was your dad's."

"Yeah." George fired back, "Sometimes in life, someone has to do the dirty work while others can get the glory. That's how it was with football. Somebody had to take the lumps so others could shine," George teased.

"That's right, boys. We can't all be stars. We need the guys on the line, someone to do the grunt work. What your dad says is true. But, it's a choice we make when we play a game, and in real life too, boys. You have choices, and you have to make decisions when you grow up. It's all part of becoming a man."

The boys were fascinated with Mr. Felton. They liked the way he talked, and he made them see things in a different way. They loved his laugh, the way he moved when he walked, but most of all they loved his laughter.

John asked, "Mr. Felton, one day, would you show me how to play football?"

George Junior spoke up. "And my brother Bill, and me? Would you show us, too?"

"Sure, I'd be glad to show you what I know. But there's one thing you must promise me, boys." His face became serious as he waited for their response.

"Yes sir, we'll promise." Now they were nervous because they had no idea what they were promising.

"I want you boys to call me, Uncle Bill. That is if your mom and dad don't object."

"Can we Mom? Can we Dad? The boys pleaded.

"I think that's a fine idea." George beamed, as Rosa nodded.

The children clapped their hands and shouted, "Yeah, we have a new uncle!"

Rosa smiled, "Thank you Mr. Felton. That's very nice of you."

"Now, I have a favor to ask of you, Mrs. Read."

"You do? What is it?" She asked, looking surprised.

"Would you please call me Bill?"

"Oh. All right, I will if you call me Rosa."

"Consider it done." Bill said smiling. He pushed his chair back from the table, got up and hugged her, and then shook each boy's hand.

The boys hadn't ever been happier than they were at this very moment. They were energized and felt alive. Uncle Bill was a breath of fresh air and had made them happy in a way they hadn't ever been before. Now they wanted to live up to their pledge to be more helpful to their mom. With a look from their older brother, they jumped up and began cleaning off the table, doing the dishes and cleaning up. John grabbed a broom and began sweeping the floor. Bill Felton watched them in quiet amazement.

"Why don't you men retire to the living room? I'm going to serve coffee, and apple pie." Rosa offered.

"Are you and the children going to join us?" Mr. Felton asked.

"Oh, you don't want us in there. I'm sure you men have lots more catching up to do."

"Oh yes, we do have lots more to catch up on. But Bill's working at Smallwood Elementary, so we'll have plenty of opportunities to visit in the future. I think it would be good if you and the children join us."

Rosa was shocked and pleasantly surprised at her husband's response. "All right, then. I know it will please the boys to no end, won't it boys?"

"Oh. Yeah! We'd like that," John replied, as the others beamed. "We'll be finished in no time." Bill volunteered.

"Then we'll see you in the living room shortly," Uncle Bill replied as the two men left the kitchen.

The prospect of sitting with the men provided an extra impetus for the boys to work even faster. Each one had a role and they worked well as a team: one washed, one dried and one put the dishes away. As soon as they finished, Rosa asked them to carry the dishes with the slices of pie to the living room. She brought in the coffee, cream, silverware and cups on a tray. The boys took seats on the floor and ate as the men enjoyed theirs in the comfort of the two large easy chairs.

Between bites of pie, Bill Felton asked, "George, do you remember the barrel at school?"

"You bet I do. My scholarship didn't allow me any extra money for clothing. But I could never bring myself to go to the barrel for shoes, or clothes. For some reason, I couldn't. Something wouldn't let me do that. Not that there was anything wrong with the clothes. It was just the idea of taking charity, I suppose. Did you use it?"

"No, I didn't, but not for the same reason. My parents were able to send me money and clothes, if and when I needed help."

"I didn't know you came from money Bill." George teased.

"I didn't, but my folks were very good to me, and I'm grateful for all the sacrifices they made to keep me in school, and able to send money enough so I could dress decently. I know they did without to provide for me. If you didn't go to the barrel, and you didn't have money, how was it that you always dressed decently?"

"Do you remember that African boy, Felix Obeoine, from Nigeria? We were roommates. I was kidding you about coming from money, but he did. His parents were well off. One winter he noticed I had holes in my shoes and was wearing a raggedy old sweater. He also knew I wouldn't go to the barrel. Well, what he did was very clever."

"How do you mean?" Bill asked.

"Well, what he did after he found out my shoe size…he would buy a pair of shoes, then he'd look all innocent, and he'd tell me they were too tight. Then, he'd ask me to do him a favor and break them in for him. Of course he never asked for them back. The boy never wanted me to think he was feeling sorry for me. But, I'll tell you, Felix would always find a way of giving me something without ever making me feel I was receiving charity. One winter, and it was a cold one, and I needed a sweater. I was really freezing my you know what off. Obviously, Felix noticed. Well, he told me his folks had sent him a sweater, but it made him itch. In fact, he said I'd be doing him a favor, if I would take it off his hands. That was the kind of guy he was."

"You had a true friend George. I'd say he was one good guy." As he spoke, Uncle Bill's eyes searched the faces of the boys, aware they had been listening to their every word. "Well, boys, I think you've heard enough from us. Why don't you tell me what's happened to you fellows that's exciting?"

The boys were surprised. No adult man had ever included them in conversation in quite this way; in a formal grown up setting like this. They looked at each other, then to their parents for guidance, not knowing if it would be proper for them to speak.

Rosa recognized their quandary, "Go ahead boys, tell Uncle Bill about your life here, or anything else you want to talk about."

John, the talker of the brothers volunteered, "Can I tell Uncle Bill about me and the rooster?" Everyone in the family knew the story, and burst out laughing at the mere mention of the incident.

Uncle Bill looked surprised. "Well, judging by that reaction, it must be a good one."

"Oh, it is." Rosa said chuckling.

Uncle Bill leaned forward, "I can't wait to hear it, son."

Never shy, and loving the sound of his voice, John began, "When I was really little, I couldn't unbutton my pants in the back when I had to 'go'. Mom would unbutton me, then, I would go to the outhouse with the flap down and my bottom showing. I was in the White House, which is what we called it, and I left the door open, when this big ol' rooster started crowing. He went 'cock-a-doodle-doo!' Well, every time he would do that, you know, 'cock-a-doodle-do', I would say, 'shuuuuuut uuuuup!"

Rosa interrupted, "John's shut ups had the same tonal quality as the rooster's cock-a-doodle-do's; therefore, the rooster took his calls as a challenge. I'm sorry to have interrupted son, I just wanted Uncle Bill to understand how the rooster interpreted your calls."

"That's all right. Anyway, I guess he did think I was making fun of him. Because he'd cock-a-doodle-do and I would call back, shuuuuuut uuuup! This calling back and forth went on for a long time. I guess I was making him pretty mad, because he came down from where ever he was, then, he stood on this little hill above the white house. That way he could see me sitting, because I always left the door open. I guess he wanted to make sure of where the shut-ups were coming from. When he crowed, and I answered back, he'd sort'a cock his head. Anyway, after he crowed a couple of more times and I answered back, he'd puff up and start scratching, and walking in circles, but I didn't pay him any attention."

"Boy, it sounds like you were playing with fire." Uncle Bill interjected.

"Yeah, I guess I was, because when I got up from my seat and left the outhouse and started walking towards the kitchen, that ol' rooster, charged towards me. I saw him coming out of the corner of my eye. He was coming at me full speed, half running, half flopping his wings and hopping up and down as he came. He looked big when I first saw him on the hill, but now that he was close to me... he looked twice as big!"

Uncle Bill's eyes twinkled, "Seems like to me, you were in big trouble, my boy."

"Yeah, I was, and I was really scared."

"So, then what happened?" Uncle Bill prompted, caught up in the boy's excitement.

"Being up high, you know up on that hill, it must have helped him go faster, because he was on me like lightening!" John exclaimed, his eyes growing wider as he relived the moment. "I started running, but he kept up with me. In fact, every time I took a step, he would jump and scratch my backsides with his claws. Mom heard me screaming, so she came out, saw what was happening and chased him away with a broom. But he scratched me bloody. Mom had a hard time cleaning my back sides from all the claw marks, and I was so sore, I couldn't sit down for a week." The boy looked exhausted from recounting the traumatic event.

His brother's laughed as they remembered how funny he looked when he came tearing towards the house and the rooster hot on his tail, then how it was afterwards when he tried to sit down. Uncle Bill grinned, "That's quite a story young man."

"I'm not through, Uncle Bill, there's more." John interjected.

"Oh, I'm sorry. I thought that was the end of your story."

"No. There's just a little bit more, then, I'm finished." John said solemnly. "The next day when I had to go to the White House, as soon as I stepped out on the porch, that big ol' rooster ran down from the hill, all the way to the house and stood below the porch glaring at me. He puffed himself up and scratched the ground, daring me to step off the porch. Well, I was afraid to get off the porch, so I had to call mom to walk me there. She walked me all the way after shooing him away, then, she had to wait outside and walk me back to the house. After a few days of that, Mom decided enough, was enough, and the ol' rooster ended up in the pot."

George had a big smile and a look of pride after John concluded his story, then added, "That's some story isn't it Bill?"

"Yes. Yes. It's quite a story. And, I must say, young man, you told it very well."

"Thanks," John said modestly.

"He gets that talent from his mother. Rosa is quite a story teller..

"Is that true Rosa?" Bill Felton asked with enthusiasm.

"I've told a story or two in my day," Rosa replied with a smile.

"Would you do me the honor of telling one of your stories?" Uncle Bill urged.

"I could, but George and the boys have heard my stories a million times."

George cleared his throat, "I think I speak for the boys, and I can assure you that we would love to hear any one of your stories. We don't tire of hearing them…right boys?"

"That's right Mom, tell the Laziest Man in Town story." Bill urged. Yeah, tell that one Mom, his brothers echoed.

"Really, that's the one you want me to tell?"

"That's the one we want to hear, Mom." George urged.

"All right then, that' the one I'll tell."

"Here Rosa, sit in the easy chair." George stood and gave her his seat, then settled back on the couch next to his college roommate. The boys sat on the floor, facing their mother.

She took the offered seat, cleared her throat, then she began. "The story starts in the rugged hills of Tennessee. So long ago, the Model T Ford hadn't even been invented yet. Now, living up in those hills was a man by the name of Will Jameson. Will and Molly, his wife owned a shack in the small mountain town of Whoa Mattie Haw. Ol' Will as he was known by local folks, was said to be the laziest man in town. He got this reputation because as far back as anyone could remember, and that was pretty far back, Ol' Will never, ever, did a lick of work in his life. Least wise, according to the men folk who would get together, chew the fat and keep each other abreast of the latest goings on in town. No sir, not a one could remember Will ever pop'n a sweat from do'n a minutes worth of work. And they knew for durn sure, he had never ever held a pay'n job. Nope, Ol' Will had been content to just sit all day in his rocking chair on his rickety front porch and just watch the world go by.

All of the other husbands and men folk in town, they found work, planted crops and shot game to provide for their families. But not Ol' Will."

And she continued to tell the story in detail, imbelleshing it as well as her dad had years before.

"What a great story, Rosa. I can see using it in my classes." Bill Felton said.

"Thanks, Rosa. That was well done." George said proudly.

"Well, thanks. But the credit goes to my father. He was a true, old time story teller, I just happened to have a good retentive memory. I was the oldest child and he would tell us children stories all the time. Then at night, when we would go to bed, I would repeat them to my younger siblings. "They were my practice audience, and I just loved to repeat his stories."

Bill Felton stood. "Well, George, Rosa, boys…I can't remember having a more enjoyable day than I've had today." Turning to his college pal, he said "Piggy, you are truly a fortunate man. You have a lovely wife and family. You are truly blessed, I hope you know that. And I thank you for allowing me to share them today."

George stood, and the two men embraced for several moments. Then, they each stepped back and playfully threw punches. Bill abruptly turned and walked outside, everyone followed him. He stood by his car as each boy walked up to him and shook his hand. He went to Rosa and gave her a hug, and kiss on her cheeks. "Rosa, it's been a real pleasure, I can't wait for you to meet my better half."

"I look forward to that too, Bill."

He opened the car door, put his foot on the running board of his Buick, swung himself in, started the engine, and in a flash, was bouncing down the road in a cloud of dust.

As they watched the disappearing car, Rosa looked over at her husband and saw something she hadn't seen since his Mother's passing. Once again, there was a spark in his eyes. The rich timbre in his voice had returned. And, he had a spring in his walk.

That night Rosa laid alongside George, watching him sleep. She had her husband back. She thought, "God does work in mysterious ways." She also knew she would be eternally grateful to Bill Felton for returning the man she thought was lost to her, and her boys.

The brothers gathered in John's room before they said their good nights to each other. After a brief discussion among themselves, they all agreed Uncle Bill was a special person, and they were glad he had come into their lives.

CHAPTER 14

The Witch's Broom

Rosa happened past the window and saw Sara coming down the walkway carrying something. She opened the door and waited for her neighbor to come up the steps.

"What have you got there?" Rosa asked with a smile.

"You'll see." Sara replied, as she placed a pie on the table.

"Oh, that looks good." Rosa exclaimed.

"It's shoo fly pie, Missus. I brought a pie over for you and your family," the little lady said with a pleased expression.

"Thank you so much. Shall I cut you a slice now? It would go well with the coffee I have brewing on the stove," Rosa offered.

"No, no. I made two pies. You, the Mister, and the boys enjoy this one, I'll have some tonight with Al. But I will have coffee if it's done."

Rosa went to the stove, "It's ready," she announced, then picked up the gray enamel coffee pot, filled two cups and brought them to the kitchen table.

Sara blew on the coffee she was handed, then carefully put the hot beverage to her lips and sipped it cautiously. "Missus, it just ain't the same, is it?" She said with a sad expression, remembering their weekly sharing of coffee and cake with Mother Mary.

"You're so right, Mrs. Gross. Before you came over, I sat out three cups and saucers, thinking she was still here and would be joining us."

Sara nodded, then, asked, "Your Mister, how is he? Some better? I know he didn't seem himself when I was here the last few times…he seemed to be grieving still."

Rosa looked at her neighbor thoughtfully, then, replied, "Mrs. Gross, you are so right. There was a time when he wasn't all right. He had lost his spirit. Now, I think he'll be fine."

"I know he was close to his mother, so now you think he will be all right?" Sara asked, looking for further assurance.

"Yes, yes I do. Thanks to seeing an old friend of his who came for a surprise visit. I think it's safe to say he's over the worst of his sorrow. I think he'll be back to his old self very soon."

"Missus, I'm so glad to hear that. I know I could see a difference in his eyes there for a while. He didn't seem to be with us in his mind. His body was here…but not his spirit, it was gone."

"You're very observant, Mrs. Gross. Nothing gets past those sharp country eyes of yours," she teased.

"What you said about your Mister getting better, that makes my heart feel warm."

"Oh, Sara. What a nice thing to say."

"Well, it does onc't, and I know Al will feel the same when I tell him the good news about your Mister."

"Thanks for your kind thoughts. You know God blessed us when he gave us you and Mr. Gross for neighbors."

"Arch, Missus. He blessed us, too when He put yuz folks next to us…that's fer sure."

“Thanks for being you, Sara. You always brighten my day.” Rosa reached across the table and took her neighbor’s hands. They sat for several minutes in silent prayer.

Finally, Sara removed her hand and stood. “Well, Missus I can’t stay longer. I have a heifer that’s due anytime now, so I bes’ get back and see how she is. We likes to be there when they drop the calf. Al’s better at help’n than me, but I still likes to be there, you know, to help and do what I can.” She took her cup and saucer to the dish pan, then placed them in the sudsy water.

“Oh, I understand. I think that’s wise. You never know when the poor creatures might need extra help. By the way, after you leave here, I’ll be running to the Fink farm to return a tool, then I expect to come right back.
The ladies hugged and said good bye.

As Sara approached the barn, she could hear the heifer’s moan. From her past experience she recognized it as a distress call. She didn’t want to panic, but knew she wasn’t capable of helping the poor thing by herself. She thought, ‘Oh, God, why is Al up in the woods today, of all days?’ For a brief moment she was tempted to go up in the woods and try to locate him, but she realized that could be just a waste of time. The woods were vast, and she could spend hours looking, then not ever find him. So, she ruled that out. It came to her that she was in a real ‘fix’.

Opening the barn door, she peered in. The heifer was down; a sure sign the impending birth was not going well. Pain and alarm showed in the animal’s eyes. Sara wanted to remain calm, but panic began settling in. She decided since she couldn’t reach Al, the next best thing would be to call the animal doctor. Yes, that would be the best thing to do. Then she remembered the Missus was going to the Fink Farm. If she hurried, she could get a ride to the Fetrows, and ring up the doctor.

As she closed the barn door, the animal let out a long mournful moan. She hiked up her dress and started running towards Twin Cedars. As she approached the house, her heart sank. She could see the Missus's car going down the road in a cloud of dust. She felt an overwhelming sense of despair as she watched the car disappear. "If only I had made up my mind sooner, I would have caught the Missus. Ach, such bad luck!" She knew she had to do whatever it took to get help for the poor creature. With the sound of the suffering animal fresh in her ear, she started running toward the Fetrow farm, a mile down the road.

She arrived at their lane out of breath, but she was determined to continue on to the big stone and frame farm house. Her breath came in short gasps; she was on the verge of collapse as she climbed the arbor steps. She walked the few paces to the house, then, leaned against the door for support before calling, "Hello! Hello! Is anyone home?" Her voice was weak, barely audible. She pressed her face against the glass portion of the door allowing her to see in. To her surprise, she could see the window shades were drawn tight. The kitchen was in virtual darkness. "Maybe they've gone to town." she thought. But she had to be sure, so she began knocking, and calling their names. "Mom! Cora! Mable! Minnie! Eddie! My heifer is due… something is wrong with her; I need to call the animal doctor! I need to use your phone!"

A voice from the other side of the door answered, "The door is open, come in onc't."

Sara was surprised. The voice seemed to come from just on the other side of the door, yet when she peeked in she didn't see anyone. Obeying, she opened it. The opened door allowed more light into the darkened room. Now she could see Mom Fetrow standing just inside, and to the left of the door. Then she could see the three daughters sitting around the table at the darkest end of the kitchen. Only Eddie Junior was missing. "Why are they all sitting in the dark, in the middle of the day?" Sara wondered. Under normal circumstances she would have asked. But at the moment, her focus was on reaching the doctor,. She didn't have time to give their odd behavior a second thought. As she stepped into the room her eyes went to the broom lying in her path. Instinctively she bent to pick it up.

A sweet voice said, "Just leave it lay, step over it, and come on in onc't." It was Mabel, the youngest sister who spoke.

"Ach, it's nothing, I'll just lean it against the door." A broom shouldn't be out where someone might trip over it, she reasoned, as she placed the broom against the door frame.

Cora screamed, "IT'S HER! IT'S HER! SHE'S THE WITCH!"

Mom yelled, "The pow wow doctor said the one who wouldn't step over the broom is the witch! The witch who made my Mister take sick and die. The one who made our animals get the sickness!" Mom was referring to the recent death of her husband, and the rash of illnesses and deaths among their animals.

The sisters sprang to their feet and charged Sara. They began cursing, striking and shoving their startled visitor. Minnie, the smallest of the three swung an open hand that caught Sara flush on the face. Cora, short and rotund, built square like her mother and weighing two hundred pounds, pushed Sara with such force, she fell backwards through the open door and onto the arbor's stone walk. Sara frantically crawled down the steps on her hands and knees. As she crawled away, Mable grabbed a nearby stick and began striking her on the back.

Sara was terrified, in a state of disbelief. These were her childhood friends, her former school mates. How could this be happening? Lying on the ground, she looked up at her tormentors and pleaded. "Mable, Minnie, Cora... what are you doing? It's me, Sara, your friend, why are you calling me a witch? I'm not a witch!"

Her plea fell on deft ears. The sisters and Mom were in a frenzied state. Their faces red and contorted with hate, their eyes blinded by rage, they didn't see Sara; they saw an evil thing that had to be destroyed. They kicked and pummeled her with unbridled fury. Scrambling to her feet, she began running down the lane, the sisters in pursuit, screaming, "WITCH! WITCH! YOU'RE THE WITCH!" The sisters picked up stones and hurled them at the fleeing woman. Some found their mark, striking her back and shoulders before she reached the main road at the foot of Fetrows hill. The hill was steep, probably a forty five degree grade. Sara's fear gave her the strength and endurance to struggle up it as her tormentors fell further and further behind. As she trudged on, she tried to get her bearings. This nightmare was too much for her to comprehend. Her face was flushed, her back and shoulders hurt. But the worst pain was in her broken heart. She continued on up the steep grade in pain, moaning and sobbing.

George Junior was working in the long laying house when he happened to glance out of one of the windows. He saw someone coming down the road. He didn't recognize the person, but he could see that there was something wrong with whoever it was. It was a woman running, walking, stumbling. He knew whoever it was, was in bad trouble. As he looked closer, he realized there was something familiar about the staggering figure. "Oh. My God!" George Junior exclaimed. "It's Mrs. Gross!" He dashed outside in search of his mother. "Mom! Mom! Something's wrong with Aunt Sara…with Mrs. Gross! She's down the road; I think she's in trouble."

Rosa burst out of the brooder house door. "George, what's wrong? What are you saying about Mrs. Gross?"

"There's something wrong with Mrs. Gross. Come, you'll see!" From where they stood, the barn blocked their view of the road. George led his mother down toward the long laying house. "See, see!" He pointed. "She's coming down the road…there's something wrong with her. Mom, I think she's hurt."

"You're right, son. She looks like she's ready to collapse. Let's go help her!"

As they ran down the road, it was obvious Sara was near exhaustion. She stumbled forward a few more steps, then collapsed into Rosa's outstretched arms. She could hardly speak, "They say I'm a witch! They hit me. They called me bad names. Missus, I ain't no witch! Tell them that I ain't no witch." She pleaded in a hoarse whisper.

"Who said that? Who said those awful things to you?" Rosa asked, horrified at what she heard.

"They said I made their Mister die and their animals sick."

"Who said that, Sara? Who said those things to you?" Rosa persisted.

"The Fetrows; the Fetrow girls…and Mom Fetrow, she said it too. They all said I was a witch because I picked up a broom that was lay'n on the floor. They pushed me out of the house…they beat me with sticks. They hit me with stones. Why did they do that? I ain't no witch."

"Oh, Sara, I'm so sorry for what they did to you." Rosa said tenderly. Sara didn't hear her comforting words; she had fainted in her arms. "Here George, take her feet, I'll carry her under her arms. Let's get her to bed." They picked up her small, limp body, and carried her from the road up the steep incline to the house. Rosa said, "Let's put her on the living room couch." She took the patchwork quilt that covered its back and spread it over her, then tucked it tightly under her shoulders.

John and Bill, working in the laying house had seen their mom and brother carrying Mrs. Gross to the house. They dropped their work tools and ran to the kitchen to find them. Not seeing them, they continued on to the living room, breathing hard and curious to know what had happened to Mrs. Gross. They were stunned to see her lying on the couch.

"What's wrong with Aunt Sara?" Bill asked.

"Hush! I'll explain later." Rosa answered curtly. "John, go get a wash pan. Fill it with cool water. Bill, you know where the wash cloths are. Bring me one." The boys quickly complied with their mother's orders. Rosa began humming softly as she placed the damp cloth on her friend's bruised and swollen face. The boys stood by, watching quietly.

Sara's tiny body seemed even smaller as she lay on the couch. She made whimpering sounds as she drifted in and out of sleep. Rosa stroked her head until she was comforted enough to stop moaning and fall into a deep sleep." Boys, stay with her. I'm going to make some soup. Call me if she wakes up." Rosa hurried off to the kitchen as the two boys took up the vigil in nearby chairs.

They watched her every move, her every breath for over an hour. They were frightened for their Aunt Sara, and felt helpless, wanting desperately to somehow make her feel better. Finally, she stirred and her eyes began to flutter. Then she tried to push herself up. The cover was tucked so tightly around her, she couldn't get up.

"Where am I?" She murmured, as her eyes searched the room.

"Mom! Mom! Aunt Sara is waking up." John yelled excitedly.

"I'll be right there. Tell her not to get up." Rosa answered. She filled a bowl with soup and hurried to the living room. Sara began struggling again to get up just as Rosa sat on the edge of the couch next to her. She handed the bowl of soup to George. "Sara, I'll help you up. You're safe now; you're with us. Just try and relax." She loosened the covers from around her shoulders, helped her up, and placed a pillow behind her back so she could sit up.

"Oh. My. What time is it, Missus? Al will be looking for me." She asked with panic in her weak voice, all the while still struggling to get up and off the couch.

"Shh. Shh. You need some nourishment first. Don't you worry. We'll get you home to Al soon. Now open your mouth," Rosa ordered as she gently push her back against the pillow.

Like a small child, she relaxed and took several spoons full of soup. The warm broth calmed her. After swallowing sever spoons full, Sara shook her head at the next offering.

Realizing that Sara needed more rest, Rosa pulled the covers back up over her, all the while suggesting she lie back down. Reluctantly she did. In a few minutes, Sara was sound asleep. After several hours, she woke up. "Oh. My! What time is it onc't? Al will be looking for me, I bes' be go'n home." She tugged at the covers, managing to pull them off, while pushing herself up to a sitting position.

Turning to Bill, Rosa said, “Get your baby brother.” Offering her hand to Sara, she said, “We’ll take you home, Mrs. Gross.” She helped her neighbor to get up on her feet, but noticed she was unsteady when she stood. “George, help me, we had better hold on to her.” They put their arms around her tiny waist, and walked her out of the house, through the field and to her home. Carrying his baby brother, Bill brought up the rear, while John trudged closely behind his mother and George Junior.

Trying to be discreet, John whispered. “Mom, what is wrong with Aunt Sara?”

“Not now, John!” She answered sharply. “I’ll explain everything, but not now! Do you understand?”

“Yes. Mom.” He replied sheepishly.

“You and Bill, look after your little brother.”

They entered Sara's kitchen and released their hold. “Are you all right?” Rosa asked her neighbor. Sara stood still, looking helpless, and lost. Rosa realized she was still not functioning properly. “I think you should go to bed, Mrs. Gross.” Rosa took her arm, then, led her upstairs. Sara offered no resistance and allowed Rosa to lead her up the steps and to bed.

Rosa helped her undress and prepare for bed. As she did, Sara continued to express her anguish. “Missus, I ain’t no witch. You tell them that. They don’t listen to me.” She pleaded, reliving her ordeal with the Fetrow women.

“Shhh, shhh, you don’t worry your head about such nonsense.” Rosa responded softly. “We love you, and we don’t want you to listen to that kind of talk. They believe in superstitions, and that’s all it is, superstition!”

As Sara stood bewildered in her own bedroom, Rosa poured water from the bedroom pitcher into the wash basin, then wet a cloth and gently wiped the welts on her back. Afterwards, she sponged her body, then helped her slip into her night gown, and into bed. Rosa tucked her in, then, hummed quietly to Sara, who promptly fell asleep.

Downstairs, the boys sat on the wooden box, waiting for their mother to return. They were startled when they heard someone stomping on the back porch. "Mister, I mean, Uncle Al must be home." George said.

When he entered the kitchen, Al's face showed a mixture of surprise and joy at seeing the boys. Before he could speak, John announced, "Aunt Sara's in bed."

"In bed! the die heinger!" Why is she in bed?" He roared.

John flinched at his outburst. He wasn't expecting such a strong response to his announcement.

Rosa heard the exchange as she entered the room. "John! That will be enough!" Turning to Al, she said, "Mr. Gross, have a seat, I've got something to tell you."

As he looked at Rosa, wrinkles formed on his brow. He knew something was wrong, but complied with her command. He sat down in his rocker, then leaned forward and spit into his spittoon. His eyes sought Rosa's, as he tried to determine what news his neighbor had to tell him.

"Mr. Gross." Rosa began softly. "Sara had a terrible thing happen to her today. She went to the Fetrows to call the animal doctor for the heifer that was due."

Al interrupted, "I should'a stayed home today, I ought not have gone to the woods," he said, berating himself. Then, he added, "I looked at the heifer before I left, and she didn't look right then. I jes' went to the barn now; an' they's both dead. Yah, I should'a stayed home.

Maybe I could'a helped the heifer," he lamented, not grasping the meaning of Rosa's statement.

"Mr. Gross, what I want to tell you is not about the heifer. It's about what happened to Sara at the Fetrows."

Al looked puzzled. "Something happened to Sara? What happened! I thought she was put out because she saw the animals is both dead, an' went to bed."

"No. She....we didn't know about the animals being dead. No, that's not what I want to tell you. It's what happened to her when she went to the Fetrows to use their phone." Finding the dead animal had upset him, and he couldn't focus on what Rosa was telling him. She continued, "The Fetrows had put a broom on the floor, and she picked it up. They said a witch couldn't step over a broom. So, when she picked it up, they said she was the witch and chased her home. Mom Fetrow and the girls accused her of causing Mr. Fetrow's death and the sickness of their animals."

Al was stunned. He jumped up, his mouth hung hanging open as he stared at Rosa.

"Mr. Gross, they beat her, they cursed her, and they stoned her as they chased her up the road. That's why she's in bed. She's in a bad way. They hurt her body badly, but more importantly, they've hurt her spirit."

Al had heard enough. He ran upstairs, stopped at the bedroom door, and looked in. His wife lay in bed, her eyes wide open. He asked in a loud whisper, "Sara, Sara. Are you hurt bad?" Getting no response he went in and sat on the bed alongside her.

His words didn't seem to register with her, as her mind seemed to be in some faraway place. Finally, she responded, "They said I was a witch. Tell them I ain't no witch." Her eyes didn't focus, and her voice and face were expressionless.

Al looked at his wife intently. He could tell she had been wounded deeply, and he became frightened for her… and for himself. "Now listen here Sara, we never put no stock in that pow-wowing business. Don't you take to heart what they said; they is ignorant. That's what." He reached out and touched her bruised face. "Now, you bes' try and get some rest." His voice was gentle as he rose to leave. He couldn't stop the tears from streaming down his weather-beaten face.

He wiped his eyes before he entered the kitchen but he couldn't control the tremor in his voice. He shook his head, blew his nose, then, in a hoarse voice said, "Missus, she's in real bad shape. I ain't never seed her like this before. How could they do that to her? They wuz her school mates; they grew up together." His eyes searched Rosa's for answers.

"I don't know. I don't know how anyone could do what they did to her." Rosa said sadly.

"They wuz her best friends, Missus; they grew up together...ach', this will take a toll on her, I know that fur sure. She is tough, but she has a frail side to her. This will take time to heal."

Rosa went to him and hugged him tightly. "Mr. Gross, we will see her though this," she said softly.

A few days later, George came home. He hadn't gotten out of his coat before Rosa began explaining what had happened to Sara. "The sad part is I missed her by seconds when she came looking for me. I had just left with the boys to return the crimping tool Mr. Fink had loaned you. We just dropped it off, then, came right back home. It must have been a matter of minutes that we missed her when she went in to the Fetrow lane, and when they chased her back. I feel so badly about that. It might have been different if I had taken her there."

George made no comment, instead asked in concern, "How is she?"

"Not good. Not good at all. The gossip is already out that Sara Gross is a witch."

George shook his head slowly, "Oh, that's terrible, just terrible."

"George, do you know only a few days before Sara went down, I had stopped by the Fetrows to use their phone, and guess what? There was a broom on the floor then. I started to pick it up…but one of the girls said, 'just leave it lay'… and so I did. I took heed and stepped over it. God knows, I had no idea what the consequences would have been had I picked it up."

"That's really a scary thought," George replied, "A very scary thought."

"I had a funny feeling when I got there that day. They were all sitting in the dark in the middle of the day. It all seemed so eerie. I bet the pow-wow doctor had told them to just sit there and wait until someone came who wouldn't step over the broom, and that person was the witch causing the sickness.

"Thank the Lord you didn't pick it up. Can you imagine what could have happened if you did?" George said. Then, he added, "That was a close call for you, Rosa."

"Not only that, I'm thankful for Sara that their brother Eddie wasn't there when they attacked her. He was home the day I went. Lord, he's so strong that had he been there, he might have killed her."

"This whole thing is hard to believe. I have to wonder how it's all going to end?"

Rosa added, "As I started to tell you before, George, in a matter of days, the gossip had spread about her. They're saying things like, "Don't look her in the eyes, she'll cast a spell on you." And they're spreading the notion that she was the cause of Mr. Fetrow's death. They're telling people she can turn their children into witches or make them go blind. My Lord, George, where will this end?"

The boys were all ears. Finally Bill asked, "Will she get better?"

Before Rosa could answer, John interjected, "I'll bet no kids will come near her." Then she added as an afterthought, "I feel sorry for her and Uncle Al."

"Boys, the sad part about the whole thing is, anyone who believes in witchcraft and has a sickness or a misfortune on their farm, they will automatically blame Mrs. Gross. And there are lots of people around here who believe in it strongly. So, I think things might turn bad for her." Rosa was concerned.

George listened solemnly, then, spoke. "Rosa. Boys, listen to me. The Grosses stood by us when the Klan burned that cross against us, and we are going to do the same thing for them. They're going to need our support and help if things get bad for them, and I think things will get worse. Right now, I don't know what we'll be able to do, but whatever is needed, we will do it. Is that understood?"

Rosa nodded, and the boys answered, "Yes, sir."

That evening, George went to see Al. He found him standing on his porch. "Mr. Gross," George began, "I can only guess how hard it's going to be for you and Mrs.

Gross along through here, but, I want you to know you can count on me, my wife and my boys for anything you and your Missus might need." Al started to speak, but George held his hand up and continued, "We're here for you, just as you were for us when the Klan burned that cross when we moved here."

Al didn't reply, he placed his hands on George's shoulders, squeezed them tightly as tears formed in his eyes. He turned away and went back inside the house.

It wasn't long before the tormenting began. It started the night Al was awakened by the barking of his dogs and the sound of a slowing car. He looked out the window, but the car continued on down the road. In the morning he found a dead black cat upon their porch, and the next night a beheaded chicken on their front yard. With Sara confining herself to the bed, Al disposed of them without her knowledge.of the nasty event. One night, Al got up with his gun because he heard a car stop and the dogs barking become intense. The car had roared off by the time he stepped outside. But the bright moon light quickly revealed the devilment they were up to. On their side of the fence, he saw a dead calf hanging on their front gate. Once the ugliness started, he got up early every day to get rid of any dead animal that had been left during the night. Al knew Sara had enough to overcome without seeing the disgusting behavior of some of her so-called friends, neighbors, and total strangers.

He had been able to shield her from the physical ugliness that was left behind; however, the nights brought out vulgarity he couldn't protect her from. When the dogs barked, he would pull her close, making her feel safe in his arms. Eventually a bunch of zealots took up the cause.

They'd stop out front, then, shout vulgar and hurtful words, "Sara Gross is a witch. Burn the Witch. Kill The Witch." Al tried to protect her from the clamor by keeping her close to his chest and pulling the covers over her head. But the wetness on his chest, and her shuddering body made him realize his efforts were in vain.

Al never mentioned the death of the heifer and its calf to Sara. But she had found out on her own when one day she felt well enough to walk outside and look in the barn and saw they were both gone. (Al had dragged them to a remote spot in the woods the very next day). Sara felt a renewed shame when she realized they had both died.

In time, despite her inability to function for Al and attend to his needs, she did (out of guilt for the death of the heifer) begin to care for the other animals. But she did her chores by rote – feeding chickens, gathering the eggs, milking the cow and slopping the pigs. Afterwards, she would disappear in the house and stare at the walls for hours on end. Her cook stove sat cold, forcing both Al and her to survive on the meals Rosa prepared, and delivered each day. Sara picked at the food, but ate very little.

Al saw how despondent his wife had become and was frantic to snap her out of her depressed state. He tried reasoning. "Now Sara, you can't just let these ignorant people get you down. We know who you are, what you stand for. The good folks don't think that way. The Reads don't think that way. It's only the fools who do, and we don't hold no stock for fools." It was a refrain he'd repeat to her daily with deep conviction.

She responded with a sad look and a voice that seemed to come from a faraway place. "I don't know what to do, I'm just so tired."

He realized he wasn't reaching her, but he knew that he had to get her attention and snap her out of whatever was consuming her mind. "Sara!" he'd boom. "We're go'n to hold our heads high and look them all in the eyes; we ain't gonn'a let these fools get us down. Now, you mind me onc't."

Her lack of response crushed him. He felt as if he was talking to a ghost. He just could not reach her and get her to focus on his words.

Her golden hair turned gray, and her infectious laugh was gone. A dull film covered her once sparkling eyes. If she happened to be outside, the sound of an approaching car sent her scurrying inside the house. And her mind couldn't get past the belief she had failed the heifer and her husband. "Why didn't I know where in the woods Al was? Why didn't I leave the broom lay? Why didn't I go see the Missus sooner? Why didn't I? If I had, things would have been different." The thoughts consumed her, repeating themselves over and over in her head.

Al came up from the fields often in order to check on her. Today he entered the kitchen, expecting to see her sitting at the table staring blankly into space. When he didn't see her, his first thought was foul play. "The gol durn dirty bastards!" He yelled. "By God, if they touched my woman, there'll be hell to pay!" He was certain someone had done her harm. He started upstairs to get his shot gun. As he passed through the darkened living room, he heard a low moaning. Looking around he saw her tiny form curled up in a fetal position, off in the far corner of the room. "Sara, Sara! What's wrong?" He pleaded. His words were soft, reassuring, but, she still didn't respond.

He helped her up, then gently led her back to the kitchen and settled her in his rocker. Al had never seen her in such a state. Just then, Rosa knocked. "Mr. Gross, I've brought you and Mrs. Gross some dinner."

"Missus, thank God you're here. I don't think my woman is going to make it. She won't talk, she don't eat, she don't hardly sleep. I don't know what to do." He confessed to his neighbor. "I just now found her all curled up in the living room."

Rosa came in, set the tray of food on the table, then took Sara by the arm and led her upstairs to the bedroom. She tucked her friend in, then, began talking about old times, reminding her of the fun they had had, repeating some of Mother Mary's stories she knew Sara enjoyed hearing. As she spoke, Rosa watched her face to see if anything ignited a spark of interest. But, nothing did. Sara continued to stare with unseeing eyes. Nothing penetrated the wall she had erected, or could reach her mind in the deep well it had fallen into. Rosa held her friend's hands, and gently massaged them as she sang lullabies to calm a mind that was obviously in torment. After several hours, she was able to leave when her friend finally fell asleep.

Descending the stairs, Rosa found Al sitting in his rocker, "Mr. Gross, she seems to be off in a world of her own. I think all we can do is be patient, talk to her, and pray for her recovery."

"She's been hurt bad, Missus. Sara has a tender side, and they has tore it open, that's what they's done. They's hurt her real bad." The shock of her childhood friends branding her a witch, and the nightly harassment had drained Sara of her will to live. Al realized he was losing a friend, lover and helpmate.

Rosa moved toward the door to leave, "Mr. Gross, I'll come over every evening and spend some time with her. I'm sure we'll reach her somehow." And she did, visiting her every day for weeks. Every evening she sat with her friend, fed, bathed and talked about anything, everything and nothing. Rosa's biggest accomplishment turned out to be getting her out of bed and back to the kitchen table again during the day. She reasoned that sitting at the kitchen window, she could see the array of colors the hollyhocks that followed the fence around the house as well as the palette of colors her flower beds presented. Rosa hoped the sheer magnificence of colors might in some way brighten her mood. However, Sara remained depressed and focused on something far away.

Rosa was busy preparing a meal for her family and the Grosses when John and his brothers came home from school and expressed their own concern about their Aunt Sara. John asked, "Mom, can I go over and visit Aunt Sara?"

She looked at her son, realizing this was something he sincerely wanted to do. The earnest expression on his face made her reconsider her first impulse to say'no.' She placed her hands on his shoulders, "John, why not? What harm could it do? You just might be what the doctor ordered. Who knows? Certainly nothing has worked so far, so why not?" she said with a smile.

"Can I go now?" He asked eagerly.

"Can we go, too?" Bill asked quickly; asking for himself and his older brother who had also been listening to the exchange between John and his mother.

"No. I think under the circumstances, we'll let John go alone. Maybe you two can go later. It was his idea, and he should be allowed to pursue it." John took those words as a yes and headed out the door. Rosa promptly called him back. "Now, don't stay more than an hour, and if she seems to get nervous, or upset, you come right home and tell me. Is that understood?"

"Yes, ma am." He quickly escaped out the door and ran across the field as fast as his legs could carry him, stopping at their gate. The dogs barked when he approached, but began licking him and wagging their tails as he unlatched the gate and went to the kitchen door. Looking through the screen door, he could see her sitting at the table, but he knocked anyway. She didn't acknowledge his presence, even though she could see him clearly. "Mrs. Gross, may I come in?" Her head turned slightly toward him, but she didn't reply. "Well, she didn't say no, so I guess I can come in," he rationalized.

Taking a seat opposite hers, he sat quietly for some time.

John wondered what he could talk about and finally decided that since he liked school so much, he would tell her what his day at school was like. He told her about his entire day, hour by hour. Starting at the time he got up in the morning, and ate breakfast. He even told her what food his mother had prepared for him that day. He described his walk to school, what he saw on the way and the conversations he had with some of his friends at school. Then he described in detail what he learned during the day, who the teacher punished, and why. However, Mrs. Gross was still unresponsive.

An hour passed before his mother and brothers appeared with dinner for Mr. Gross, and soup for her, the only thing Sara would swallow. Mr. Gross was pleased to see them all when he came in. Rosa set the food on the table, and told him about John's desire to visit with Sara and hoped it was all right with him.

“Oh, Missus, that’s fine. I worry, she’s alone so much during the day, I gott’a do my work and tend market and all…I can’t…” He apologized.

“Mr. Gross, I understand. You have no reason to explain anything to me. Anyway, John would rather talk than eat, so it’s not a hardship for him.” Her comment provoked laughter from his brothers.

Soon, the days turned into weeks. Every day John brought his school books and read to her from them. Sometimes a problem arose that he couldn’t solve quickly. If that happened, he’d discuss it with her as if she understood what he was attempting to do. After he worked on the problem and solved it, he would act as if she had participated in its solution. Sometimes he would ask her a question, then, pause as if he expected her to give him the answer. Sara’s response continued to be a blank stare. After one particular visit, he told his mother when he returned home that Aunt Sara had smiled when he knocked to come in.

“Maybe, just maybe, she might be coming around, John. You keep it up. I’m sure in her own way she appreciates your company.” Rosa said, encouragingly.

Al enjoyed seeing the boy come on a regular basis, too. Some days he would stand quietly on the porch and listen as he narrated stories, or read to his wife. One afternoon he heard John say, “Aunt Sara. One day my mom said to me,” ‘John, when you come in the house, bring the basket of laundry that’s out on the porch in with you,’ “I don’t know why I said it, but I answered, 'No I won't!' Well, my Mom came flying out of the door. ‘What did you say, young man?’ She yelled. 'You heard me,' I answered, and then I took off running as fast as I could. I jumped off the porch, and ran down the road. Well my

Mom jumped off the porch right behind me. But she got tired, and stopped. So, I stopped, too. Then, I started laughing at her. She said, 'Boy, you come back her and take your lick'n.' I said, "You make me!" Mom said, 'All right young man, I will.' I saw her start picking up rocks 'What are you going to do with those?' I asked. She yelled, 'If you don't start walking back to me boy, you'll see!' I began laughing, and laughing. That's when Mom started running towards me. So, I started running away from her again. I hadn't run far when all of the sudden, rocks started whizzing past my head. They came closer and closer. Then, I remembered; mom had told us kids, when she was young, she could throw rocks as far, and straight, as any boy. Well, she sure told the truth! Cuz, the rocks kept coming closer and closer, and that's when I really got scared. So, I turned around, went back to her, and took my lick'n. And, I've never told my Mom, 'no I won't' ever again," he concluded.

The story over, Al walked in and heard an unfamiliar sound…Sara's laughter. Her shoulders shook, and tears from laughter, filled her eyes.

Rosa came to the door just then with dinner. "Come in, come in Missus," Al urged. When she stepped in, she found a smiling Sara, a happy Al and a proud son.

"Missus, the boy, the boy got her to laugh! She's back, my Sara is back! See, see!" He almost did a jig as he paced back and forth, and pointed to his recovered wife.

John had a smile that spread from ear to ear. Sara put the boy on her lap, and held him close to her, then began smothering him with kisses. Rosa turned to Sara. "Hello, Mrs. Gross. How are you?"

"Better, Missus, better. Your boy here, he's an angel. He made me laugh." Sara continued, "He came over so many times, I heard him onc't, I saw him, but I couldn't talk. I don't know why. It was like I was asleep, and couldn't wake up. I heard him so clear when he talked to me, and when he read to me. But when he told me that story, Missus, it woke me up. The boy, he woke me up," Sara exclaimed beaming brightly.

"Well, welcome back Mrs. Gross. You had us worried sick. It's so good to see your smile again." Turning to Al she said, "How do you feel, Mr. Gross?"

"Missus, I can't tell you how much I thank the boy. I was standing outside and heard him tell'n the story…it made my Sara laugh. Missus, I can't tell you how happy the boy has made me." As he spoke he walked over and shook John's hand. "Thank you my boy," He said as John beamed

Sara stood, and walked to Rosa, "Missus, thank you for feeding us. I'll do better. I'll be a wife to Al again. I'll do better now." The two women fell into each others arms.

Summer arrived and George was off from work for the next two months. He felt strange sitting at the breakfast table with his family, knowing he wouldn't have to leave on Sunday and make the drive to Delaware for the next two months. He had begun to feel like an absentee husband, father and business partner. Settling back in his chair, he sipped his second cup of coffee. Feeling totally relaxed, he turned to his wife, "How are things over at the Gross's. Is she doing better?"

Rosa stopped putting dishes away and sat down next to him. "You'll be proud to know your son, John, provided the miracle. You know he had been going over for weeks, talking to her about anything and everything, and doing his homework in front of her. Well, and don't ask me why, but one day he decided to tell her what he must have known would be a funny story about me throwing rocks at him. Well, the story made her laugh, and the laughter seemed to snap her out of her depressed mood."

George went to his son who was sitting nearby, and put his hands on the boys shoulders, "Good for you son, I'm proud of you for being so persistent in your desire to help her. And you did a very, very good job."

"Thanks, Dad," John replied, beaming.

Rosa continued, "Mrs. Gross is more like her old self. She's cooking for him now. She even came over for a visit and had coffee and cake. But, if she's outside, and hears a car she still runs into the house and hides. Things have settled down in terms of the real nasty stuff like throwing dead animals on their property. But, there are still some low life's that come by at night and yell nasty things… that sets her back."

"Do you know how often that happens?"

"Mr. Gross said they come by once or twice a week. Why do you ask?"

"I'm going over to see Mr. Gross. Maybe I can return a favor. After I see how he feels about my idea, I'll fill you in." George said smiling.

As soon as breakfast was over, he walked over to see Mr. Gross and found him in the barn, cleaning out the horse stall. "Good morning, Mr. Gross."

Al looked up and gave George a big smile,

"Morning, Mister, it's good to see ya'." He offered his free hand.

"How's Mrs. Gross? Some better I hope."

"Yes, some better, but she still has a way to go." He said, looking serious.

"My wife said you still have some lowlifes coming by at night, yelling filthy stuff. Is that still happening?"

"Yah, not every week, but every onc't and a while they come by and yell. It upsets Sara. She gets quiet and nervous like. It sets her back, onc't."

"Do you think it's the same ones doing it?"

"Yah, I do. It's the same bunch. I recognize the car's motor and their voices, yah, it's the same ones. They come after they get liquored up, mostly on Friday, or Saturday nights. They gets brave after they has downed a few," Al said in disgust.

"They come about the same time of night?" George asked, wanting to get a clearer picture of what was happening.

"One or two in the morning. That's when they do their dirt," Al said angrily.

"Mr. Gross, why don't we sit up tonight, and if need be, tomorrow night, too, and give those no goods a hot reception?" George said with a mischievous wink.

Al answered with a broad smile, and a wink in return. He got George's meaning immediately.

It had been months since the two families had had their ice cream and pretzel night together. That afternoon Sara ventured over and suggested they resume it this evening. Rosa was delighted that her neighbor was feeling well enough to begin having their Saturday night fun night again.

Rosa told her she would make the custard and have George buy the ice. She didn't want Sara to overdo herself.

At six, They walked over to the Gross's. Al and George began chipping and crushing the ice, placing the custard container into the oak bucket, then filling it with crushed ice and coarse salt. The boys did all of the cranking, while Al and George sat off to the side, watching the boys as they talked.

Inside the ladies placed soup bowls on the table for the ice cream and several platters with thick salty Dutch pretzels. Sara was able to help, but Rosa noticed she moved a bit slower than normal. She was still not her old self. George reminded Al that they had an appointment at eleven that night. A faint smile crossed Al's face as he nodded.

Because it was cooler outside, the ladies had the men bring the ice cream container into the kitchen where they spooned it into the bowls. Everyone took a handful of pretzels, and stuck them into the soft ice cream. The boys went back outside to eat on the porch. By the time the boys had seconds, the night air had cooled, and everyone went back inside. As he adults sat around the kitchen table and talked, the boys sat lined up on the wood box, amusing their baby brother by making shadow faces on the walls from the light cast by the kerosene lantern. Their little brother was fascinated by the " magic."

At ten o'clock, George and Al exchanged nods and George suggested they say good night. Once the boys were in bed, George took Rosa by the arm and led her to the kitchen. In a hushed voice he said, "Tonight, Mr. Gross and I are going to sit up and wait for the guys who are still coming by and shouting those insults at Sara. We want to give them a real good scare if they show up"

"I hope you can. She's been through enough. That woman just doesn't need any more of that kind of nonsense. She's doing better, but she's still fragile. And those men are setting her back. We don't want them to undo all the work that John, God bless him, has done. George, I'm telling you, I'm so proud of that boy. He was really determined to help his Aunt Sara, and he was finally able to reach her, and get her out of her shell."

"The boy did do well, Rosa. I'm proud of him, too. Now we'll never be able to tell him he talks too much," George joked.

Rosa laughed, "That's true. George, speaking of talking, do you know what he reads after he does his homework?"

"No, I can't say that I paid that much attention to what he's reading." He confessed.

"Well, he reads the dictionary. George. He reads it for hours on end. Can you imagine? He sits and reads words as if he's reading a novel."

"Maybe the boy will be a teacher like me," George joked.

"That could be, or maybe a farmer. He'll be able to impress the animals with his vocabulary," Rosa kidded. "But back to Mrs. Gross, George. You saw her tonight. She is functioning better, but I think she still has a way to go."

"I can see that this whole episode has caused her to age."

"You've seen her hair. It's almost all gray, and her eyes aren't bright anymore. She seems to be living with a shadow over her. I hope you and Mr. Gross are able to scare the daylights out of whoever is still doing this to her."

"I hope so, too. I really want them to show up tonight. If they do, we'll give them a reception they won't forget." George said with a chuckle. "You can go up and tell the boys not to worry if they hear guns going off tonight."

"As soon as you leave, I will. But be careful." Rosa planted a kiss on his cheek.

The two men met in front of Al's home. Each brought a double barrel shot gun and a pocket full of buck shot shells.

"I set up a couple of logs for us to sit on just off in the woods there." Al pointed, then led the way to the two stumps placed just across from the house in the deep shadow of the woods.

"Did you tell your Missus what we were up to tonight?" George asked.

"Yah, I told her. I had to. I don't want to scare her to death if we start shootin' our guns off tonight…this way she knows what's going on."

"That's good. I told my wife to tell the boys so they wouldn't be frightened."

The men sat talking quietly, occasionally slapping at mosquitoes until Al said, "I think I hear a car com'n…yep,

I sure do…see the car's lights coming down the road from your way."

The car came up the rise in front of Twin Cedars with its lights on. As soon as it reached the top of the rise, the car's lights went off. "Oh, oh, I bet this is them," Al whispered, "Mister, get ready." Both men stood and moved a few feet apart from each other; holding their guns at the ready.

As the vehicle approached the house, the car slowed and the dogs began barking. The moon's bright light outlined the form of three men in an open sided car which came to a stop in front of the house. One called out, "Sara Gross is a witch!" Another yelled, "Kill the witch!" A third screamed, "Burn the witch!" Their laughter was raucous.

Pointing their guns in the air, George and Al looked at each other and nodded, "On three." George whispered, then did a fast count, "One, two, three!" The guns roared, Boom! Boom! Boom! Boom! in quick succession. The men reloaded quickly, and fired off a second salvo.

A man screamed, "Holy shit! They's trying to kill us!" Another yelled in terror. "Let's get the hell outt'a here!" The driver pushed the gas pedal to the floor, and the car roared off down the road.

Al and George walked from the woods to the road. They faced each other for a moment, smiled, then, shook hands. "Good job, Mister." Al said beaming.

"I think it was a good night's work, Mr. Gross. I don't think they'll be returning anytime soon."

"Mister, I think you're right. Me, and my Missus will be sleep'n a lot better now." And, Al was right. Their sleep was never disturbed again after that night.

CHAPTER 14

Saying Goodbye

Al and his friend, John Ness walked down the road toward Twin Cedars. Opening the gate, Al led the way through his neighbor's yard, to the back porch, and then knocked on the door.

George was home alone, watching his youngest son. His wife and the other children had dental appointments with Doctor Kimbrow, in York. He heard the knock and went to see who was there. When he opened the door, Al said, "Mister, you remember my old neighbor, John Ness."

"Oh, yes, yes." George answered. "It's good to see you again." He offered his hand to John, who shook it vigorously.

Al continued, "John was out visit'n and I remembered you said you wuz look'n fer someone to do some electrical work. Well, John here, he's done become a first class electrician since he gave up farm'n. So, I brung him over so you two could talk."

"Well, thank you, Mr. Gross. I haven't decided exactly what I want to do just yet. Maybe talking to John will help me decide." As he spoke, his three year old son, Dick, and his dog, Dixie pushed their heads between the door and George's leg to satisfy their curiosity.

John patted the boy's head, then the Collie's, since she wanted to share in the offered affection. "Well, hello. Looks like you two are real buddies." John said laughing.

"We got the dog on his first birthday and they've been together ever since." George explained.

"Well, I bes' be get'n home." Al interrupted, "I got chores to do, I bes'get go'n now. See ya when yur done here, John." He called over his shoulder as he walked away.

Dick and the dog disappeared back into the kitchen and resumed their routine of chasing each other from one end of the room to the other. They had bonded and were very close; the dog tolerated all of the boy's tugs and pinches when he was a toddler, and now, his rougher play as a three year old. They always chased each other until exhaustion overcame them both, then, they'd curled up together and fall asleep on the floor.

"Maybe we can talk better out here." George suggested, pointing to the porch steps, away from the dog's yapping and his boy's happy squeals.

"Now, what was it you had in mind, Mister?" John asked.

"I'd like to expand the capacity of my two brooder houses. I know it will require some electrical work, maybe we can walk up and you can take a look, that way you can see for yourself what I have in mind."

A scream from the boy caused the men to jump up and rush back into the kitchen. They found him sitting under the large wooden kitchen table, yelling his head off, his small hands holding his blood covered forehead.

"What happened?" George asked as he knelt next to his son, all the while pulling the child's hands away in order to see where the blood was coming from.

The boy pointed an accusing finger at the kitchen table above him. "He must'a run into the corner of the table, Mister." John suggested.

" Yes, I think you're right." George said as he picked the boy up, then, sat him in a kitchen chair. "Let's see if a cold cloth will stop the bleeding." Hurrying to the corner table where the water bucket sat, he picked up the nearby wash pan and poured several dippers full of water into it. He took several out, wet one, then knelt next to the boy. "Don't cry." He took several kitchen towels, wet them, and gently began wiping blood from the boy's face. George pressed the damp cloth against the inch long gash for several minutes. Much to his surprise, blood continued to ooze from beneath the cloth. Eventually, George became concerned. He looked up at John, "The boy is losing a lot of blood. Normally pressure against a wound like this would stop the bleeding." George said perplexed.

"Mr. Read, let me say this. I wuz out visit'n my sister the night your boy here decided to get born. I wuz among those that helped shovel the snow to get Doc Meckley through the drifts, so I got a stake in the boy, and some say, too. Now, I wann'a try something. It'll just take me a second, if it's all right with you."

"If you feel you can help, by all means…"

John took a knife out of his pants pocket, opened one of the blades, then took a match out of his shirt pocket and lit it, holding the flame against both sides of the blade.

"What are you going to do with the knife?" George asked in alarm.

"Well, fur one thing, I ain't gonn'a hurt the boy none. Just give me a minute." Kneeling in front of them both, he took George's hand away from the still bleeding wound, and placed the flat side of the knife's blade against the open wound. He placed his other hand on top of the boy's head and muttered a few words in Dutch. Within minutes the bleeding stopped.

"What did you do?" George asked in amazement. "I don't understand what you just did."

A pleased John Ness replied, "Mister, a pow-wow doctor showed me how to do that. Now, you can say your boy has been pow-wowed over…which I guess makes him a fur sur' Dutchman." John said, feeling proud and very pleased with himself.

"I don't know what you did, but I certainly want to thank you." George stood and patted John on the back. "To be safe, I'll wrap a damp towel around his head and let him lie down until his mother comes back from town." George explained.

"My head hurts." The boy complained, as his father wet another towel, then wrapped his head with it. George lifted him and laid him on the nearby wood box.

"Rosa will probably fire me for doing a poor job of looking after the boy." George chuckled.

"I'm sure your Missus will want to rewrap that there bandage you put on him. He looks like one of them swami fella's, or whatever they call them." John commented with a laugh, shaking his head in disbelief at the huge wrapping George had put around his boy's head. "I'll come back another day and take a look at your brooder house. You've got your hands full here. Is that all right with you?"

"Yes, that's fine. You're right, I better stay put until my wife gets back." George replied as John left to go back to Al's house.

Shortly after John left, Rosa came home. She parked the car near the back door to make unloading the day's purchases easier. The boys loaded the wheel barrow with items intended for the animals, then, pushed the loaded wheel barrow up to the barn. The things intended for the house, were carried to the kitchen porch and dropped there. George watched the unloading from inside, reluctant to go outside and explain the misfortune that had befallen their number four son. "Oh well, I might as well face the music," he muttered as he stepped outside to the porch, knowing he had some explaining to do. "Ah, Rosa," He began, "Dicks had a slight accident." Then he added hastily, "But he's fine."

"He had a what?" Rosa replied, as she rushed up to him. "Dick had an accident? What kind of accident? Where is he?" Before he could answer, she entered the kitchen and saw the boy lying on the wood box, an oversized 'bandage' wrapped around his head. "Oh my Lord, look at him…what did he do, split his head open? Did you call the doctor?" Her words tumbled out.

"Now, Rosa, calm down. He's fine. He just bumped his head on the corner of the kitchen table. I just put that damp towel on his head to keep him cooled off and to catch any bleeding if it started again, that's all, the boy's fine." George explained, feeling like a total failure. "John Ness was here, he pow- wowed over him to stop the bleeding." As George spoke, Rosa, unwrapped the oversized towel. "How do you feel, son? Oh my, that is a deep cut. I'll put some iodine around it and a smaller bandage." Then, what George said earlier, sank in, "John Ness did what?" Rosa looked up at her husband who was trying hard not to let his embarrassment show.

"I couldn't get the bleeding to stop, Rosa. John offered to help. So I let him." George then explain-ned everything John did with the knife, then continued, "He said a few words in Dutch, and I'm telling you, the bleeding stopped! Then, he said, 'Now your boy's a for sur' Dutchman.' I really can't explain it, but I'm telling you, Rosa, I tried, and tried to stop the bleeding, but it just wouldn't stop. What do you think of that? I mean, what John did?"

"I'm grateful for his help, even if you can't explain it. Anyway, I guess it does make our boy the Black Dutchman, at least an honorary one. You weren't there, but that's what the name the farmers gave him in Dutch the night they opened the road for the doctor. This is confirmation, I suppose."

"Not to change the subject, but with all the excitement, John didn't get a chance to finish up the business he had come over for." George added.

"I didn't know we had any business with John. What business are you talking about, George?"

"Well, I've been thinking, we could expand the capacity of the brooder houses, he was going to give me an idea of what it would cost and…"

"George. Before you find out the cost for the brooder houses, I suggest you find out what the cost would be to run electricity to our house. To the house we live in, George!"

"I didn't ask him about our house, I figured we would get to that after the brooder houses were done, the extra chick capacity would pay for itself in less than a year, then I could…"

"George, I don't know how to say this, other than to just say it. But I want you to listen to me. I'm sick and tired of the chickens getting everything. Do you know they live better than your wife and children do?"

"How can you say that?"

"How can I say that? Quite easily! The chickens have running water; they've had that for years. Yet, we pump, and cart water to wash ourselves, and our clothes. The chickens have electricity, they've had it for, Lord knows how many years, and now you're talking about expanding, expanding what they already have, while we're still burning kerosene lamps. The boys are doing homework by lamp light, George. Something is wrong with that picture!"

"Rosa, look, it would only be a matter of another year or…"

"George, I've had it! You seem to not want to get it! want to get it. The boys and I, we work like dogs, I really mean that, like dogs. And, I've told you this before. You aren't around enough to appreciate what goes on around here. Besides, I need some conveniences so I can feel like a human being again, not a work horse. We don't have an indoor toilet; we have to go to a smelly outhouse. Don't you know we could be more productive if we didn't have to spend time pumping, and carting water to the house to do the laundry, for drinking, for bathing and for cooking? Can't you see it's a big waste of time and energy? Which by the way, I'm running out of."

George had his heels dug in. He had his own way of seeing things. "Now, look, Rosa, as I keep trying to tell you, it's only a matter of a few more…"

"I don't want to hear it, George. You obviously just don't want to get it, and this isn't the first time you've played deaf, blind and dumb when it comes to your family. Well, let me put it in a way you will understand. I'm sick and tired of chickens having running water, electricity, insulation, timers, you name it; the damn chickens have it. No doubt about it, the investments in them have paid off. Now it's time for you to invest in your family!"

"Rosa, why won't you listen to me? It will only be a matter of…" George continued to try push, and explain his position.

"I don't want to hear 'in time' because these damn chickens are going to continue living better than the boys and me. Well, maybe you'll understand this, George. I quit! Do you hear me? I quit! If you can't do what I've asked you to do for your family, then I've had it, I'm done. Even if it means we have to close down the business." She turned and ran out the door past the boys who had taken positions so they could hear everything that was being said.

They were shocked. They had never heard their mother confront their father in such a forceful way. "Mom was really mad. I wonder what she meant when she said, she quit?" Bill wondered aloud.

"Maybe she will just stay inside and cook, you know and do things like that, and…" George Junior stopped mid-sentence as their father walked past them, his face set in stone as he headed to the garage, backed his car out, then roared off down the road.

"I heard her say if he doesn't give her electricity and running water in the house, then he should close down the business," John added as the boys looked to each other, totally confused.

Their mother returned, walked past them without saying a word and began doing her household chores. John said, "We need to go in and talk to mom. Let's find out what's going on." The boys went inside. "Mom, can we talk to you?"

She had regained her composure and looked at her children as they filed in. "All right boys, take seats at the table." They took seats; their faces reflecting the confusion they felt. "Now, I know you boys heard what your father and I were discussing, didn't you?"

They all nodded. "But you said you quit. What happens if you quit?" Bill interjected.

"We heard you say you would." John added.

"Boys, your father and I don't agree on how to proceed at this stage of our lives. We have a good business, thanks to all of you and your willingness to work hard. Now, I feel we need, and deserve, some rewards for those efforts. We need electricity and running water in the house, things that you know he's installed in the barn, and chicken houses. Something he did for the chickens years ago, because it was important for the business. Well, the business is a success. Now, I feel it's time for us to reap some rewards. I think we need running water, and electricity which are just minimum things as far as I'm concerned. The problem is your father doesn't agree with me."

"But you said you quit. What does that mean?" John persisted. "You didn't answer that."

"You know, I don't really understand what it means other than we will not continue in the chicken business; at least not unless your father changes his mind. What it probably means is we'll start selling off the chickens, and the equipment, then go into some other kind of work to make a living. But, to be perfectly honest, boys, I don't know, at least until your father and I come to some kind of an agreement, and he's not around right now. So, until he comes back and we talk things through, everything is up in the air. But we'll be fine, don't you boys worry about anything." Rosa concluded, trying to sound more confident than she actually felt.

Over a week went by and there was no sign of their father. Each day was more somber than the last. The day and meals were no longer pleasant; their mother bore a sadness that reflected onto the boys.

John jumped out of bed and ran to his older brother's room, "George, George!" He whispered as he shook his sleeping brother. "I hear Dad. He's back. He and Mom are talking. Come on, let's go downstairs and listen." They let Bill sleep as they tiptoed downstairs and went into Mother Mary's old room. They pressed their heads against their parents' bedroom wall, so they could hear more clearly.

"I tell you Rosa, it's the best thing for us…I'll be hired as a principal, teacher and you'll be hired as the kindergarten and first grade teacher. It will mean two incomes, and we'll have summers off."

Rosa had been asleep when he returned. He had lit the kerosene lantern and had taken a seat on the edge of the bed. She had remained lying down while he first spoke; now she sat up with the pillow pulled up behind her back against the headboard. The flickering lantern cast their shadow against a far wall.

She looked at her husband with a steady gaze. Her voice was even and calm. "You mean you'd uproot us, move to another state and start a whole new life, rather than fix this place up? I don't believe you. Where is your logic? Or is it you just want out of the chicken business and you don't want to say so, and this is your way of doing it? There must be a reason you're not telling me." George looked at her, but remained silent. Rosa continued, "You know the boys love this place, and so do I, but I will not put up with the inconveniences we have on a day-in, day-out basis. George, why in heavens name won't you give in and fix this place up?" She was almost ready to break down and cry, but she refused to.

"Rosa, I will, but not now. We need to expand our capacity, then we could afford to fix the place, just the way you want it, if you would just wait."

"Oh, shit, George. I'm sick and tired of hearing you say, wait. Wait a few more months, wait a few more years. Weight is what broke the wagon, and this wagon is busted." Rosa pulled her pillow from behind her, put it under her head and slid back under the covers, then, turned her back to him.

The next morning, George drove off and didn't return for two weeks. When he did, he had a letter from the school board of a small town in New Jersey. The letter stated that both of them had been accepted for positions at the school. Rosa's heart was heavy when she called her family to have seats in the living room. "Boys, your father and I have something to tell you," she began, then,sat down.

The brothers looked at each other. They knew what was coming. George stood in the doorway and began, "Boys, in view of the fact that we aren't doing as well as we might with the chicken business, your mother and I have decided to sell it off and move to New Jersey where we can both teach and make an income. I'll be the principal of the colored school, and teach the sixth, seventh and eighth grades. She'll be the kindergarten and first grade teacher. We'll be leaving in a month or so."

The silence was oppressive. Rosa's head dropped. Tears slid down Bill's cheeks. George stared at his father with cold eyes, John's face began to puff up; the veins in his forehead began to swell. "I'm not going, I'm not leaving here." The thirteen year old boy said in a low voice. "The business is doing fine; you just won't fix the house up for Mom, that's why. Why won't you, why won't you, Dad? Why won't you fix up the place! We love it here. This is our home! We don't want to move to some dumpy town!" His voice rose, as he challenged his father.

"Now, you see here, young man, I won't have you talking that way. You don't know what you're talking about…so be quiet!"

"I won't be quiet. I'm telling the truth, I know what's going on, you…"

George was across the room and in a second, his large open hand landed full force across the boy's face.

"You can hit me all you want, but I know the truth! You're just too cheap to spend any money on Mom!" George's other hand caught the opposite side of John's face. The boy bit his lip and glared at his father with steely eyes.

" Stop it! Stop it!" Rosa screamed. "What are you doing? What are you trying to prove? Leave the boy alone!" She went to comfort her boy, but he ran past her and out of the house.

"Well, I hope you're happy, George."

"No son of mine is going to talk to me that way, I just won't have it," he said as he stormed out of the room.

Dick, sitting between Bill's legs was too young to comprehend what was happening. But he felt the tension, heard the angry voices, and witnessed his father's violence against one of his brothers and started screaming. Bill pulled him onto his lap and hugged him tightly, trying hard not to cry himself.

The process of dismantling the business began the next day. Unknown to Rosa, George had placed an ad in the local paper. * TWIN CEDARS FARM * GOING OUT OF POULTRY BUSINESS FARM SALE * GOOD LAYERS * BROODERS AND EQUIPMENT *

The ad was successful. Farmers began showing up before breakfast. George greeted every potential buyer with a warm hello and a hardy handshake, then gave each farmer a 'cooks' tour in order that every item that could be sold, was sold. One by one, the farmers left with chickens, equipment, sometimes both.

Watching from the top floor of the barn, the boys could see their father and the farmers loading crates of chickens and equipment into trucks. "I hate him, I really do hate him." John said to himself as much as to his brothers.

"I guess he's doing what he thinks is best." George Junior replied in a conciliatory tone, anxious to head off any confrontation between the two of them.

"Bullshit, George." John snapped. "He's just a stubborn, mean bastard, and a lazy one to boot. Who does the work around here? Who does, George? Mainly Mom, you, me and Bill, that's who! All he ever did was come back on Fridays, spend Saturday seeing what needed to be done and tell Mom, or you what to do, then, leave on Sunday. I think he lost his job in Delaware and doesn't want to be a farmer and get his hands dirty Thats what I think." Before George could reply, their father called.

"Boys! Boys! I need you to catch some chickens."

"To hell with him." John snarled. "Let him go catch them himself."

"You stay here. Bill and I'll go." George said, trying to head off a confrontation.

"Yeah, stay here, no point in getting slapped again." Bill said matter-of-factly.

As the boys approached, he made no mention of John's absence. "A few chickens got out into the field when we loaded the truck. See them out there?" George pointed to several roaming around well down in the field.

"Yes, sir," George Junior replied. "We see them."

"Catch them, and put them in the upper laying house."

"We will. Come on, Bill." The boys walked down the field to the chickens and herded them toward the hedge row which separated two fields but had thick briar patches mixed in the rows of small trees. They shooed them towards the hedge row where they soon entangled themselves in the briars and were quickly cornered and caught. However, two chickens didn't cooperate; they ran toward the nearby walnut tree and flew up to the lowest branch.

"Did you catch all of the chickens?" George asked the boys as they exited the upper laying house.

"All but two, they flew up into the walnut tree. You know the one, the big one in the middle of the fence row."

"Tell your brother John, I want him to get those chickens."

"Dad, they'll just fly higher. He won't be able to catch them in the tree."

"You tell him I want him to get those two chickens. Had he been there earlier to help you, they probably wouldn't have had the chance to get away and fly up there." George groused.

The boys went back to the upper part of the barn to relay the message to John. "We caught all but two of the chickens; they got away and flew up into the walnut tree. Anyway, Dad wants you to catch them."

"He's just looking for an excuse to belt you again." Bill observed.

"That's all right, I'll get them. He didn't say when I had to catch them did he?"

"No, He just said to tell you to get those two chickens. That's all he said. Right, Bill?"

"Yep. That's what he said."

"Then I'll get them tonight. "John said with a smile. "They're easy to catch in the dark."

Dinner was eaten in silence. Rosa wore a resigned expression, and the boys, (except for their baby brother) picked at their food and had sad faces, too.

Their father broke the silence. "John, did you get those chickens out of the tree?"

"No, Sir. I did not."

"Did you brother tell you that I wanted you to get them?"

"Yes sir, they did."

"Well?"

"Well what?"

"Boy, don't get fresh with me, you hear?" He said through clenched teeth.

"May I be excused from the table? John asked.

"Yes, you may." Rosa answered quickly.

John jumped up and went outside.

"That boy has a fresh mouth." George grumbled.

"That may be, but just remember he's a carbon copy of you." George said nothing, but looked at her with disbelief.

John stayed outside and out of everyone's sight. When darkness fell, he went to the barn and got a burlap feed bag, then headed to the walnut tree. The moonlight clearly revealed the two white Leghorns perched close together on a branch, about twenty feet off the ground. He made his way up the tree, using the sturdy branches as steps. The chickens sat quietly until he grabbed one, then the other by the legs. They squawked, but fell silent when he stuffed them into the burlap bag.

He climbed back down and headed to the upper laying house. Then he had a thought, 'I'd better protect myself.' Instead of going to the upper laying house he went to one of the empty brooder houses and put the two hens in there. Then he went back to the house where he silently slipped into bed.

The next morning, the atmosphere at breakfast was the same as the night before, except there was an air of anticipation for what everyone knew was coming when their father confronted John. The wait wasn't long. George cleared his throat, then said, "John, I told you to get those two chickens and you didn't. You deliberately disobeyed me, and I'll not have that. I'll see you after breakfast."

George Junior and Bill looked at John. Had he forgotten? They wondered. But they couldn't read him. He sat silent and solemn faced.

Rosa, trying to head off a confrontation, spoke up, "George, you know it's almost impossible to catch a chicken in a tree. Just wait until they come down, I'll just throw them some corn. We can catch them that way. Why are you making it such an issue?"

"Because the boy is deliberately disobeying me, that's why." He stood abruptly, and turned to his son. "All right, John, you come with me."

The two left the table and headed to the barn. As they walked, George began taking his belt off. When they reached the apple tree he said, "Go over to the barrel and bend over." Without a word, he complied with his father's orders. George swung the folded belt and hit his son full force on his backside; once, twice, three, four, and finally, five times.

John's fury was full blown; his face became discolored, and swollen. Tears welled up in his eyes, but none fell. He straightened himself, faced his father, and then spoke. "This morning at breakfast you said you told me to get those chickens and YOU said I didn't. You never asked me if I had. You just assumed I hadn't because I didn't do it when YOU thought I should. Look in the brooder house. That's where they are... can I go now?"

George was speechless. He looked at his son, walked to the brooder house and opened the door. There were the two chickens. He turned to face his son, but John had gone back to the house and disappeared through the kitchen door.

For the next several days, John avoided any contact with his father.

In a short while, the poultry stock, equipment and the farm animals were all sold off. Then one day before anyone realized how quickly the time had gone, a moving truck pulled into the yard.

Rosa had had a hard time explaining to Sara why they were leaving. It was hard because it didn't make any sense to her, or to her boys. The move was total insanity, Rosa knew it was, but she had no choice. George was the man of the house, and had the final say in such matters. He and Al stood by the car, talking, shaking hands, saying good bye. Nearby, Sara and Rosa held on to each other, crying silently.

It was a hot August day and the world seemed to have come to a complete stop as the boys climbed into the rear of the big Jewett car. George walked to the back and checked the luggage tied down on the rear carrier. He went to Mr. Gross and said good bye once more, then climbed into the driver's seat. The moving truck had already left.

Rosa climbed into the passenger seat. Now she held her hand out to Sara who stood looking up at her, her pale blue eyes full of tears. "Ya, take care, and come back onc't." She pleaded.

"We will. And you and Mr. Gross take care, too." Rosa answered as George started the car. The sound of the starting engine jolted Rosa. She realized this insanity was real. They were leaving their home for no good reason. They were leaving because of his stubbornness. "Wait" She shouted as she opened her door, jumped to the ground and wrapped her arms tightly around Sara. "I'm going to miss you so much." Rosa sobbed.

"I will miss you too Missus. I don't know what we will do with you folks gone."

George called out, "Rosa, we have to get going. Get in the car!."

Rosa felt numb as she climbed back in. She stared straight ahead. Once the car moved, her emotions erupted.

"Oh, God, oh God, what are we doing?" Then she let her emotions erupt into full blown sobs. Her outburst caused Dick, who had no idea of what was happening, to begin howling. Then George and Bill began to cry. Only John sat grim faced and dry eyed. No one spoke during the four hour trip to the small New Jersey town.

CHAPTER 16

Starting Over

The day before school was to open, George stood before his staff of three. They sat around in a semi-circle in straight backed oak chairs in the front of what would be his classroom. His staff was made up of Rosa (assigned to teach kindergarten and first grade), Miss Baskerville, a young athletic dark brown skinned woman (second and third grade), and Miss Frisby (a small woman who defied age determination). She wore the high top shoes and the clothes of an old woman, yet her skin was wrinkle -free, and she had not one gray hair, a total contradiction in terms of her attire and her actual physical appearance. In any event, she was assigned to the fourth and fifth grades. George would teach sixth, seventh and eighth grade, and serve as the school's principal. The last staff member was the janitor, Mr. Ham. He tended the furnace in the winter, kept the school yard free of any paper and the school's floors, swept and mopped.

George began the meeting. "First of all, I expect the school to be kept neat and clean, not just by Mr. Ham, but by the teachers and students as well. We will address each other as Mr. or Mrs. or Miss as the case may be. There will be no use of first names. We will conduct ourselves in and out of the classroom in a dignified and proper way. That means out in the community as well as well as in the classroom. Is that understood?" There were nods of agreement.

"I have a philosophy that will be used as the school's mantra for our children. And it isn't complicated. So far as the children are concerned there is no such word as CAN'T. I don't want to hear that word used by a student, or a teacher. Is that clear?" Again there were nods of agreement and murmured, "Yeses," He added, "We want our students to feel that nothing is impossible." Warming to the group he continued, "We will dress properly, and we will require that of our students as well. Lastly, slang will not be tolerated in the classroom. Is that clear?" Again, there was total agreement. "If there is a problem you can't handle, come and get me. That's why I'm here." That said; he adjourned the meeting.

The teachers went to their respective classrooms and began setting out books and supplies for opening day. The sight and sounds of school on opening day were far different from the quiet, orderly atmosphere of the day before. The building vibrated with the screams of children. They ran, pushed, squealed as they scurried up and down the hallway, opening doors, and poking their heads into the class rooms, anxious to see what the new teachers looked like. At 8:45 George rang the bell, indicating that school was now officially open.

He stood at his classroom door and greeted each student as they entered. Most were polite and returned his greeting. However, some ignored him, and gave him blank stares. If a child's hat was on, George reminded the student to remove it. Finally, three older boys sauntered in. Two were George's size, one several inches taller. Each wore a cap. "Please remove your hats." The principal said as they walked past him, all three exhibiting 'attitude.' Two of the youths muttered something under their breath as they passed, but took their caps off. The taller boy glared at the teacher, then, swaggered to his seat, his cap still on his head. He slouched down low in his seat, then stuck his long legs out into the aisle.

After the last student filed past, George left the door and walked to the front of the room to greet his student. “Good morning, boy and girls. I’m your teacher, and principal, Mr. Read. Some returned his greetings. Others merely stared back with blank faces. All were keenly aware of the boy who sat in class with his cap still on, wondering what the new teacher was going to do about this defiant youth.

“Boys, girls; before we get started I want to explain something to you. Getting an education is the most important single thing that you can do for yourselves. It is important because without it, you will not get ahead in the world. You will not be able to get a good job, a job that pays well, a job that will give you personal satisfaction and respect in the community. That’s why I’m here. I want to help you achieve any goal or dream you may have for your future life. But you must have a goal, you must have a dream, you must have something you want to achieve with your life. It won’t come to you You will have to work hard for it, you have to want it badly, and you must be willing to apply yourself. You will not be able to become a professional person without an education. And, by the way, who knows what a professional person is?” George surveyed the room, no hands went up.

The children looked at each other with puzzled expressions. After a few minutes of silence, he continued. “Who can tell us why we are here? Why do we come to school?”

Three hands shot up. "Yes, Miss?" He pointed to a brown skinned chubby girl. "Please stand and tell us your name."

The girl stood. "My name is Madeline Stokes, and we are here to learn, to learn how to do arithmetic and history and to learn good English."

"Thank you Miss Stokes. You may take your seat, and you are correct. Now, after you learn all of those things, what do you do with that knowledge?" He pointed to another student.

"My name is Blanch Jones. You learn these things so when you grow up, you can get a job, right?" The tall thin girl said, then, slid back into her seat.

"Yes, Miss Jones. But, what kind of job do you want? Do you want a job digging ditches, or a job as a professional…a doctor, a lawyer, a teacher, or a dentist. Those are professional occupations. They allow you to make more money, and give you standing in the community. People will look up to you." His rich voice held their attention. He asked, "Have any of you thought of becoming a professional?" Ever so slowly a hand went up in the back of the room. "Yes. Mr.?"

"My name is Herbert Simmons, Mr. Read."

"What did you want to say Mr. Simmons?"

"Well, I was thinking about becoming a cook. Is that being a professional?"

"That's an excellent question; however, before I answer your question, I think we should all get acquainted. Let's start here." The teacher pointed to the student sitting in the first seat in the sixth row. "Please stand and tell the class your name and what it is you want to be when you grow up."

One by one the children stood and told the class their name and what they wanted to be. Many of them said, "I don't know." Others said, "I haven't thought about it." A boy said he wanted to be an artist, a girl said she wanted to become a nurse, another boy said he'd like to be a farmer. But most said they didn't know. When the hat-wearing youth's turn came, all of the children sitting in front turned around to see how this drama would play out. The boy stared into space, slouched way down in his seat, a look of defiance still on his face. His cap pulled even lower on his head.

"Young man, it's your turn to stand and tell us your name. The boy refused to respond. "All right, I'll skip over you for the moment. Maybe you've forgotten your name, because it's obvious you've forgotten your manners, since your hat is still on." The teacher's barb provoked snickers from his class mates, which irritated the youth. He didn't want to let on that the teacher had actually gotten to him, had embarrassed him in front of his classmates. To compensate, he shrugged his shoulders. "All right, let's continue, we will come back to the young man who seems to have forgotten his name." Again the children snickered. The roll call continued until the last student stood, gave a name, and made a statement about his, or her future plans, if any.

After the last child spoke, George pointed to the defiant boy. "Well, young man, have you remembered your name? Are you going to stand and tell the class what it is you want to be when you grow up?" The boy stared straight ahead, except now he wore an angry scowl on his face.

George walked to the front of the class room. "Boys. Girls. I have a request to make of you. I want you to go outside, and stand in an orderly manner over by the playground fence. Everyone, except the young man who's forgotten his name. The children had never been asked to leave a class room before, except for a fire drill. George stood by the door until the last child left. He then locked it, took off his coat and tie and placed them neatly over the oak chair back. He unbuttoned his collar, rolled up his sleeve, then walked over to the sullen boy, who now wore a look of utter disdain.

"Young, man." The teacher began. "This is my classroom and I'm the boss. There can't be two bosses here. If you think you're the boss you're wrong." Before the boy knew what had happened, he grabbed the youth around the neck with an arm lock, and dragged him out of his seat and up the aisle to the front of the class room. He threw the kicking boy to the floor and sat on his stomach, holding him by the wrists with powerful hands. The boy was taken totally by surprise. He couldn't have known that the man in the suit and tie, as a teenager had been a gang member, and was more 'street' wise than he would ever be. "I'll fight you fair and square if that's what you want, boy, but I can guarantee you one thing; you will lose. So why don't you give up the tough guy act and join in with the rest of the class?"

"You get off me…I'll tell my father an' he'll…" His voice trailed off.

"Do that, you just do that. In fact I'll send him a note and tell him I want to meet with him, so I can tell him all about his son's behavior…you be sure and tell him about our little get-together today."

The boy struggled and squirmed to get his tormentor off, but George had the strength of a bull.

Finally, he realized he had met his match, and gradually the look of anger gave way to a look of hurt.

"Boy let me tell you something, I know what you're going through. I know what it feels like to be poor and raggedy, to be too big and feel out of place. But that's not your fault. You can be whatever you want to be. I'll help you, but you're going to have to meet me half way. I can look at you, I know there's a lot of good in you, a lot of potential; you can amount to something." As he spoke, he could feel the boy's body relax; as it did, he released his hold. "So what do you say? Let's forget this ever happened, let's start over and start from scratch...is that a deal?"

The boy was shocked, and for reasons he couldn't quite understand, near tears. He looked up at the man sitting on his stomach, and didn't know what to make of him. Slowly he nodded his head, "All right, all right…I'll try to do better. I'll act right."

"Good, good, that's the ticket." George stood and offered his hand. The boy started to ignore it, then, reluctantly accepted his help.

"By the way, I still don't know your name." The teacher asked as he pulled the boy up.

In a low, shy voice the boy answered, "It's Alonzo Perry."

"I'm pleased to meet you, Alonzo Perry." George placed his hand on the boy's shoulder. "What happened here is between you and me as far as I'm concerned…it ends right here. It ends right now if you want it to. If it gets out, it's on you. Either way, is fine with me. Understood?"

"Yes, sir, I understand what you're saying." Alonzo stooped down, picked up his cap and stuck it in his hip pocket.

George brushed off his knees, buttoned his shirt collar, put his tie and coat back on, then, turned to the youth, "Well, how do I look, Alonzo?"

The boy was shocked by the question. The past few minutes had been surreal. Finally, he got it. The teacher was for real. Slowly a broad smile spread across his face, revealing two rows of gleaming white teeth, and an award - winning smile.

"Well?" The teacher persisted. "I asked you, how do I look?"

"Oh, Uhhh, you look just fine…just fine, sir." Then Alonzo laughed in spite of himself. The tough guy act had just evaporated.

"Good." George patted the boy on the shoulder as he walked to the door and unlocked it. He then proceeded to the outside door. "All right, you all may come back to class!" He called in a loud voice.

The children returned to the classroom with wide eyes. There was a vast range of speculation among them as to what awaited them inside. Would the teacher be packing to leave? If he was, he wouldn't be the first one to leave after a few days. One year a boy punched the teacher after they got into an argument. The students were accustomed to teachers being bullied and chased away by the bigger, older boys. Would the class room be wrecked if the two of them had gotten into a fight? Once they entered the room, they saw there wasn't any sign of a brawl. They had to use their imaginations when they saw Alonzo sitting at his desk, hatless, dignified, straight and tall. What happened

between Alonzo and the teacher remained a mystery, since neither of them ever mentioned what happened.
Once the students settled into their seats, the teacher said, "We have one more student to hear from. Young man, will you stand and tell us your name and what you would like to be when you grow up?"

Slowly, ever so slowly, Alonzo uncurled his six foot frame from his small desk, pushed himself up and stood, looking very uncomfortable. "My name is Alonzo Perry." That said, he started to sit down. But his teacher reminded him that he hadn't told the class what he wanted to be when he grew up. "Oh, I haven't thought about that yet…I don't know." With those softly spoken words, he was allowed to sit down.

The children could see the change in their classmate's demeanor, and appreciated the struggle he went through to stand up and speak. They didn't laugh at him as they might have in the past; in fact, their hearts went out to him.

"Thank you, Mr. Perry. Now, class, what did I say to Herbert Simmons before I sent you outside? Who remembers?" Several hands went up. "Now, let me see if I remember your name... Miss Duckenfield, is that correct?"

"Yes, Mr. Read, that's my name. You said you would answer Herbert Simmons about being a cook. He wanted to know if being a cook meant he would be a, a, professional, and you would tell him when we came back in."

"Excellent, Miss Duckenfield; that is precisely what was said. Now I want to live up to that promise. Mr. Simmons, there are special schools where you can learn a trade. Being a cook does require additional special education and training. You can make an excellent living as a cook. In fact there is an industrial training school in Borden Town, where you can learn that trade." The teacher pulled a chair to the front of the room and sat down. "You will not get a four year college degree, that is to say a Bachelor's degree. But you will receive a certificate of completion, and you will have the needed training to obtain a good job in a restaurant, or a hotel. I think it's a fine ambition, Mr. Simmons, and we will talk more through the year about how to get enrolled there."

The next morning the children entered the building in a more orderly manner. They did so because their teacher had on the afternoon of the first day gone to each classroom and told the children what he wanted and expected of them. "I expect you all to behave like young ladies and gentlemen. Running is to be done during recess, in the play yard. And when you play, I want you to play hard---outside. Inside, you are to talk, and walk quietly. Is that understood?"

There was a chorus of "Yes, Mr. Read."

He continued, "And you are to help keep the school, and its grounds clean. Pick up paper, and anything you see that doesn't belong on the ground, and put it in one of our trash baskets. Can you do that?"

Again there was a chorus of "Yes."

On the second day, Alonzo was among the first to return his teacher's greeting as he entered the room. However, the two boys who muttered a greeting on the first day had decided they would test the teacher, and kept their caps on. At his desk, one of the boys ran his hand up a girls dress as she passed by. "Mr. Read, Thomas grabbed my ass!" She screamed. "And Bob squeezed my tits."

George whirled around, "Thomas Marr. Is that not correct!" He said, pointing.

Thomas muttered, "Yeah that's me."

"And you are Bob Jones. Is that not correct?"

"Uh, huh, that's me."

Both boys had sat down quickly, smirks on their faces.

However, they were both surprised that he knew which one was which in only one day. The boys were stocky muscular fifteen year olds, who like Alonzo, felt totally out of place in their current setting. Both had been held back several times because there were no special classes for slow learners in the white high school. "All right, you two come with me." George said as he pointed to the cloak room door.

The boys swaggered to the front, scuffing their feet as they moved forward. Turning to the class, George said, "Your lessons are on the black board. You may begin them now." Before entering the cloak room, George took his coat off, and draped it over the chair back. He opened the door, then, ushered the boys in ahead of him.

The room was a long narrow affair, so narrow the two youths facing had to stand slightly one behind the other. George's eyes bore into theirs, "Boys, you're going to learn a lesson today. You see, I'm the boss, and I intend to remain the boss; therefore, you will abide by my rules. "His voice was controlled, his words measured. Then he barked, "Take off your caps....NOW!" The boys flinched at the ferocity of his command, but remained defiant. Neither made an effort to comply with his demand. "If you don't take them off, I'll take them off for you."

The boys considered themselves tough guys; they had bullied, and frightened other teachers off in the past. This dude would be no different, they thought. Thomas said, "We don't think so, teach, 'cuz we be bad sons of bitches, and we gonn'a whup your butt." Their faces were menacing as they stepped towards George. However, he was prepared. He had hidden a three foot hickory stick on the top shelf that ran the full length of the cloak room. As a teacher, he had faced similar situation in Delaware.

In a flash, George reached up, grabbed the stick, and used it as a ram rod. He jammed the stick into Thomas's stomach with his full might. Thomas screamed in pain and went down to one knee. He then jabbed Bob in the chest as he stepped forward, and then another fast thrust to the stomach. Bob stumbled backward, tripping over Thomas's foot. His body made a loud thud as it hit the floor.

"Now, boys, I'll fight you fair, one on one any time you feel you can take me, or, I'll do my best to break this stick over both your heads if you want to try me. But, I'll guarantee you, either way, I'll win. Now drop your attitudes and let's try to get along with each other and do what it is we are here to do...and that's to learn. Go take your seats... NOW!" He ordered in an icy voice.

Despite his order, they stood frozen in place. They were in pain from his jabs and thrusts. Both boys were bent over, groaning while they rubbed the spots where the teacher's stick had landed. They were in a state of total shock. This was not what they were accustomed to. No teacher had ever stood up to them this way. Neither boy was willing to take his 'one on one' challenge. Their sore, throbbing bodies were a reminder that they were dealing with a different kind of teacher. Thomas growled, "I'm gonn'a tell my ol' man what you did, and you gonn'a be in a lot of trouble."

"I look forward to meeting your father, and you be sure and come with him, too. Now! I'm going to speak to you two about grabbing girls in an inappropriate manner. You both will write the young lady a note of apology. If I approve of it, you will give it to her, then, you will also tell her to her face that you are sorry for what you did…you got that? And both of you will apologize to the class for not taking your hats off when asked. Now take your seats! I won't repeat myself." His voice sounded like a clap of thunder to the hapless boys.

The class had heard enough to understand what had happened behind the closed cloak room doors. Their suspicions were confirmed when they saw the hang doggy, gloomy faces of the once swaggering boys as they emerged from the cloak room, then took their seats.

That afternoon George ordered the boys to begin their notes of apology. Thomas was the first to complete his. After raising his hand, he offered his note to the teacher. George was pleasantly surprised to see the flow of words Thomas had put together. Despite the poor grammar and misspelling, he realized the boy had a gift for writing. He smiled because it was obvious; Thomas had a crush on the girl and didn't know how to express it properly. George read the note as Thomas stood beside him at his desk. "I'm going to correct some of your spelling; you may rewrite it, and then give it to her. I think the young lady will be very pleased." He said with a smile.

"Really?" Thomas said in genuine surprise.

"The pen is mightier than the sword." George teased. The boy gave George a puzzled look. "Do you know what I mean by that?" He asked the surprised youth.

"No, I don't." The boy confessed.

"Well, I'll make that a lesson for the whole class one day."

Bob raised his hand, "Yes, Mr. Jones?"

"I done wrote my note."

"You may bring it to me."

The boy presented the paper to his teacher. After reading it, he realized Bob was at least three or four grade levels below the eighth grade, where he found himself struggling to keep up, trying to fit in. He wasn't able to express himself at all. "Get a chair and sit next to me, Bob." The boy quickly complied. "Now, we will discuss what you want to say to the young lady. You can tell me by speaking softly so the others don't hear."

"I is sorry for what I done, and I ain't gonn'a do it again." Bob whispered.

"All right, I'll write it out. Then you can copy it. But we will not say it exactly the way you just said it. You have made some errors in grammar…in English. And we're here to learn how to speak and write correctly. Aren't we Bob?"

The boy was surprised at the question, then stammered, "Ahhh, yes, yes sir, that's why we is here."

George redrafted the note, then, went over it word for word, explaining what he had done. The youth went to his desk and copied the words, then shared it with his teacher. "I think you can give it to the young lady. But first, you will apologize to the class for keeping your cap on. "George went to the front of the room and announced. "Mr. Jones and Mr. Marr want to speak to us."

The two boys walked to the front of the class, but, the swagger was gone. Instead, two shy youths stood before their classmates. Bob cleared his throat; his hands shook as he held the paper in front of his body. In a small voice he read, "I'm sorry for what I did, and I won't do it again." Then, added. "Thank you." The young man was so nervous he had read the note he was to have given to the girl he had grabbed. George smiled and overlooked his error.

The class erupted in cheers and hand clapping. Bob shyly took his seat, pleased with himself for the first time in a long time.

"Mr. Marr. You have the floor."

Thomas stepped forward. He was secure with himself, and stood easily in front of the class, "I'm sorry I didn't listen to my teacher." There was polite applause for his statement. As he walked back to his desk, he gave Geraldine his note of apology.

When recess time came, the children were dismissed to go outside and play. All were excused except Thomas, Bob, and Geraldine. Each boy, stood in front of her and in turn apologized, and promised, "It won't happen again." The young girl lowered her eyes and smiled. Their apology had made her feel like a lady.

She replied to each one, "I accept your apology."

After that, the class settled down for the balance of the day. There was no more drama, and the afternoon passed uneventfully. In fact, so did the next day, the next day and the next. The days turned into weeks, the weeks into months. There were situations in some of the other classes that demanded the principal's attention, but soon the whole school settled into an orderly routine. The bad boys had been tamed, and that created a ripple of calm to spread throughout the school. The teachers and students were relieved to finally have someone with a firm hand in charge. They responded positively to his no non-sense leadership. He had indeed proven he was the 'boss' and the children and faculty loved it.

School was over for the day. George was locking the outside door when he saw two men cutting across the playground yard, walking toward him, "Mr. Read?" The tall man called.

"Yes. Yes, that's me. What can I do for you?"

"I'm Mr. Marr, Thomas's father." He responded as he approached.

"I've been expecting you for some time. Where's your boy?" George called.

"Oh, he won't be coming. No need to have him here. By the way, this here is Mr. Bob Jones; the Jones boy's dad." Mr. Marr pointed to his shorter companion lagging a few steps behind.

George tried to read the men as they walked across the playground toward him. As they came nearer, he scrutinized their faces, even the way they walked; he wanted to determine if they were going to be hostile, or, if they had come in peace. He remained standing on the step's landing, rather than go down to their level. If they had come to fight, George reasoned, he would have a slight advantage from his higher spot. His 'street' smarts were always with him. George deftly unbuttoned his coat, then, checked to see if he was wearing his heavy belt buckle, a good weapon, and he knew how to use it. The men stopped in front of him. Mr. Marr looked up, and studied the teacher for a few moments, then offered his hand.

"Mr. Read, I want to tell you something."

George, still cautious offered only the tips of his fingers instead of his whole hand; once the man squeezed them he pulled his arm back quickly. "Yes, and what's that?" He wasn't sure what the men's intentions were, and he wasn't going to get suckered and let his guard down, not just yet.

Mr. Marr began. “Mr. Read, I want you to know that you have my permission to do whatever it takes to knock some sense into that boy of mine. I been see’n he is headed down the wrong road, sure as anything. I know’d he was headed for jail. He’s been plain pig headed, an’ don’t listen to noth’n his mother, or me tell him.”

Mr. Jones coughed, “Mr. Read, I want to say amen to what brother Marr just done said, and I agrees with him, one hundred percent. I knows my boy was head’n for trouble sure as anything, and anything you can do to put him on the straight and narrow, is fine with me.”

For the first time since the men appeared, George relaxed. “I’m glad to hear that. I want you men to know I didn’t use my stick without reason. The two boys were going to jump me.” He began coming down the steps to face them. “So I had no choice. I…”

Mr. Marr interrupted, “Mr. Read, my wife heard exactly what happened from some of the other children. We got the whole story. They heard what them boys said to you, and exactly what happened. So, we understand. You got no cause to explain to us.”

He realized his caution had been unwarranted. He saw that these fathers had come in peace, and wanted the best for their sons. “Well. Good. So long as you understand what I’m trying to do here…” George paused, as he gathered his thoughts. He wanted these men to understand what he felt his mission as a teacher was, “Let me put it this way. These Negro children don’t stand a chance in life, in this country, if they don’t learn some discipline, and get a good education…that’s why I’m here, to see that they do… even if I have to knock it into some of them.” The men laughed in appreciation of his frankness.

"We understand what you're up against. Some of these boys don't have no respect for anything, or anybody." Mr. Marr complained. "But, you know what? I already see a change for the better, and you got our support, you remember that. You can call on us anytime." When the men offered their hands, this time George returned the gesture with a firm grip. As the men walked away, Mr. Marr called over his shoulder, "You just give us a yell if you need anything, you hear?"

With a smile, George called, "I'll remember that, gentlemen. Thanks."

Rosa had stood just inside the door, listening and watching, ready to call the police if they had started trouble. She came outside and joined her husband as the men walked across the playground to their homes. "Well, that should make you feel good." Rosa said with a big grin.

"Actually, it does. At least I know I've got some support from parents who want something better for their children. I've seen it go the other way, too. Sometimes the parents are worse than the kids. That's when it's a no-win situation. It gives the student a reason to act out when the parents support their bad action. But that's rare. Usually it goes the other way, and the parents will support you."

"Thank goodness for that." Rosa sighed.

Mornings in every class room began with the Lord's Prayer, the singing of "My Country 'Tis of Thee" and the Pledge of Allegiance. Every so often a half hour was devoted to discussing current events. Often there would be an issue in the colored papers that the children were excited about: Joe Louis winning a fight, a lynching down South, a case of police brutality, the brilliant Paul Robeson setting records as a football player at Rutgers University, or the treatment of the potato picking migrant workers, brought up from the South, then, shipped back at the end of the harvest season. These topics gave George insights into the children's concerns, interests, and their thought processes. He also felt public speaking was important, and he let the children select any topic they chose to address. He reasoned they would do better and be more motivated if they chose their own subjects.

His rules for speaking before the class were simple; Stand straight, project your voice, and no fidgeting. Hand gestures were allowed to dramatize a point. He demonstrated the proper way to use your diaphragm in order to make your voice bigger, and how to project it. And of course, no mumbling allowed.

Mr. Shook, the superintendent of schools was invited to a play about Harriett Tubman and the Under Ground Railroad that the children put on. He sat in the back of the room with George and watched the performance. The girl that portrayed Harriett, carried a stick to represent Harriett's ever present rifle. The children had memorized their lines, and delivered them flawlessly. The performers sang spirituals coded to set the time and place to meet for their journey North, and freedom. George explained to his visitor, "Often, they sang these songs in the presence of the overseers, rejoicing as they did, because the overseer hadn't a clue as to the meaning of the song." The children sang "Steal Away" to illustrate the lesson, then tiptoed into the cloak room through its open door, and symbolically to freedom, led by 'Harriett.'

At the conclusion of the play, the whole class sang the Negro spiritual “Down by the Riverside” with exuberance. At the end of the song, the class was dismissed to enjoy recess.

After the room emptied, the superintendent turned to George, “Mr. Read, I want you to know I’ve seen a change in the short time you’ve been here, and it’s been nothing short of remarkable.”

“Thank you Mr. Shook. I appreciate your kind words.”

“Well, it’s the truth. What’s your secret?”

“Well, sir, in my life I’ve learned a few things, and two remain paramount with me as a teacher. For my people to get ahead in this country, we educators must stress these two things. Education. Education. Education. And, Learn, Learn. Learn. It’s just that simple.”

Mr. Shook smiled, “Mr. Read, I can say from first hand observations, you have turned the learning switch on in the brains of these children.”

“I hope so, Mr. Shook.” The men got up and walked to a window that overlooked the playground. George gestured. “I hope I’m reaching them, I see so much potential among these boys and girls. The problem is they haven’t been motivated to want to learn. That’s what I’m trying to do, keep them motivated, make them want to learn.” As the men chatted, a student burst into the room.

“Mr. Read, there’s a big dog running around loose on the other side of the playground fence. He keeps trying to get over on our side.” The boy was visibly upset. “An’, he, he looks real mean. An’ foam is coming out of his mouth.”

“Thanks for telling me, son.” George knew instantly, the boy had described a rabid dog. He raced to the outside and yelled. "Everybody, children come into the school at once!" As he called the children in, he saw the dog running back and forth on the opposite side of the chain link fence which separated the school's property from a private home's yard. The dog needed to go only a bit further to where the fence ended, and he would have access to the children. He yelled as loud as he could, "The dog is sick, don't let him near you, come in, come inside at once! Stay calm, but hurry." He pointed to several of the older boys, "Help the little ones, and you boys." He pointed again, "You fellows check around the side and the back of the building, make sure there are no children there. If there are, bring them in…but hurry and don't let that dog near you!"

Donald Lewis, Joe Conover and Alonzo ran around the building. Alonzo spotted two little girls, busy playing under a tree. "You girls, come with me!" He shouted. But before the startled girls knew what happened, he had scooped them up, one under each arm and delivered them to the open door where George and Mr. Shook stood. "Mr. Read…no one is left alongside the building," he managed between deep breaths. Joe and Donald had checked the rear of the building and followed Alonzo to the doorway. "We looked in the back, and there ain't no more kids outside, Mr. Read."

"Good work, boys." The children safe inside, George hurriedly closed and locked both outside doors. He went to the other class rooms, and explained to the teachers and children what was happening. "There's a rabid dog outside the school. Everyone must stay inside until we can do something about it. The dog is sick, and can make anyone he comes in contact with it sick as well. So stay inside until I tell you it's safe to go outside." The children sat wide eyed. A few began to cry. "Don't be afraid, children, you're safe as long as we all stay inside, and you listen to your teacher." George's voice was calm and reassuring.

As he and Mr. Shook walked back to his class room, he saw the dog had managed to come around the fence and was crossing the playground, heading toward the rectangular shaped building. He seemed to be in a trance as he began plodding methodically around the building again, and again. In a low voice Mr. Shook said, "I have a pistol in the glove compartment of my car parked in the street. Do you think one of your boys could get it? I'm a good shot, but I'm not agile enough to run to the car and bring it back."

"Mr. Shook," George answered, "The shortest distance to your car is out of my classroom window. It would be a much longer run if we were to leave by this door. The problem is the ground slopes away severely from the building at that end. It's too far to the ground to jump out of the window."

"Let's go see what it looks like, Maybe there is a way," the superintendent offered.

As the men hurried back to the classroom, George suggested. "I know what we can do. I'll call the police. They could send an officer to shoot the animal."

"That's a good possibility. Do you want me to call? I know the chief."

"Sure. My phone is in the cloak room closet."

The superintendent dialed the police station. "This is superintendent of Schools, John Shook. Chief? Oh, I'm fine…look, I'm at the colored school, and we have a problem. There's a rabid dog here. We have the school locked up, the children are safe, but the dog is a danger to others who would encounter him." The superintendent began shaking his head as he listened to the lengthy reply. Finally, he hung up.

"No, he can't send anyone for a couple of hours. The two officers on duty are at a three car accident, and he can't pull them. And, he can't leave. He's expecting a couple of prisoners to be brought in, and he has to book them."

"We really have to shoot that animal. We're safe, but if that dog leaves here, he could bite some unsuspecting person." George looked at the older boys. "I have an idea. Bob and Thomas are strong young men, I'll have them lower me to the ground, and pull me back up. Let's see if they feel they can do that."

The men walked to one of the four large windows that faced the street where Mr. Shook's Ford coupe was parked. George raised the window most in line with the car. Both men poked their heads out of the raised window. Just then, the dog trotted past beneath them on unsteady legs, as he continued his ritualistic pattern of circling the building. George turned to face the students; "Bob, Thomas Alonzo would you come here?" The boys hurried from their seats, and crowded around the men standing by the window. They sensed the urgency in his voice. "Now, we know the dog is rabid. If he were to bite someone, it would mean painful shots in the stomach to prevent the disease. Now, Mr. Shook can shoot the dog if I can get his pistol out of the car. Do you think two of you could lower me to the ground, then, pull me back up? Do you fellows think you can do that?"

Without hesitation, Alonzo protested, "No, Mr. Read, you shouldn't do it. I'm taller and I don't weigh as much as you. They can lower me, and get me back in much easier than they can you. Let me do it!"

"This is serious business. It's a dangerous task, young man." Mr. Shook added.

"I know, but they can lower me down and pull me back easier than they can Mr. Read…right?" Alonzo replied as he looked for support from his two buddies.

"Yeah, we can, and he's right, he don't weigh as much as you, Mr. Read. We can do it."

Mr. Shook smiled, "I must agree with the boys. This young man is taller and a lot lighter than you. With those long legs, he'll hit the ground sooner, and get to the car quicker than you can. No disrespect intended, Mr. Read. But I think Alonzo here has a good point."

A brief smile crossed George's face at the reference to his weight. "The boys may be right." He finally admitted.

"They'll be able to grab him easier because of his height and long arms. I say yes, let the three of them do it." Mr. Shook added firmly.

A flicker of disappointment crossed George's face. Then he looked earnestly at the three boys. "All right, what you say makes sense…are you fellows sure you can and want to do it?"

"Yes, sir, we do. We can do it." The boys agreed.

"All right, then, let's get started. First, we should time the dog and see how long it takes him to circle the building." George suggested.

The superintendent pulled his pocket watch out, then, leaned out the window. "No, he's not here yet. Not yet, not yet, not yet." He muttered. "Now! He just turned the corner, and he's passing underneath the window right now."

The children sat wide eyed as they listened intently, but remained quiet as mice. They recognized the seriousness of the situation. The superintendent kept his eyes on the ticking hands and the ground beneath him. "Here he comes again. It took him three minutes; he turns the corner in exactly three minutes.

"Now we know how much time you have, Alonzo, so we'll tell you when to head back once you get to the car. Understood?" George asked.

"Yes, sir." Alonzo replied.

Mr. Shook looked grim as he spoke, "The gun is in the glove compartment. Get it out, then, wait in the car until the dog passes under the window, and turns the corner. That's when you should head back. We'll yell to you when it's time. Once you get under the window, toss the gun to me."

That's when Tom and Bob will pull you back up. If it's close to the time for the dog to return, we'll tell you to run back to the car." George added.

"The gun's in a holster, but it's loaded...don't take it out." Mr. Shook added.

"Yes, sir. I understand what you want me to do."

"Tom, Bob we will hold your legs as you boys lower Alonzo. That way you won't lose your balance, because you're going to have to lean pretty far out of the window, so Alonzo won't have too far to drop."

"Yes, sir, we understand" The boys echoed.

Alonzo sat on the window ledge, his long legs dangling outside. He turned to his friends as each took one of his arms. They waited for the dog to pass. Once he showed himself, Mr. Shook looked at his watch. "I clocked him on his last pass, he's still running at the same pace."

"All right, Alonzo, you can start down." George said.

Alonzo slid off of the window ledge slowly. The boys held his wrists tightly. As he slid off the ledge they felt his full weight. The Superintendent and George were on their knees, each holding one of the boys tightly by their legs. As the boys leaned further and further out the window, the men rose slowly, allowing the boys to stretch themselves to their full lengths. "OK, let me go!" Alonzo yelled to his buddies. They released their grip and he dropped to the ground. The men quickly pulled the two boys back in and stood next to them, their eyes on Alonzo. They watched as his long legs took him across the short grassy yard, over the sidewalk, then, down the steep six foot embankment. He slid down the grade on his rear. He went to the passenger side of the car's door and yanked on the handle. "It's locked." Alonzo yelled."

"Go to the driver's side!" The superintendent called back.

Alonzo scurried around the car. Thankfully, the door opened. He leaned across the seat, pulled the glove compartment door open and groped for the pistol. His hand went this way and that. At first felt he nothing. Finally his fingers touched the gun's handle. Stretching his body even more, he wound down the window, and yelled, "I got it!"

"Stay inside the car. Wait until the dog comes back around and turns the corner." George yelled as Alonzo pulled himself fully into the car.

The youth placed the .32 caliber revolver's handle in the palm of his hand and looked at it in awe. He had never touched a gun before. It was a thrill he hadn't expected to experience when he came to school earlier in the day. Then he remembered he had to watch for the dog.

He began looking at the corner of the building, expecting the dog to turn the corner and come into view at any moment. As he watched, the boy was unaware how hard his heart was pounding.

Suddenly, the dog appeared. As soon as it turned the far corner George yelled, "Come back, Alonzo!"

The boy jumped out on the driver's side, slammed the door and started up the embankment. His smooth leather soled shoes had no gripping power. Before he knew what was happening, he fell to his knees. The slip caused him to lose grip on the gun. He watched in anguish as it slid to the bottom of the incline. "Shit" Alonzo hissed. He scrambled back down to retrieve it. On his second try, he got up the embankment easily. He ran back to the building, and looked up at the men leaning out the window.

"Toss the gun up." Mr. Shook called as he extended his body as far as he could.

With a smooth underhand motion Alonzo tossed the pistol up to the man's outstretched hands. But, Mr. Shook was over-anxious, and closed his fingers too soon. The gun fell back to the ground with a thud. "Try again, I'll get it this time." He promised. Alonzo repeated his underhand toss. This time the superintendent caught the gun and quickly placed it on the floor between his legs.

The children reacted as if they were watching a movie thriller and cheered at the accomplishment of these real life actors.

"All right boys, let's get Alonzo back inside. Lean out as far as you can. We'll hold you the same way as before." George ordered. The boys stretched their bodies and arms as far as they could while spreading their fingers wide in order to grab Alonzo's wrists.

"OK, Jump, Alonzo. Jump, man! Tom yelled. And he did, but he missed both boys. He couldn't quite reach them.

"We'll lean you further out, but if he doesn't grab you on this try, tell him to go back to the car." George told the boys, his voice sounding urgent.

"Time is running out, that dog is due back in seconds." Mr. Shook was alarmed.

This time the tall youth jumped as hard as he could and managed to grab their wrists. Bob and Tom locked their other hand on his wrists. "On three!" Tom yelled. Then, he counted quickly. "One. Two, Three!" With all their might, they began pulling with strength they didn't know they had. Just as they completed their first tug, the dog rounded the corner. His yellow eyes instantly locked on the struggling form hanging outside the building. With a burst of speed, the dog leaped at the boy's flailing legs, its jaws snapped shut with a click at the apex of its jump.

Luckily, Alonzo had decided to help his own cause by digging his feet into the side of the brick building, desperately trying to get a toe hold in order to gain some upward momentum. That decision moved his legs out of harm's way, and just in time.

With another mighty tug, the boys raised Alonzo to the level of the window. The children squealed and stamped their feet in delight when Alonzo's head poked up above the window sill, a broad triumphant smile on his sweaty, handsome, ebony face. When he slid off the window sill, and into the room, the children cheered even louder.

"Good job, Alonzo! Good job, boys." George said as both the superintendent and he patted them on their backs and shook each boy's hands.

"Now, I've got a job to do." The superintendent said. "Maybe he's still outside the window and he'll give me a stationary target." His voice was hopeful as he looked out the window. "No, he took off again. I just hope he continues circling. Let's pray he won't break his routine because he lunged at the boy. I'll just wait here and see. Please, everyone stand back now." The tall man took a shooting stance at the window. His elbows resting on the ledge, his left hand holding his pistol hand to further steady it. In a low voice, almost a whisper, he said, "Here he comes. OK. Steady, steady now, steady."

Bang! Bang! The gun cracked. "Awooo." The dog cried. "Got him. By gosh, I got him!" The man exulted.

"Good shot, Mr. Shook. Good shooting." George praised as he patted the man's back.

"Can we see? Can we see?" The children pleaded.

"Yes, you may. First I want to tell you how proud I am of all of you for being so calm and listening so well. What we were able to accomplish is in large part due to you being such good boys and girls, and I want to thank you for listening so well. Now, what we will do is start with the first desk on the sixth grade row, then work through the seventh and eighth grade. You may begin now. Walk by the window single file, then, return to your seats. We'll open the rest of the windows so more of you can see the dog at the same time." Tom and Bob quickly opened the other three windows.

The children stopped at the open window to get a look at the dead animal. The dog's foam-covered tongue extended from his open mouth. Blood oozed from the two bullet wounds in its side.

"Oooh, he looks awful." Look at the blood." "I think I'm going to vomit." Each child had his or her own reaction to the dead animal. Some took a fast look, then turned away. Some stood transfixed, and had to be told to move on. It was an event that no child would ever forget. After everyone had had a chance to look and had returned to their seats, George went to the front of the classroom.

"Who knows what rabies is, and how you can get it?" Several students raised their hands. "Yes." He pointed to a seventh grade girl.

"You catch it from a dog bite…and it can make you go crazy… and I think you will die."

George nodded. "It can kill you, and can make you become mad if you don't get the rabies shots, which are quite painful. But if you are bitten and get the shots, you will not die. That is why we wanted to keep everyone safe and away from the dog. That's why it was important we not let the dog get away, and possibly bite some unsuspecting person off the school grounds."

An eighth grade boy raised his hand and asked, "Is he going to be left there?"

"No, we'll call the dog catcher. He'll dispose of the animal the proper way, in the ground, it could give you the disease, could give you rabies. I don't want anyone to go near that spot for any reason, not until I say it's safe. Is that understood?"

John Shook and George walked to the class room door. The superintendent extended his hand. "Well, I can't remember when I've had a more exciting day." He smiled as he and George shook hands. He turned to the class.

"Children, I'm proud of you, too. Just keep up the good work. You'll go far in life if you listen to Mr. Read. Alonzo, Bob, Thomas. You boys did a very good and brave thing today. You were all exceptional." He took a few steps, then, turned to the class again. "Good bye, boys and girls, I'll see you again."

"Good bye Mr. Shook" They replied. One boy called out, "Thanks for being a good shot." The comment made the superintendent smile, and the class applauded as he went out the door.

On the front page of the weekly local paper, *The Freehold Transcript,* there was a featured story about a rabid dog that had appeared at the colored school during recess period. The article went on to extol the sound leadership exhibited by the Negro principal, George Isaac Read, and the bravery and courage of several students. One boy in particular; Alonzo Perry, had put himself in harm's way to retrieve a gun that was used to destroy the dog. The article went on to praise the strength and level-headedness of two other boys, Thomas Marr and Bob Jones, who used their strength and determination to pull Alonzo to safety The article was written and submitted to the paper by John Shook, Superintendent of Schools.

Notes

C.Richard Read, author and graphic designer verbally paints pictures for his readers, enabling them to follow and experience what happened in the turbulent years of the era in which he has lived.

This is his first book of his two-part series of *The Black Dutchman.* This first part was revealed to him by various members of the family because it covers the times before he was of an age to remember. His second book is written in first person and narrates what he experienced.

His vivid descriptions of the characters, their thoughts, their lifestyles, and the experiences are honest, raw and objective, and read like fiction. Nonetheless, the readers feel an empathy as they travel through the years with an extraordinary author who pulls the readers into the story and into his life.

CPSIA information can be obtained
at www.ICGtesting.com
Printed in the USA
FFOW04n1553080115
10073FF

9 781940 2246